THE PRIVATE WORLDS
OF DYING CHILDREN

The Private Worlds of Dying Children

Myra Bluebond-Langner

PRINCETON UNIVERSITY PRESS

Princeton, New Jersey

Copyright © 1978 by Princeton University Press

Published by Princeton University Press, Princeton, New Jersey
In the United Kingdom: Princeton University Press,
Chichester, West Sussex

Library of Congress Cataloging-in-Publication Data
Bluebond-Langner, Myra, 1948-
The private worlds of dying children.
Bibliography: p.
Includes index.
1. Terminally ill children—Psychology. 2. Socialization.
3. Leukemia in children—Psychological aspects. I. Title.
RJ47.5.B58   618.9'21'55   77-85529
ISBN 0-691-09374-1
ISBN 0-691-02820 pbk.

Publication of this book has been aided by a grant
from The Andrew W. Mellon Foundation

This book has been composed in Linotype Caledonia

Printed in the United States of America

Princeton University Press books are printed on acid-free paper
and meet the guidelines for permanence and durability of the
Committee on Production Guidelines for Book Longevity of the
Council on Library Resources

Portions of chapters five and six previously appeared as "Meanings
of Death to Children," in *New Meanings of Death*, ed. Herman Feifel,
copyright © 1977 by McGraw-Hill Book Co.
Part of the appendix appeared as "How I Came to Study Dying
Children," in *Rhetorical Considerations*, ed. Harold Brent and
William Lutz, Winthrop Publishers, Inc., 1977.

Most of the final scene in chapter two is quoted from "The Last Day,"
from *Charlotte's Web* by E. B. White.
Copyright © 1952 by E. B. White. Reprinted here by kind
permission of Harper & Row, Publishers, Inc.

First Princeton Paperback printing, 1980

7   9   10   8   6

FOR THE CHILDREN

"... *All men struggle against powerful odds to define for themselves a constantly threatened and therefore all the more precious identity within that brief span of time that is their own.*" (Berger 1963:160)

CONTENTS

CONTENTS

viii

PREFACE

This study of awareness and communication in terminally ill children represents an effort to gain insight into two significant problems in social science: childhood socialization and social order. It begins by asking how terminally ill children come to know that they are dying when no one tells them, and how they conceal this knowledge from their parents and the medical staff. I argue that the children's acquisition of information about their world and their place in it is best understood as a socialization process, and that their decision not to reveal their awareness reflects their knowledge of the order to which they have been socialized, of how it is acceptable to die in this society.

Chapter one revolves around the questions of what is a child and, by extension, what is childhood socialization. A discussion of the relevant literature shows why a study of awareness and communication in terminally ill children is particularly well suited for the investigation of childhood socialization and social order.

The life of such children is presented in chapter two, a five-act play, "The World of Jeffrey Andrews." Focusing on what children see, feel, and put together at each step of their finite journey, we realize how children in a sometimes strange and often threatening world become aware of what is happening to them.

The universality of "The World of Jeffrey Andrews" is revealed in chapter three, where the question of what terminally ill children know is dealt with in detail. Attention is given to the range of the children's knowledge of the hospital structure, personnel, disease-treatment process, and prognosis.

The children do not learn everything at once; their awareness is not suddenly that of dying children. The acquisition of information is a long and difficult process, involving experiences in the disease world and changes in self-concept. The structure and content of this process is examined in chapter four, and analysis is based on a theoretical position outlined in chapter one.

Attention is then directed to the problems of how and why dying children choose to conceal their awareness from adults. These problems are dealt with in chapters five and six, respectively, through an examination of the fabric of social order and the individual's relation to it. This requires consideration of what it means to be a child, a parent, or a physician in the American society. Here, a fundamental question of the human condition arises: Why, even in the face of death, do people behave in socially acceptable ways, maintaining solidarity with those from whom they will soon be separated?

The research for this book was conducted over a nine-month period in the Department of Pediatrics of a large midwestern teaching hospital, the site of two other important studies of terminally ill children and their families (in order to preserve anonymity the names of these studies are not given).

The children ranged in age from eighteen months to fourteen years; but unless otherwise noted, the subjects of this book were between the ages of three and nine. Of the forty patients regularly seen in the pediatric oncology out-patient clinic, thirty-two were major informants (observed in the clinic for at least ten visits and in the hospital for at least ten consecutive days), and of these thirty-two, eighteen were primary informants. Six primary informants were alive when I left the field; none survive.

Basic data about the children came from observations and my own conversations with them. Detailed accounts were kept of interactions observed between the children and significant others—family members, staff members, visitors, strangers, and school teachers; in a variety of settings—hospital rooms, treatment rooms, clinic waiting rooms, and, when possible, the homes of the children themselves; at a variety of times—weekdays and weekends, holidays, early morning, midday, evening, late at night.

In my conversations with the children, I used a modified form of play therapy (cf. Axline 1947). This technique allowed the children to reflect on their own behavior without undergoing direct questioning, which destroys the integrity of the phenomenon (see chapter one). Furthermore, children, particularly these, do not often respond to direct questions. My aim was to get as close as possible (realizing, of course, that I influenced the situation) to their thoughts, their interactional strategies, and their structuring of the situation.

Supplementary data about the terminally ill children came from informal interviews, conducted throughout the project with parents and staff, as well as from charts and case histories.

By observing the families and staff in such settings as the hospital, pediatric out-patient clinic, homes, funeral parlors, cemeteries, and also by attending staff conferences, hospital rounds, and various social gatherings, I acquired information about family and staff attitudes toward death, dying, and those terminally ill, as well as the adults' perceptions of what was happening and being communicated to the children. A representative, but by no means exhaustive, sample of the data collected is presented in the play.

In an effort to control for biases of various sorts, I kept running introspective accounts of what I was thinking and feeling during any interaction and in my rudimentary analysis. This was necessary because of our culture's pervasive sensitivity to death. My choice of methods, the problems that I had in using some of them, the inability to use others due to the field conditions, and the more general problems of doing fieldwork with children in a taboo area are discussed in the appendix.

ACKNOWLEDGMENTS

This book is based on my doctoral dissertation, the field research and writing of which were supported by a fellowship trainee grant from the National Science Foundation and by a summer stipend from the Department of Anthropology of the University of Illinois, Urbana, Illinois.

I thank the members of my committee: Professors Jan Brukman, Edward M. Bruner (chairman), Clark Cuningham, Norman Denzin, Harold Gould, David Plath, and Norman Whitten for the help that each gave at various stages of my research. I am grateful to Professors Brukman and Bruner for the support and intellectual stimulation they offered me throughout my graduate career. Special thanks are due to: Marian Brinkerhoff, Barbara Schockett, Diane Bosch, and Beatrice Saler for typing from my many illegible drafts; Nancy Newhouse for copyediting the final draft of the dissertation and Hope Hillman for assistance in proofreading; Carole Joffee and William D. Amis, the readers for the Press, for helpful comments and criticisms; Robert Brown for copyediting the final manuscript for the Press, and finally Sanford Thatcher, my editor at Princeton University Press, for the invaluable assistance and encouragement he offered at various stages in the preparation of the manuscript.

For various kinds of support, tangible and intangible, I owe a great deal to: my friends David Rosen, Enid Schildkrout, Sibby Whitten; my sister Judith Bluebond Seelig; and my niece Lara Emily Langner; and especially my husband, Richard Woods Langner, without whom neither the research nor the book would ever have been completed.

I appreciate all the assistance that the pediatric hematologists, house staff, nursing staff, occupational therapists, and leaders of the parents' group (all of whom must remain nameless to protect the anonymity of the parents and children) gave me. Most importantly, this research would not have been possible without the cooperation of the parents and of the children, to whom this book is dedicated.

May, 1977

ABBREVIATIONS

BIA—Bureau of Indian Affairs
C.B.C.—Complete blood check
C.N.S.—Central nervous system
FATIS—Family Adaptation to Terminal Illness
I.V.—Intravenous
L.P.N.—Licensed practical nurse
N.A.—Nurse's aide
O.T.—Occupational therapy
R.N.—Registered Nurse
WBC—White blood cell

THE PRIVATE WORLDS
OF DYING CHILDREN

CHAPTER ONE

Children as Actors

A child lies in bed, a white sheet drawn taut under his chin, staring out through the slightly open doorway. Outside, a doctor informs the parents, in hushed tones, that their child has leukemia. Questions race through their minds: "What am I going to do? What does it all mean? Will he die? What am I going to tell him?"

The physician's answer to this last question will depend upon his beliefs about the thoughts and feelings of young children. These beliefs are informed by what is to date a rather small and diverse literature on awareness and coping in terminally ill children.[1] The contributors are generally the physicians themselves, social workers, and psychologists, whose concern about what to tell a dying child led to an examination of the behavior of these children.

Noting the failure of terminally ill children to ask questions about their illness, some researchers believe that such children do not know the gravity of their condition.[2] Some feel that no good would be served by telling the children; in fact, it would probably make them more depressed and anxious.

Others interpret the children's silence differently. They attribute the lack of questioning not to an ignorance of the condition, but to the children's perceiving that adults are reluctant to talk about it.[3] But these researchers fail to understand the complex relation of these two factors, and this

[1] For a review of literature on awareness, communication, and coping in terminally ill children, see Bluebond-Langner 1975:1–16.

[2] See Agranoff and Mauer 1965, and Richmond and Waisman 1955.

[3] See Easson 1970, Hoffman and Futterman 1971, and Karon and Vernick 1968, 1965.

then leads them to one-sided solutions. For example, they suggest that groups led by health care professionals be formed so that children can talk freely about their condition with their parents and the physician.

There is a third group of physicians who advocate neither silence nor disclosure.[4] They start from the premise that children, in contrast to adults, have rather limited linguistic, intellectual, and emotional capacities. Children under ten are not capable of understanding their condition as adults do,[5] therefore the notions of "seriously ill" or "dying" just do not have the same import for them. Without clarifying in what way the children view their conditions, these authors go on to recommend that disclosure of information be left to the discretion of the parents and physician.

The literature is, I believe, inconclusive, and its recommendations problematic. It is not clear whether the children know, and if they know, what the precise nature of their knowledge then is, or how they come by it. Much of the problem, I submit, lies with the theories and methods these authors employed. Implicit in all of the work discussed is a view of children and their socialization common to both structural- and psychological-functionalism.

Socialization studies conducted from the structural- or psychological-functionalists' viewpoint tend to focus on situations in which the child is the patient and the caretaker is the agent.[6] For the most part these study child-rearing by the society's adult members. Other areas of childhood (e.g., peer relations, play, even the child's manipulation of the adults under study) are neglected. The understanding of and approach to childhood socialization that result are not

[4] See Kliman 1968, Natterson and Knudson 1960, Morrissey 1965, Solnit and Green 1959, 1963.

[5] For a full discussion of the problems inherent in these assumptions, see Bluebond-Langner 1977.

[6] See Elkin 1960, Aberle and Naegele 1968, Brim 1966, Maccoby 1968a and b, Kaplan 1961, Kardiner 1945, Linton 1945, Mead 1928, 1930, Mayer 1970, Richards 1970, and Whiting and Child 1953.

4

very different from the layman's. Attention is directed to the same areas of behavior that parents focus on. Traditionally oriented researchers concentrate on education, child-rearing, sexual identity, goals, internalization of norms and values; in brief, what is necessary for competent performance as an adult, according to their definition of adulthood.

In such studies, children are defined in terms of what they will become; childhood is viewed in terms of its bearing on future activities and status. Adults hold up a preexisting image to children, and measure them according to that standard, yet the children's definition of themselves and their world remains unexplored.

Critics of this approach argue that the very area of study, socialization, is neglected. Socialization is a negotiated two-way process involving the self and others over time (cf. Mead 1970, Blumer 1969). It is not simply "putting in" information at one end, and "getting out" a finished product, the adult, at the other (Inkeles 1968:77). Research that proceeds from a view of children as recipients of action from an external agent, or an internal force beyond their control, that approaches them in terms of an image to which they are being reared to conform, loses sight of the dynamic and functional character that marks socialization and, in fact, all interaction. As Denzin (1973:7–8) writes of structural-functionalist and psychological-functionalist approaches, "[they] fail to grasp the shifting, unfolding, creative aspects of all human behavior."

Finally, in their failure to respect children and their world, these studies do not comprehend the child's role in the initiation and maintenance of social order, to which adults respond with things like child-rearing practices. Researchers in structural- or psychological-functionalism mistake for socialization one of the many interactional strategies used when dealing with children. Child-rearing is only one aspect of interaction between parents and children, let alone of socialization. How children initiate such actions, their responses to the action taken, its consequences for the parents' or children's succeeding act, and for the parents' view of themselves and of the children—these are some elements ignored by traditional studies. As Inkeles (1968:103) points out, "All 'views' and 'perspectives' are inherently one-sided."

Whatever the merits of these general criticisms, the view and approach common to structural- and psychological-functionalist perspectives is unsuitable for studying terminally ill children.[7]

How can one use a model that presumes a future, that presupposes adulthood, for children who will never reach adulthood, particularly when everyone associated with these children is acutely and painfully aware of the fact? Leukemic children's knowledge of their condition colors their entire world view (see chapters two, three, and four).

The consequences of using the traditional model can be seen in the work of physicians, psychologists, and sociologists who have studied dying children's understanding of their terminal condition and prognosis. Richmond and Waisman (1955), and Solnit and Green (1963), for example, though studying such children, based their conclusions on the observed interactions between parent and child and doctor and child. Since the children did not ask adults about their condition, researchers assumed that the children either did not know, or were not interested in finding out, about their condition. Children would indicate their awareness, felt the researchers, by discussing it with adults, as many older children did. These investigators did not entertain the possibility that perhaps the children obtained information

[7] Considerations of space and continuity preclude further discussion of this model, but the reasoning behind such criticism and the ensuing choice of an alternative perspective is more apparent in the work of the symbolic interactionists and ethnomethodologists who study children when one sees what problems are solved there that could not have been solved using the perspective common to structural- and psychological-functionalism.

from other sources; or that they were in fact expressing awareness, but in a symbolic way that adults did not understand; or that by not talking about their condition, the children were observing social taboos, and attempting to save others' face (chapters six and seven).

These alternatives do not occur to one who fails to see children as willful, purposeful individuals capable of creating their own world, as well as acting in the world others create for them. Had the researchers entertained such a view, they would have sought out and investigated those possibilities by studying the children's peer-group interaction, their use of symbolic expression in art and play, and their knowledge of cultural norms and values, before concluding that only some older children become aware of their prognosis. They would also have formulated the problem of acquisition of information differently. It would not have been looked at as a simple process of learning from adults. We must employ an alternative view and approach; this may be found in the more recent work on childhood socialization done by those who share the symbolic-interactionist or ethnomethodological perspective.[8] Both of these rest on the premise that children possess a self, and are, therefore, purposeful, willful individuals capable of organizing their own behavior toward others. Children are able, as Denzin (1973:9) states, "to take one another's roles, present definitions of self, construct elaborate games and manipulate adults into desired directions." They can initiate and sustain prolonged interaction (e.g., play) without adult intervention; they can also participate in worlds that adults create for them, and initiate action in those situations.

Possessing a self, children can interpret the behavior of others and act on the basis of their own interpretations (cf.

---

[8] For examples see Denzin 1970–1973, Joffee 1973, Speier 1970, Cicourel 1970, and most recently the contributors to Dreitzel 1973. Dreitzel's book appeared after I wrote the first drafts of this work. While many of my ideas appear there, I was not aware of his work until I had completed my own.

7

Mead 1970 and Blumer 1969).[9] For example, Faith (age three) interpreted the hospital as a threatening place. Those associated with it, identifiable by their uniforms, inflicted pain. Whenever anyone in white approached Faith, she dove under the covers. Jeffrey (age five), like Faith, saw the hospital in terms of "us" and "them." He made his primary cut (major category division) on the basis of those in uniform vs. those not in uniform. He later moved to a more behaviorally based interpretation—those who took orders and spoke only when spoken to versus those who came and went when they pleased, sometimes with and sometimes without explanation, a practice usually reserved for adults. On the basis of these interpretations, Jeffrey refrained from questioning the medical staff about his condition and assumed a supplicant position (see play, below, Act i).

Interpretations of the self, others, and objects are made in the course of interaction.[10]

> The meanings of such things [self, others, objects] is derived from, or arises out of, the social interaction that one has with one's fellows. (Blumer 1969:2)

The interpretations become available through action and are the basis for consequent action. For example, a five-year-old boy interprets his mother's crying as indicating that he is very sick. "See my mommy's red nose, that's from me. Everybody cries when they see me. I'm pretty sick." He also notes that he is getting more presents than his sister. "I get more presents than when I had my tonsils out. My sister gets the same." Finally, he has been behaving in

[9] "Interpret" is used here and throughout not in the sense of giving meaning to something recondite, but as giving *any* meaning, the basic act that all language-users must perform.

[10] According to Blumer (1969:10), "an object is anything that can be indicated." There are three categories of objects: physical (e.g., drugs, bone marrows, lab results); social (e.g., mother, doctor, anthropologist); and abstract (e.g., illness, the word *sick*, death, taboos). In this chapter, I refer to social objects as "others."

8

ways that are ordinarily cause for reprimand and finds that he is not reprimanded. In fact, he is rewarded. Following his interpretation of others' behavior toward him, he sees himself as very ill, and he forges a line of action in accord with such a view. He acts the sick role and claims his right on the basis that he is truly ill. For example, Beth, snatching a toy from her sister, said, "Gimme that, I'm the sick one, not you."[11]

In arriving at a certain self-image, children interpret not only the behavior of others toward them, but also their own behavior toward other objects. For example, Scott (age five and a half), seeing his mother crying after the doctor told her that Scott would need a bone marrow (a diagnostic aspiration of the marrow), and knowing that the bone marrow was not expected (it was not four weeks since the last one), deduced from his mother's behavior that he was not doing well, and that unexpected bone marrows are not a good sign. His behavior after leaving the doctor's office indicates he did not interpret his mother's tears as concern over the pain of the procedure. He chose to postpone his lunch until he heard the results of the bone marrow. "The worst part is waiting for the results," he said (see play, below, Act II, Scenes 5 and 7).

Children are capable of choosing behavior so as to affect the way others see them. Children who know they are dying but wish to conceal this knowledge from their parents can, by doing some of the things that normal children do, momentarily change their parents' view (see chapter five).

A form of behavior common among terminally ill children, "exhibition of wounds" (see chapter four), underlines how children try to affect not only the way others see them, but also how they see themselves. By showing where and how they have been poked and prodded, children present themselves to others as sick and find their self-image con-

[11] This kind of interpretation and consequent action is also seen in normal children when they are sick. Children often play sick because they know that rules will be relaxed and they may get more attention.

firmed. This is further evidenced by the fact that once children internalize this view of self, they no longer use this strategy, except when meeting someone for the first time and wanting, for any number of reasons, to affect the stranger's view of them (see chapter four).

This use of behavior can also extend to affecting others' actions. For example, by crying in the face of a procedure in the terminal phases of the disease, the child may change the nurse's view of him ("He's ready to die") as well as her behavior (she will not administer the drug).

The children's interpretation of themselves, others, and objects, and the consequent action taken varies with the social, physical, and temporal settings. A child's failure to discuss his or her prognosis in the presence of adults, compared to open discussion in the presence of other children, is one illustration of the effect of social setting. Since the children interpret death as an inappropriate topic of conversation with adults (evidenced by the adults' reactions when children try to discuss it), and as an appropriate topic with other children (evidenced by their willingness to offer information and answer questions), they refrain from discussing the subject in the presence of adults, but pursue it with peers. This is also true of sex discussions among normal children. Leukemic children often discussed their condition in the place children often go to discuss sex—the bathroom, where adults cannot hear them. Looked at another way, then, we can say that children's pretense in one social setting and their candor in another indicates their ability to make judgments about a situation and to act appropriately.

The role of physical setting in the interpretation of self was shown in the different way children viewed themselves in the clinic, as opposed to in the hospital. Regardless of whether the children were sicker when they came to the clinic than they had ever been when hospitalized, they saw themselves and were seen by others as being in better health than when they had been hospitalized. The hospital was "where people go to die." There was a feeling among the parents, children, and staff that no matter how sick children might be, if they were not in the hospital, they were not going to die. This interpretation of the self had consequences for people's actions in both settings. For example, parents and children could separate far more easily in the clinic than in the hospital.

As discussed in detail in chapter four, terminally ill children's view of themselves, others, and objects also changed over time. They first defined themselves as well, then, by degrees, as ill, seriously ill and will get better, always ill and will get better, always ill and will never really get better, and, finally, as dying, with noticeable changes in their behavior at each stage. The children's view of nurses ("others") changed from all nurses are threatening all of the time, to all nurses are threatening some of the time, to some nurses are threatening some of the time, to nurses are not threatening at all. They acted toward each on the basis of these definitions. For example, those whom they viewed as nonthreatening, "on their side," they tried to solicit help from to get out of medical procedures. "I bet if Elsa were here she wouldn't let them do this to me." It should be noted that this shift in view of certain nurses from threateners to protectors or nurturers came at about the time that children ceased to see their mothers as the authorities, protectors, and nurturers, and began to see them as the ones to be protected or whose authority could be disobeyed (see chapter six).

Similarly, children's interpretation of the illness ("abstract object") changed from acute to chronic to fatal. Even the definition of concrete objects, like drugs, changed from healing agents to just something that prolongs life; from always effective, to effective some of the time, to not really effective at all. Children's behavior changed accordingly, from passive acceptance of the drugs to refusal to take them. "They don't do nothin' anyway."

The children's view of time itself changed (see chapter

11

four). It was no longer, as it is for most other children, endless. It became finite, marked by relapses and remissions. One consequence of this changed view was that the children no longer spoke of the future. Above all, time was not to be wasted.

The following points can be made about children, based on this research:

1. They are willful, purposeful creatures who possess selves.
2. They interpret their behavior and act on the basis of their interpretations.
3. They interpret their own self-images.
4. They interpret the behavior of others to obtain a view of themselves, others, and objects.
5. They are capable of initiating behavior so as to affect the view others have of them and that they have of themselves.
6. They are capable of initiating behavior to affect the behavior of others toward them.
7. Any meaning that children attach to themselves, others, and objects varies with respect to the physical, social, and temporal settings in which they find themselves.
8. Children can move from one social world to another and act appropriately in each world.

It is not true, then, that a child's view of himself is "x" and therefore he does "y"; or a child sees her mother as "z" and therefore she does "b"; or a child's view of a certain object is "f" and he therefore acts towards it with "g." Each interpretation of self, others, and objects varies with the physical, social, and temporal settings in which it occurs, and with the individuals' views of themselves and their relation to the society of which they are members. These interpretations and consequent actions become available to us through participant-observation. To duplicate this process, the data are presented in the form of a play.

"The World of Jeffrey Andrews" (chapter two) was written to give a sense of the everyday life of terminally ill children, their emotions and thoughts at each step of a finite journey from diagnosis to death. It recreates the dramatic, living quality of that which is taken apart, analyzed, and used to illuminate theoretical issues in succeeding chapters. To construct the play, I went through my field notes (a combination of taped transcriptions and recorded observations) and wrote a play for each child from these. Then I assembled them to form the composite play, "The World of Jeffrey Andrews." In this way I could include a sufficiently wide range of characters and experience to sustain a broad analysis. Preserving the anonymity of a few individuals who might have been recognizable was also facilitated by the composite characterization.

Often, I created a single character from two different children. However, one can also separate the two children without doing violence to characters or my conclusions, because the children were not combined to make an ideal type. Similarly, in other cases several characters were created from a single child, since using the same name more than once would have made it easy for others to recognize the child. Age, sex, and circumstances have been altered when necessary to protect a child's or adult's identity. Dialect has been removed altogether for the same reason. I have tried to present the information without compromising scientific validity, while preserving the anonymity of informants.

Being terminally ill, living with dying, is an extended process, and the acts reflect the length of the various aspects of the disease. The longest act, Act IV, deals with a series of relapses and remissions, as this is the longest aspect of the process in actual time and the patients' view. Act V, the death, is the shortest. The five acts also reflect the five stages of the socialization process. Each act represents what occurs at a stage in the process that is discussed from a more theoretical perspective in chapter four. To replicate as closely as possible the data-sorting process, the data taken from the dialogues in the plays and necessary for the analysis in chapters four through seven is presented in chapter three. In brief, the play immerses one in the fieldwork experience; analysis begins in the succeeding chapters.

CHAPTER TWO

The World of Jeffrey Andrews

PERSONAE

(In order of appearance)

JEFFREY ANDREWS: *Five-year-old boy with leukemia**
MRS. ANDREWS: *Mother of* JEFFREY ANDREWS
MR. ANDREWS: *Father of* JEFFREY ANDREWS
NURSE RICHARDS: *R.N. on pediatric ward*
NURSE STEVENS: *R.N. on pediatric ward*
RECEPTIONIST ON PEDIATRIC WARD***
"DR." SID COLE: *Third-year medical student*

("Heme Team")

DR. ABRAMS: *Chairman of the department of pediatrics, and hematologist*
DR. ELLIS: *Pediatrician, hematology fellow*
DR. WESSON: *Pediatrician, hematologist*
DR. WESSLEY: *Pediatric hematologist/director of pediatric oncology clinic*
DR. CELLARS: *Pediatrician, hematology fellow*

STUDENT AIDE***
TV MAN***
DR. ESTERSON: *Resident in pediatrics*
DR. MC PHEARSON: *Intern in pediatrics*
FAITH WELDER: *Three-year-old girl with leukemia**
MRS. WELDER: *Mother of* FAITH

* Age when the character first appears in the play.
** When no name is given, it indicates that neither the children nor the parents ever learned that person's name, who then remained nameless throughout the course of the illness.

ROBERTA SUMMERS: *Medical technologist for pediatric hematology*

NURSE LYONS: *R.N. on pediatric ward*

MEDICAL STUDENT°°

MYRA BLUEBOND: *Anthropology student conducting research with terminally ill children*

NURSE WALTON: *R.N. on pediatric ward*

TWO SURGEONS°°

NURSE LOCKNER: *R.N. on pediatric ward*

AIDE WASHINGTON: *Nurses aide on pediatric ward*

RECEPTIONIST IN THE ONCOLOGY CLINIC°°

MRS. STALLER: *Mother of* KATHERINE, *six-year-old girl with leukemia*

DR. ISSACS: *Family therapist and coleader of the "parents' group"*

MRS. BAXTER: *Mother of* LAURA, *ten-year-old girl with cancer°*

NURSE GREEN: *R.N. in the oncology clinic*

MRS. RICHARDSON: *Mother of* PAULA, *infant girl with cancer*

MISS KOHNE: *Psychiatric social worker and coleader of the "parents' group"*

MRS. HERBERT: *Mother of* MARTIN, *eight-year-old boy with leukemia°*

MRS. MINDY MYERS: *Mother of* ELLIOT

MRS. ALICE HANDELMAN: *Mother of* JENNIFER

MRS. MARTIN: *Grandmother of* LYNN WELDER

SETH WELLER: *Five-year-old boy with leukemia°*

MR. WELLER: *Father of* SETH

O.T.S. 1: *An occupational therapy student°°*

SCOTT HELLER: *Five-and-a-half-year-old boy with leukemia°*

AARON THOMAS: *Three-year-old boy with leukemia°*

MRS. HELLER: *Mother of* SCOTT

ERICKA ANDREWS: *Four-and-a-half-year-old sister of* JEFFREY°

ELLIOT MYERS: *Eighteen-month-old boy with leukemia°*

SHARON MULLEN: *Occupational therapist assigned to pediatrics*

16

LISA PHILLIPS: *Seven-year-old girl with leukemia**
MICHAEL SHEPARDS: *Seven-year-old boy with leukemia**
MRS. SMITH: *Mother of* MARK, *seven-year-old boy with leukemia**
JILL KLEMONS: *Eight-year-old girl with leukemia**
NURSE IN ONCOLOGY CLINIC
SANDY RODWAN: *Six-year-old boy with leukemia**
MRS. PHILLIPS: *Mother of* LISA
MR. PHILLIPS: *Father of* LISA
TOM REEDER: *Seven-year-old boy with leukemia**
AIDE THOMAS: *N.A. on pediatric ward*
ELIZABETH JONES: *Eight-year-old cardiac patient**
MRS. REEDER: *Mother of* TOM
KITCHEN AIDE****
MATHEW SPENCER: *Seven-year-old urology patient*
MAN FROM THE X-RAY DEPARTMENT****
NURSE BING: *L.P.N. on pediatric ward*
NURSE RHONDA EDWARDS: *R.N. on pediatric ward*
AIDE LEWIS: *N.A. on pediatric ward*
DR. ELWOOD: *Intern in pediatrics*
O.T.S. 2: *Another occupational therapy student*
PETER FRENCH: *Six-and-a-half-year-old boy with leukemia**
JENNIFER HANDELMAN: *Seven-year-old girl with leukemia**
NURSE SINGLETON: *R.N. on pediatric ward*
MRS. COSTIN: *Mother of* MARY
MARY COSTIN: *Eight-year-old girl with leukemia**
IAN HELLER: *Eight-year-old brother of* SCOTT
LAURA BAXTER: *Ten-year-old girl with cancer**
NURSE DICKERSON: *L.P.N. on pediatric ward*
JACK COSTIN: *Twenty-two-year-old brother of* MARY
O.T.S 3: *Another occupational therapy student*
MAN FROM THE EYE BANK****
NURSE BARTON: *Student nurse assigned to pediatrics*
MR. AND MRS. ANDREWS: *Grandparents of* JEFFREY ANDREWS

ACT I: THE DIAGNOSIS

SCENE 1: *The nurses' station on the thirteenth floor of a metropolitan medical center, Monday, 4:00 p.m.*

A small, pale, dark-haired boy, holding his parents by each hand, steps off the elevator. He walks to their bewildered and hesitant step. In his mother's free hand is a sheaf of papers and in his father's is a small overnight bag. As they make their way to the nurses' station—smiling back at the stares of children in various stages of dress and undress, who race back and forth in wheelchairs and tricycles, screaming to one another; carefully walking around those children coloring in the middle of the floor with mothers, grandmothers and aunts seated on the couch looking over them—two nurses move from the back of the nurses' station and position themselves to either side of the reception desk, behind the glass. They know who this five-and-a-half-year-old boy is and why he is here. They have been told by the morning shift that JEFFREY ANDREWS, *a "possible leukemic," would be arriving sometime in the afternoon. He was being sent in by one of the suburban pediatricians, and the hematologists should be called when the* ANDREWS *arrive.*

(THE ANDREWS *reach the desk.*)

NURSE RICHARDS: Hello (*smiles*).

MRS. ANDREWS: (*Smiles*) I'm Mrs. Andrews, Jeffrey's mother. We were told to come up here to be admitted.

NURSE RICHARDS: Do you have your admission slip?

MRS. ANDREWS: (*Releases* JEFFREY'S *hand, pulls out the slip, hands it to the nurse, and takes* JEFFREY'S *hand again.*)

NURSE RICHARDS: (*Glances at the slip*) OK. Has Jeffrey been exposed to any childhood diseases within the last three days?

MRS. ANDREWS: (*Shakes her head quickly and answers quietly*) No.

18

NURSE STEVENS: (*Smiles down at* JEFFREY.)

NURSE RICHARDS: (*Hands* MRS. ANDREWS *a plastic vial*) Please see that when Jeffrey has to urinate he does so in this container. We will need a urine specimen.

(NURSE STEVENS *comes from behind the desk and leads the* ANDREWS *to* JEFFREY'S *room*.)

NURSE RICHARDS: (*To another nurse*) Enter it in the cardex as "possible WBC."

SCENE 2: JEFFREY'S *room, 10 minutes after admission.*

(THE ANDREWS *enter the room and stand awkwardly in the entryway.* MR. ANDREWS *takes a few steps forward and places the overnight bag on the floor against the wall. He walks over to the window, raises the shade halfway, and stares out.*)

NURSE STEVENS: (*Hands the mother a child's hospital gown from the linen cart outside in the hallway.*) Please see that Jeffrey puts this on. The doctor will be in shortly to examine Jeffrey and take a history. I'll be back to take his blood pressure and temperature.

(NURSE STEVENS *leaves.*)

MRS. ANDREWS: (*Begins to unbutton* JEFFREY'S *coat.*)

JEFFREY: (*Pulling away*) I can do it myself. (*He continues to undress between the two beds, placing his clothes at the end of the small unmade-up bed to his left. He silently dons a blue hospital gown, decorated with ships and trains, his black and blue legs plainly visible.*)

MRS. ANDREWS: I think that you can leave your underpants on for now.

JEFFREY: (*Mounts the bed.*)

MRS. ANDREWS: (*Sits down in the straight chair against the wall facing Jeffrey's bed, coat in hand and stares at Jeffrey.*)

JEFFREY: (*Looks up at the TV above her head*) I want the TV on.

19

MR. ANDREWS: (*Who has been staring out the window the entire time glances up and walks over to the TV*) There's no hookup. I guess you have to wait until you get one.

(NURSE STEVENS *enters the room.*)

NURSE STEVENS: Is everything all right? (*Walks over to* JEFFREY's *bed, puts the thermometer in his mouth, and takes his wrist.*)

JEFFREY: (*Lies back.*)

MRS. ANDREWS: (*Steps forward and smiles at the nurse.*)

NURSE STEVENS: (*Removes the thermometer after awhile and smiles.*)

MR. ANDREWS: (*From the foot of the bed*) Do you know anything about getting these TVs hooked up?

NURSE STEVENS: A man comes at about five every day. You can have it plugged in for about two dollars a day. He collects every day or you can pay him a week or so at a time.

MRS. ANDREWS: (*Smiles*) I don't think we'll be here that long.

NURSE STEVENS: (*Takes the blood pressure with a sphygmo-manometer, then uncuffs it.*)

JEFFREY: (*Sits up.*)

NURSE STEVENS: Is there anything I can get you, Jeffrey? Would you like some juice or some milk?

JEFFREY: (*Shakes his head*) Thanks.

MR. ANDREWS: (*Nods.*)

(NURSE STEVENS *leaves the room.*)

MRS. ANDREWS: (*Sits down facing* JEFFREY.)

(THE ANDREWS *sit in silence.*)

("DR." COLE *enters.*)

"DR." COLE: Hello. I'm Dr. Cole. I'm here to examine Jeffrey. (*Smiles somewhat nervously and walks over to* JEFFREY.)

MRS. ANDREWS: (*Stands up and moves to the foot of the bed.*)

20

MR. ANDREWS: (*Turns around in place.*)

"DR." COLE: Hello, Jeffrey.

JEFFREY: (*Lies down.*)

"DR." COLE: (*Conducts examination in silence.*)
                        (*Five doctors appear in the doorway.*)

"DR." COLE: (*Swallows and stands as if at attention. Moves aside as the other five position themselves around the bed.*)

DOCTORS: (*Nod and smile in varying chorus.*)

DR. ABRAMS: Mr. and Mrs. Andrews. I'm Dr. Abrams. Hello, Jeffrey.

JEFFREY: Hi (*lies down*).

DR. ABRAMS: (*Lifts JEFFREY's gown to feel abdomen*) How have you been feeling?

JEFFREY: (*Shrugs*) Mmm, OK I guess.

MRS. ANDREWS: He's been acting kind of tired and fairly quiet the last few days.

DR. ABRAMS: I see. Dr. Ellis. (*Steps aside and faces mother more directly.*) Anything else?

MRS. ANDREWS: Well, he also started running a temperature and that's when I called the doctor and he saw Jeffrey and sent us here.

DR. ELLIS: (*Feels around JEFFREY's abdomen*) Hi, Jeffrey.

DR. WESSON: (*Walks over to the door, looks at the temperature chart*) He's about 99 now.

DR. ABRAMS: (*Turning to parents*) We are going to do some tests, some of which Jeffrey may have already had, but which we may want to repeat here; and as soon as we have some results, probably tomorrow afternoon or so, we'll let you know. Do you have any questions now?

MR. AND MRS. ANDREWS: (*Shake heads.*)

MR. ANDREWS: Thank you, doctor.
                        (*Doctors smile and leave:* ABRAMS *with* ELLIS, *followed by* WESSLEY *and* WESSON, *then* CELLARS, *followed by* COLE.)

21

SCENE 3: *In the hallway outside* JEFFREY's *room after the examination.*

DR. ABRAMS: (*Motions the doctors down the hallway.*)

DR. ELLIS: (*While walking*) Well, what do you think?

DR. ABRAMS: We'll have to wait for the results of the bone marrow, but from the count that Dr. Manley called in (*shaking his head, downcast expression*) we have another one. Ada, are you going to take him?

DR. ELLIS: Yes.

DR. ABRAMS: I'd also order some cultures for that fever, so we can see what we have. Who else do we have to see this evening?

DR. WESSLEY: I think that's it.

(*The doctors proceed down the stairs.*)

SCENE 4: JEFFREY's *room, 10 minutes after the doctors have left.*

MRS. ANDREWS: Well, it looks like your dinner is here.

(STUDENT AIDE *with tray enters the room.*)

STUDENT AIDE: (*Takes the tray from the side of the night table by the bed and sets it up for* JEFFREY. *Places the tray on it.*)

(STUDENT AIDE *leaves.*)

MRS. ANDREWS: (*Walks over to the bed*) That looks good. You have spaghetti and salad and bread and milk and Jello.

JEFFREY: Yuk!

MRS. ANDREWS: Oh come on, Jeffrey. Try and eat at least some of it.

JEFFREY: (*Shakes his head.*)

MR. ANDREWS: Jeffrey.

JEFFREY: (*Unenthusiastically picks up the fork and picks at the food.*)

MRS. ANDREWS: (*Opens the milk*) Would you like me to butter your bread?

JEFFREY: OK.

> (TV MAN *knocks on the opened door and steps into the room.*)

TV MAN: Do you want the TV?

MR. ANDREWS: (*Walks over to the doorway.*)

TV MAN: It's two dollars a day or you can pay for a week in advance.

MR. ANDREWS: (*Reaches into his pocket and hands the man $2.00.*)

TV MAN: (*Walks over to the TV and plugs the hookup in. Walks over to* JEFFREY's *bed and demonstrates use of the remote control without a word. Leaves the control on the bed by the pillow. Writes a receipt and hands it to* MR. ANDREWS.)

MR. ANDREWS: (*Takes the receipt*) Thanks.

> (TV MAN *leaves the room.*)

MRS. ANDREWS: Well now, Jeffrey, do you think that you could eat a little?

JEFFREY: (*Shakes his head in an unspecified direction and nibbles at the bread.*) I have to go to the bathroom. (*Puts the bread down in the spaghetti.*)

MRS. ANDREWS: Do you need some help?

JEFFREY: No.

MR. ANDREWS: (*Picks up the tray.*)

JEFFREY: (*Climbs down and goes into the bathroom, next to the bed.*)

MRS. ANDREWS: Don't forget to use the container. (*Walks around to the bathroom*) Wash your hands.

JEFFREY: (*Comes out of the bathroom and shakes out his hands.*)

MR. ANDREWS: (*Holds up the tray.*)

JEFFREY: (*Crawls up onto the bed.*)

MRS. ANDREWS: Do you want any more?

JEFFREY: Uh uh (*shaking his head*).

MRS. ANDREWS: (*Lifts up the tray and puts it at the end of the unmade bed*) I guess someone will come for it.

(THE ANDREWS *sit silently and watch the TV for an hour.*)

23

VOICE OVER LOUDSPEAKER: All children in their rooms. (*Lights in the hallway go off. Children can be heard talking in their rooms; the TVs are still on.*)

MRS. ANDREWS: I think that we are going to go home now, Jeff.

JEFFREY: (*Whimpers.*)

MRS. ANDREWS: Ericka has been with the neighbors all day and I should get home. Daddy and I haven't had any dinner yet either. We'll be here first thing in the morning. Is there anything I can bring you?

JEFFREY: (*Shakes his head.*)

MRS. ANDREWS: (*Stands up, picks up her coat, and walks over to the bed. Bends over and gives* JEFFREY *a hug and kiss.*)

MR. ANDREWS: (*Walks over to the bed. Bends over and kisses* JEFF *on the forehead*) Good night, son.

MRS. ANDREWS: (*Walking to the doorway*) Do you want the light out?

JEFFREY: (*Shakes his head.*)

(MR. AND MRS. ANDREWS *leave.* MRS. ANDREWS *looks back.*)

JEFFREY: (*Turns over away from the doorway and cries himself to sleep.*)

SCENE 5: *Outside* JEFFREY'S *room, the next morning, Tuesday, 8:30 a.m.*

(JEFFREY *is sitting up in bed watching a morning children's show. A group of unfamiliar hospital personnel stand outside the room, pulling carts of dangling metal charts behind them. Some wear short coats, some long coats, some white pants and coats, and one wears a light green nurse's uniform.*)

DR. ESTERSON: That's Jeffrey Andrews, a possible leukemic. Heme is going to do a bone marrow later this morning. Sid, do you want to give us a little of the history and the results of the physical?

"DR." COLE: Well, I didn't get to finish it. The hematologists came and then his dinner came. I did talk to the mother some though, when they were leaving. I'll finish it today.

DR. ESTERSON: Lynn, do you have anything to add?

DR. MC PHEARSON: Well, when I went in to do the physical he was already asleep and I didn't want to wake him. His parents had already left for the night.

DR. ESTERSON: See that you look at him today, preferably before the hematologists make their rounds or do the marrow. I'll make my comment then. I did see him before he went to sleep. (*Pause. Then, as they move down the hall*) The next patient is Faith Welder.

"DR." COLE: "Heme" is certainly packing them in.

DR. ESTERSON: How is the abscess?

DR. MC PHEARSON: The surgeons are coming up again today to look at it.

DR. ESTERSON: (*Shaking her head*) So soon after diagnosis. Not a good sign.

(*The group of personnel walk on down the hall.*)

SCENE 6: FAITH'S *room, moments later,* 8:45 *a.m.*

(FAITH *is propped up in bed looking out the door. The TV is on, but neither she nor her mother, seated near the bed, seem to be watching it.*)

(*The personnel that were standing outside* JEFFREY'S ROOM *now enter.*)

FAITH: (*Whimpers and looks over to her mother.*)

DR. ESTERSON AND DR. MC PHEARSON: (*Approach the bed*) Hi, Faith.

FAITH: (*Starts to cry.*)

MRS. WELDER: Oh Faith, they're only going to look. She always cries when anyone in white comes to the door.

DR. ESTERSON AND DR. MC PHEARSON: (*Lift up* FAITH'S *gown and look at the dressing, then look up at each other. Pull the gown down*) All right, Faith. Thank you.

25

FAITH: (*Stops crying.*)
(*The group of personnel leaves the room.*)

SCENE 7: JEFFREY's *room later that morning,* 9:30 *a.m.*

(JEFFREY *is sitting up in bed watching TV and drawing on the back of an old flow sheet.*)

(MRS. ANDREWS *peeks in and enters.*)

JEFFREY: Hi.

MRS. ANDREWS: (*Comes over to the bed and bends over to kiss* JEFFREY) How do you feel?

JEFFREY: (*Looking up at the TV*) OK I guess.

MRS. ANDREWS: I bought you something.

JEFFREY: (*No response.*)

MRS. ANDREWS: Do you want to open it? Here (*places the package on the tray to* JEFFREY's *drawing*).

JEFFREY: (*Casually opens the package while looking at the TV.*)

MRS. ANDREWS: Do you like it?

JEFFREY: (*Turns from TV*) Where's daddy?

MRS. ANDREWS: He's at work. He'll be here after lunch. He had to go in and check on some things. Maybe later you and your father could work on it.

JEFFREY: (*Looks back at the TV.*)

MRS. ANDREWS: Ericka hopes you are feeling better. Grandma called to see how you were doing. Did you have a good breakfast?

JEFFREY: (*No response.*)

MRS. ANDREWS: What did you have?

JEFFREY: (*No response.*)

MRS. ANDREWS: (*Takes off her coat and puts it on the empty bed. She pulls the chair over next to the bed and sits beside* JEFFREY.)

(ROBERTA, *carrying her tray of equipment, enters.*)

ROBERTA: Hello, Jeffrey. I want to do a finger stick.

JEFFREY: (*Whimpers.*)

26

ROBERTA: It won't hurt. I just need some blood to look at (*takes* JEFFREY's *hand and washes it with an alcohol wipe*).

JEFFREY: (*Watching her every move*) Tell me when you are going to stick me.

ROBERTA: Now. (*Sticks* JEFFREY's *finger and squeezes the blood from it into small pipettes.*) OK, Jeffrey. Thank you.

(ROBERTA *leaves.*)

MRS. ANDREWS: Now that wasn't so bad now, was it?

JEFFREY: (*No response.*)

MRS. ANDREWS: Has anyone been in to see you yet today?

JEFFREY: (*Shrugs.*)

MRS. ANDREWS: Were any of the doctors in today?

JEFFREY: Yeah.

MRS. ANDREWS: What did they do?

JEFFREY: Nothing.

MRS. ANDREWS: Oh (*voice fades off*).

(DR. ELLIS *enters.*)

DR. ELLIS: Hi, Jeff. Hello, Mrs. Andrews, could I speak with you?

MRS. ANDREWS: (*Quickly rises and follows* DR. ELLIS *out into the hallway.*)

DR. ELLIS: There is one procedure that we must do here to be sure of what Jeffrey has, and to rule out other possibilities. The procedure is known as a bone marrow. A needle is inserted into the hip to aspirate a small part of the marrow and then we examine it under the microscope.

MRS. ANDREWS: I see.

DR. ELLIS: We'll do the procedure in the treatment room up here. After we have the results, sometime after lunch, we will talk with you. Is your husband coming up today?

MRS. ANDREWS: He'll be coming in after lunch.

DR. ELLIS: Good; have the nurses let us know when he arrives. I'll be back in a few minutes to get Jeffrey.

(DR. ELLIS *walks down to the nurses'
station.* MRS. ANDREWS *enters the room and sits down next
to the bed.*)

JEFFREY: What did she want?

MRS. ANDREWS: They are going to do a test to see what is
wrong with you.

JEFFREY: Will it hurt?

MRS. ANDREWS: I don't know, Jeffrey. (*Rubs* JEFFREY's *forehead and brushes away his hair.*)

JEFFREY: (*Turns away and stares fixedly at the TV through
the rest of the program.*)

(*After awhile,* NURSE LYONS *enters with a wheelchair.*)

NURSE LYONS: OK, Jeffrey, I'm going to take you down to
the treatment room.

JEFFREY: (*Whimpers*) What are they going to do?

NURSE LYONS: A bone marrow.

JEFFREY: Will it hurt?

NURSE LYONS: Well, maybe a little at first. But they will give
you something. (*Lifts* JEFFREY *out of bed and into the
wheelchair*) All set? Mrs. Andrews you can wait here
or in the hall if you want.

MRS. ANDREWS: I'll wait here (*smiles*).

(NURSE LYONS *and* JEFFREY *go down
to the treatment room.*)

SCENE 8: *Treatment room on the thirteenth floor, later
that morning,* 11:15 *a.m.*

(DR. ELLIS *is standing at the examining table with assorted
medical students and interns gathered about her.*)

(NURSE LYONS *wheels* JEFFREY *into the
treatment room and closes the door.*)

DR. ELLIS: OK, let's get you up on the table and over on
your tummy.

JEFFREY: (*Whimpers as two students walk over to lift him
onto the table.*)

(NURSE LYONS *leaves.*)

28

DR. ELLIS: This won't hurt. All I'm doing is feeling around your hip and then I'm going to wash it up. (*Turns from* JEFFREY, *puts on gloves, turns back and begins to wash hip area with iodine*) I'll tell you when I put the needle in (*gets syringe ready*).

JEFFREY: (*Begins to howl.*)

DR. ELLIS: OK, Jeff. (*The needle is in.*)

JEFFREY: (*Bellows*) Take it out!

DR. ELLIS: I'm just numbing it. It will be out soon.

JEFFREY: Is that all now?

DR. ELLIS: (*Feels around*) No, not yet. (*Makes aspiration.*)

JEFFREY: (*Shrieks.*)

DR. ELLIS: (*Nods to a* MEDICAL STUDENT.)

MEDICAL STUDENT: (*Holds* JEFFREY's *arms down.*)

DR. ELLIS: OK, now, Jeffrey, you really have to hold still now. (DR. ELLIS *removes the needle and hands it to the technician.*)

ROBERTA: (*Splatters some slides with the contents of the syringe.*)

DR. ELLIS: How is it?

ROBERTA: It should be OK.

DR. ELLIS: (*Turning back to* JEFFREY) Do you want a Band-Aid?

JEFFREY: (*Nods yes.*)

DR. ELLIS: (*Takes a Band-Aid from the procedure tray and puts it on* JEFFREY) I think you can take him back to his room now. Thank you, Jeffrey. Why don't you see that they give him some juice or something when he gets back? (*Turning to* JEFFREY) Would you like something?

JEFFREY: (*Sniffles and passively nods.*)

SCENE 9: *Later, in* JEFFREY's *room.*

(MRS. ANDREWS *is standing next to the bed.*)

        (*The* MEDICAL STUDENT *wheels* JEFFREY *into the room, lifts him onto the bed, and leaves.*)

MRS. ANDREWS: It looks like your lunch is here, Jeffrey. Are you hungry?

JEFFREY: Where's Dad?

MRS. ANDREWS: He'll be here after lunch. Why don't you eat some lunch?

JEFFREY: I don't feel like it.

MRS. ANDREWS: OK. I understand. Why don't you watch the TV. Bozo should be on now; or color. Maybe when I come back you'll feel like eating. (*Lifts the tray off the bed table and places it on the empty bed. Puts the crayons and the coloring book before him.*)

JEFFREY: Where are you going?

MRS. ANDREWS: Just to get a cup of coffee. I'll be back shortly.

(MRS. ANDREWS *leaves the room.*)

SCENE 10: *Hallway near the nurses' station, immediately following.*

(MRS. ANDREWS *passes by and the anthropologist steps forward.*)

MYRA: Hello, Mrs. Andrews, I'm Myra Bluebond. I'm doing a study of children in the hospital and I'd like to know if I could talk to Jeffrey.

MRS. ANDREWS: Yeah, sure. He'd probably enjoy the company. He's in his room coloring and watching the TV. I was on my way to get a cup of coffee.

MYRA: Well, take your time.

(MRS. ANDREWS *walks to the elevator.*)

SCENE 11: *Back in* JEFFREY'S *room later.*

(JEFFREY *is coloring and watching TV.*)

MYRA: (*Knocks on the opened door*) Hello, Jeffrey.

JEFFREY: (*Looking over to the door*) Hello.

(MYRA *enters, stands near the foot of the bed.*)

MYRA: I'm Myra Bluebond. I'm an anthropologist and I study children. I am interested in what they think about and what they talk about.

JEFFREY: (*Counting and pointing to fingers and hip*) One, two, three, four. I had four pricks. Two were for a bone marrow and two were blood tests. (*Pause*) Do you want to color?

MYRA: OK. For a little while.

JEFFREY AND MYRA: (*Color in silence for a while.*)

(MRS. ANDREWS *enters later.*)

MRS. ANDREWS: (*Coming over to the bed*) You seem· to be enjoying the company. I spoke to Dad and he'll be here soon.

JEFFREY: Good (*goes back to coloring*).

MYRA: I have to go now, Jeffrey. I enjoyed visiting with you.

JEFFREY: Will you come back tomorrow?

MYRA: Yes, if you want me to.

JEFFREY: Uh huh.

MYRA: OK. See you then.

(MYRA *leaves the room.*)

SCENE 12: FAITH's *room, later that afternoon,* 4:30 *p.m.*

(FAITH *is sitting up in bed peering into the hallway.* MYRA *is about to enter.* NURSE WALTON *walks by.*)

NURSE WALTON: Isn't she cute? It's such a terrible thing for them and their families.

MYRA: What is?

NURSE WALTON: This disease, you know. She was just diagnosed a few weeks ago and now she's back again. That's not good. She cries whenever we come in to do something, even make the bed; and the medicine—forget it! But she'll learn. She'll get used to it. They all do, poor things. (*Walks on down the hallway, shaking her head.*)

31

MYRA. (*From the doorway*) Hi, Faith.

> (MYRA *enters the room, goes over to the bed.*)

FAITH: Mommy went to dinner and she didn't ask me.

MYRA: She didn't ask you?

FAITH: (*Shaking her head*) No!

MYRA: Should she ask you?

FAITH: Yes. (*Pause*) I get medicine in my ice cream.

MYRA: You get medicine in your ice cream?

FAITH: And I take pills too. (*Pause*) I don't go potty. I go potty in Band-Aids. (*Points to the black and blue marks on her hands and then looks over at* MYRA's *hands*) You don't have any. (*She quickly turns her head to the doorway. Her brow begins to furrow.*)

> (NURSE WALTON *enters with a urine bag.*)

FAITH: (*Shrieks and cries.*)

NURSE WALTON: Oh, come on Faith. (*Takes off the used bag and puts on a new one*) There now, was that so bad?

FAITH: (*Nods.*)

NURSE WALTON: (*Laughs*) OK.

> (NURSE WALTON *leaves.*)

FAITH: (*Whimpers, then quiets down.*)

> (NURSE WALTON *reenters with a heat pack.*)

FAITH: (*Starts to cry again.*)

NURSE WALTON: (*Over by the bed lifting up* FAITH's *nightgown*) This is going to make it feel better. (*Places the heat pack on* FAITH) See? (*Pulls nightgown down.*)

FAITH: (*Begins to calm down*) Thank you, it made my boobie feel better.

NURSE WALTON: (*Smiles*) I saw your mom, she's on her way in, so I'm going to borrow Myra for a while. Is that all right?

FAITH: (*Nods.*)

MYRA: I'll see you tomorrow, Faith. 'Bye.

FAITH: (*Waves.*)

> (NURSE WALTON *and* MYRA *leave.*)

SCENE 13: JEFFREY'S *room, later that afternoon,* 5:00 *p.m.*

(JEFFREY *is propped up in bed. The TV is on, but he is look-ing out the doorway.*)

JEFFREY: (*As* MYRA *passes by the doorway*) My mom and dad went to talk to the doctor. They're going to tell them what's wrong with me and when I can go home, maybe. (*Looks down.*)

(MYRA *enters.*)

MYRA: (*Walks over to the bed*) Do you want to talk or anything?

JEFFREY: No (*Pause*) Please stay with me. Please.

MYRA: For a little while.

JEFFREY: (*Drifts off to sleep.*)

MYRA: (*Writes him a note.*)

(MYRA *leaves.*)

SCENE 14: JEFFREY'S *room, the next morning, Wednesday,* 9:30 *a.m.*

(JEFFREY *is propped up in bed playing with a stamper set on his tray and watching TV while being transfused.* MRS. ANDREWS *sits by the bed.*)

NURSE STEVENS: (*On entering the room*) Good morning, Jeffrey. Just want to check how the blood is doing.

JEFFREY: See my mommy's red nose? That's from me. That's from crying. Everybody cries when they see me. I'm pretty sick, you know.

NURSE STEVENS: (*Checking blood pressure*) But you'll be better soon.

(*Silence.*)

MRS. ANDREWS: And then we'll go home and you'll see Ericka and . . .

JEFFREY: (*Interrupts*) I got lots of presents last night. I got a truck and a stamper set from my grandma and I

33

got Candyland from my other grandma. Do you want to play?

NURSE STEVENS: Well, I have some things I have to do first this morning, but I'll come back later, maybe after snacktime, and we can play.

JEFFREY: (*Grimaces in disappointment and returns to the stamper set.*)

(NURSE STEVENS *leaves*; MYRA *enters the room, several minutes later.*)

MYRA: Hi, Jeffrey.

JEFFREY: (*Puts down the stamper*) See my mommy's red nose? That's from me. That's from crying. Everybody cries when they see me.

MRS. ANDREWS: Oh, Jeffrey. (*Aside, to* MYRA) I try not to cry in front of him. But he knows. I hope I did the right thing by coming here. My girlfriend said that we should have gone to Crickstone Memorial, but I don't know. It all happened so quickly and I didn't think it would be anything like leukemia. My mother says we're here already and they treat Jeff really nice. All the doctors and nurses have been really good. They let us stay as long as we want to. I have to go home, though, and take care of my other one. Ericka. I think I have a picture of her. (*Digs in her purse for the wallet and shows the picture.*)

MYRA: She's really cute.

JEFFREY: Let me see.

MRS. ANDREWS: (*Holds up the picture for* JEFFREY *and then closes the wallet and puts it back in her purse.*)

JEFFREY: (*Continues to stamp.*)

MRS. ANDREWS: (*To* MYRA) Well, I have to take care of her too. She's our baby. It's too much for my mother. I was suspicious, but I never thought it was really leuk— (*catches herself*). A neighbor's child died from it and it started the same way. (*Cries and wipes eyes*) I wonder how much I should say in front of him. He probably doesn't understand all of it though. But there are lots of sick children around here. A lot of them look a lot worse than Jeffrey, like those two boys across the hall. Is it curable? (*Before a response can be made*) I told Jeffrey not to make fun or stare at them, but you know how kids are. My mother is coming up later.

JEFFREY: (*Seemingly so engrossed in what he is doing that he isn't listening*) She cries a lot too.

MRS. ANDREWS: (*Embarrassed*) Oh, Jeffrey.

VOICE ON LOUDSPEAKER: Myra, you're wanted on line 1.

MYRA: Jeffrey, you'll have to excuse me. I'll be back this afternoon if you want me to.

JEFFREY: OK. 'Bye.

MRS. ANDREWS: 'Bye. (*Stares at* JEFFREY.)

(MYRA *leaves.*)

SCENE 15: FAITH's *room, later that afternoon,* 3:00 p.m.

(*Crowded around* FAITH's *bed are two surgeons, working on the abscess, a resident holding her legs, a nurse holding* FAITH's *arm, and a* MEDICAL STUDENT *on "stand by."* FAITH *still manages to thrash a bit and scream for her mother.*)

(*The procedure complete, all leave the room en masse except for the nurse, who tucks* FAITH *in and then leaves.* MRS. WELDER *enters, obviously upset, and walks past* FAITH's *bed to the chair by the window.*)

FAITH: (*Cries, opening and closing her outstretched hands*) Mommy! Mommy! Mommy! Mommy!

MRS. WELDER: (*Does not look at* FAITH, *but buries her head in her hands, then looks alternately at the ceiling and the floor.*)

(NURSE LOCKNER *enters.*)

NURSE LOCKNER: (*Comes over to* MRS. WELDER) Would you like a glass of water?

MRS. WELDER: (*Shakes head.*)

(NURSE LOCKNER *leaves, and returns later with a glass of water. She brings it over to* MRS. WELDER *and helps her out of the room.*)

FAITH: (*Cries*) Mommy! Mommy! (*more loudly, as the movement of her hands quickens*).

35

MRS. WELDER: (*Outside the room with* NURSE LOCKNER) It's times like this when I think about what she knows, and I know how sick she really is. She's in there, screaming her head off, and there's nothing I can do!

NURSE LOCKNER: It's good to cry. Everybody has to.

MRS. WELDER: (*Deep sigh.*)

NURSE LOCKNER: OK?

MRS. WELDER: (*Nods.*)

(MRS. WELDER *enters* FAITH'S *room, stands by the bed, leans over the rail, and brushes the sweat-soaked strands of hair from* FAITH'S *eyes.*)

FAITH: (*Pants and finally calms. Looks up at her mother*) Why did they do it, Mommy?

MRS. WELDER: Because your boobie was sick and they had to get the sickie out.

FAITH: Why did they hurt my boobie?

MRS. WELDER: Because your boobie was sick and they had to get the sickie out.

FAITH: Why did they hurt my boobie?

MRS. WELDER: (*Getting less and less patient*) Because your boobie was sick and they had to get the sickie out.

FAITH: (*More emphatic, less whiney*) Why did they hurt my boobie?

MRS. WELDER: Because your boobie was sick and they had to get the sickie out.

FAITH: (*Voice raised*) Why did they hurt my boobie?

MRS. WELDER: (*No response.*)

FAITH: (*Voice raised*) Why did they hurt my boobie?

MRS. WELDER: When you're older then I'll tell you why.

FAITH: (*Begins to relax, then drifts off to sleep.*)

SCENE 16: *Doctors' conference room (located next to the nurses' station), an hour later, 4:30 p.m.*

(*Doctors and medical students are giving reports on various patients as part of "house staff" afternoon rounds. There is intermittent scolding, joking, and chiding.*)

(*The "heme team" enters.*)

DR. ELLIS: Have you gotten to Jeffrey Andrews yet?

DR. ESTERSON: No, not yet.

DR. ELLIS: Well, he had his first dose of vincristine and we're starting him on the prednisone. He got the blood all right?

DR. ESTERSON: Yes, and he looks a good deal better.

DR. ELLIS: How is the mother doing?

DR. ESTERSON: The nurses say that she cries a lot but seems to be adjusting. There seems to be some disbelief, though.

DR. WESSLEY: That's to be expected. There is usually some denial and that is coupled with or quickly followed by guilt. Might even occur during the first hospitalization. We explained to them that it is in no way their fault, that they couldn't have prevented it, that they did the right things, but (*puts up hand and shrugs*).

DR. ESTERSON: The nurses say that the mother seems concerned about whether they came to the right hospital.

"HEME TEAM": (*Exchange knowing smirks.*)

DR. ELLIS: Wait 'til she gets to the "parents' group."

DR. WESSLEY: Well, be supportive. Often the guilt turns to anger. This can last even after the child dies, or quiet down when the child is in the terminal stages and re-emerge after the child dies. But with these parents— well, it's hard to say now.

"DR." COLE: Do they ever reach a point of acceptance?

DR. WESSON: Some do. Some people in psychiatry did a study of some of the parents here. There must be a copy of it around somewhere.

DR. WESSLEY: I have one if you want to take a look at it.

"DR." COLE: (*Nods.*)

DR. ELLIS: I think that we can let him go home tomorrow if he doesn't run a temperature.

DR. ESTERSON: He's been normal since yesterday.

DR. ELLIS: OK. I'll talk with the parents today and if there are any problems let me know. Make sure that they understand about the medication and the clinic on Monday.

(*The "heme team" leaves the doctors' conference room and continues down the hall.* DR. ELLIS *stops in* JEFFREY'S *room.*)

SCENE: 17: JEFFREY'S *room after the conference, Wednesday, 5:15 p.m., the time late-afternoon rounds occur.*

(DR. ELLIS *is standing at the side of the bed,* MRS. ANDREWS *is at the foot.* JEFFREY *is propped up.*)

DR. ELLIS: Well, Jeffrey, I think that we are going to let you go home tomorrow, if you don't run a temperature or anything. How would that be?

JEFFREY: OK I guess.

DR. ELLIS: Lie back for a minute, Jeff, and let me feel your tummy. (*Feeling* JEFFREY'S *stomach*) Mrs. Andrews, has he been eating at all?

MRS. ANDREWS: Not very well.

DR. ELLIS: Well, with the new medicine that we'll be giving him his appetite should pick up a little. Do either of you have any questions?

MRS. ANDREWS: (*Looks at* JEFFREY) No, thank you.

DR. ELLIS: OK. Jeffrey, I'll see you in the morning before you go home. The nurse will explain about the medication and the clinic.

MRS. ANDREWS: (*Nods.*)

(DR. ELLIS *leaves the room, passing* MYRA, *who is just entering.*)

MYRA: Hi, Jeffrey.

JEFFREY: I'm going home tomorrow.

MYRA: You are? That's really good.

JEFFREY: Yeah.

MRS. ANDREWS: I'm really pleased. He's looking better already. That blood really seems to have perked him up a bit.

38

JEFFREY: (*To* MYRA) Do you want to play Candyland?

MYRA: OK.

JEFFREY: What color do you want? I'm blue.

MYRA: I'll be yellow.

MRS. ANDREWS: Since Myra's here, I'll go out and call your father and tell him the good news.

(MRS. ANDREWS *leaves the room as they continue the game for a while.*)

JEFFREY: I got blood today. It only hurt when they put the needle in.

MYRA: It didn't hurt when it was going in?

JEFFREY: No. I didn't cry.

MYRA: You didn't cry at all when it was going in?

JEFFREY: I only cried a little when they stuck me. That lady stuck me today, too. You know who I mean.

MYRA: The one with the white coat and the tray?

JEFFREY: Yeah. But she's not a doctor.

MYRA: How do you know?

JEFFREY: I don't know, but she's not a doctor. That I know. (*Pause*) Your move.

VOICE ON LOUDSPEAKER: All children up and about to the dining room for supper.

JEFFREY: That's not for me. I can only go out for rides sometimes.

(MRS. ANDREWS *appears in the doorway.* KITCHEN AIDE *is standing beside her with a tray.*)

MYRA: It looks like your dinner is here and so is your Mom.

MRS. ANDREWS: I saw the cart and came back (*takes the tray and walks over to the bed*).

MYRA: I'll go now, Jeff, and let you have your dinner.

JEFFREY: But I want to finish playing.

MRS. ANDREWS: But I think that you should try and eat some dinner before it gets cold. You'll need your strength. (*Sets up tray.*)

MYRA: I'll try to stop by tomorrow before you leave.

JEFFREY: OK. 'Bye.

(MYRA *leaves.*)

39

SCENE 18: JEFFREY'S *room, the following morning Thursday,* 9:00 *a.m.*

(JEFFREY *is sitting up in bed looking out the door.*)

(MRS. ANDREWS *enters.*)

MRS. ANDREWS: (*Walking toward the bed*) Good morning. You're dressed already.

JEFFREY: Yeah, the young man doctor said I can go home today so I got dressed. I dressed myself.

MRS. ANDREWS: How do you feel?

JEFFREY: Much better.

MRS. ANDREWS: Did the doctor say anything else?

JEFFREY: No (*quizzically*).

MRS. ANDREWS: Well, maybe I should go out and check when you can leave. I didn't expect you to be going home this morning and Daddy won't be here to take us home 'til this afternoon.

JEFFREY: But I want to go now.

MRS. ANDREWS: Well, I'll go check.

(MRS. ANDREWS *leaves.*)

JEFFREY: (*Jumps off the bed and stands for awhile in the doorway.*)

(AIDE WASHINGTON *walks by the doorway.*)

JEFFREY: I'm going home today.

AIDE WASHINGTON: Well, that's real fine.

(AIDE WASHINGTON *continues on down the hall.* MRS. ANDREWS *returns.*)

JEFFREY: Can we go now?

MRS. ANDREWS: Well, soon. We have to wait for your medicine to come up.

JEFFREY: And then can we go?

MRS. ANDREWS: I think so, whenever Daddy gets here. I'll go and give him a call. And if he can't come, maybe Grandpa can come down.

40

(MRS. ANDREWS *walks down the hall-way to make the phone call.* NURSE RICHARDS *walks by and stops at the doorway.*)

NURSE RICHARDS: Jeffrey, is your mother here?

JEFFREY: She went to call my father so we can go home. And if he can't come to get us, Grandpa is gonna come.

NURSE RICHARDS: Well, when she gets back have her stop by at the desk.

(NURSE RICHARDS *turns and walks down the hall. Later,* MRS. ANDREWS *returns, after making the call.*)

JEFFREY: (*Steps back into the room.*)

MRS. ANDREWS: Dad can't make it, but Grandpa is coming.

JEFFREY: Is Grandma coming?

MRS. ANDREWS: No. She has to wait for Ericka to come home from nursery school.

JEFFREY: (*Turns and walks around*) The nurse wants you.

MRS. ANDREWS: Where?

JEFFREY: (*Exasperated*) At the desk.

(MRS. ANDREWS *leaves.*)

JEFFREY: (*Paces around for awhile.*)

(MRS. ANDREWS *returns.*)

JEFFREY: When are we going to leave already?

MRS. ANDREWS: As soon as we can get your things together.

JEFFREY: (*Begins to gather up his toys and "stuff."*)

(NURSE RICHARDS *enters, carrying a large paper bag.*)

NURSE RICHARDS: I thought you might need this.

MRS. ANDREWS: (*Chuckles and takes the bag*) He seems to have accumulated a lot more stuff. Jeffrey, why don't you put your toys in here?

MRS. ANDREWS: (*Picks up the clothes and somewhat carelessly puts them in an overnight bag.*) Well, I think that's it.

(JEFFREY *and* MRS. ANDREWS *leave the room,* MRS. ANDREWS *carrying the suitcase and* JEFFREY *carrying his bag of "stuff."*)

41

SCENE 19: *Nurses' station moments later, Thursday,* 10:30 *a.m.*

(JEFFREY *and his mother stand before the nurses' station as they had when they entered the hospital.* NURSE RICHARDS *walks forward with a bottle of pills in her hand and stands by the receptionist.*)

NURSE RICHARDS: (*Holding out the bottle*) You know that Jeffrey is supposed to get four of these four times a day, it's on the bottle. He's to go to the oncology clinic on Monday morning. Here is your clinic card (*hands* MRS. ANDREWS *the clinic card and the medication*). You stop at 103 first and they will do a blood count. Then you go to the pharmacy line and wait for the prescription. Wait a minute, let me check on that. (*Walks to the back of the nurses' station and talks to* DR. ESTERSON *and returns*) No, you don't have to go to the pharmacy; his doctor, Dr. Ellis, will have it. Then you go up to the tumor clinic. It's on the third floor, past X-ray. There'll be signs when you get off the elevator. I guess that's it then. Do you have any questions?

MRS. ANDREWS: No. Thank you.

NURSE RICHARDS: Jeffrey, goodbye.

JEFFREY: (*Looks up*) 'Bye.

MRS. ANDREWS: Is there anything else we have to do?

NURSE RICHARDS: No, that's it.

MRS. ANDREWS: Jeffrey, do you want to wait here or downstairs for Grandpa?

JEFFREY: Downstairs.

(MRS. ANDREWS *and* JEFFREY *turn and walk toward the elevator with a purposeful step.*)

NURSE RICHARDS: I wonder how long it will be before we see him again (*reaches for a chart*).

RECEPTIONIST: (*Raises her eyebrows and nods knowingly.*)

ACT II: THE FIRST REMISSION

SCENE 1: *The oncology clinic waiting room, the following Monday, 9:30 a.m.*

(JEFFREY *and his mother pass through the double doors.* MRS. ANDREWS *holds* JEFFREY *with one hand and in the other she clutches a sheaf of papers.* MRS. ANDREWS *looks about the waiting room, bewildered. She sees groups of parents standing and talking, some sitting and talking, some sitting in silence looking rigidly at a blank wall. A group of children are seated around a table in the middle of the circle of chairs where most of the parents sit. One little boy, about* JEFFREY'S *age, is bald, two others coloring with him are extremely pudgy. There are children in the aisle playing catch and another group of children off to the side playing with Lincoln Logs. One boy, too big for his mother's lap, is lying there uncomfortably, while another boy, looking quite pale and crying, is on the couch.*)

MRS. ANDREWS: (*Smiles to a woman seated next to the empty chair she is standing in front of speaks to* JEFFREY.) You wait here, I'll be right back.

JEFFREY: (*Whimpers.*)

MRS. ANDREWS: OK. Come on with me (*holding his hand*).
                    (*They move out of the waiting room area to the receptionist's desk;* JEFFREY *draws closer to his mother.*)

SCENE 2: *Receptionist's desk near the treatment and conference room area.*

MRS. ANDREWS: (*Hands the card to the receptionist over the divider.*)

RECEPTIONIST: (*Takes the card*) Hello, Jeffrey. When the doctor is ready we'll call you. Did you stop for the blood test?

43

MRS. ANDREWS: Yes.

JEFFREY: (*Looks down at his pricked finger.*)

RECEPTIONIST: OK. We'll call you.

>(JEFFREY *and* MRS. ANDREWS *return to the waiting room area where they had entered.*)

SCENE 3: *Waiting room of the oncology clinic, moments later.*

MRS. ANDREWS: (*Takes* JEFFREY *over to the seat where they had first stopped and unbuttons his coat*) Jeffrey, I think that you can take that off now (*sits down*).

JEFFREY: (*Takes off the bandage and hands it to* MRS. ANDREWS, *gets up on her lap.*)

MRS. ANDREWS: (*Looks about and over to the woman sitting next to them* [MRS. STALLER].)

MRS. STALLER: There is a trash can over there.

MRS. ANDREWS: Thank you. Jeffrey, why don't you go over there and throw it away?

JEFFREY: (*Gets off his mother's lap somewhat hesitantly, and walks over to the trash can. On the way to and from he steals looks at the children playing. Immediately upon return, he climbs back up on his mother's lap.*)

MRS. STALLER: Is this your first time?

MRS. ANDREWS: Yes. Eh hem. (*Fondles* JEFFREY's *hair*) We just found out on Tuesday. Jeffrey, wouldn't you like to go over there and play with those children?

JEFFREY: Uh un (*shaking his head*).

MRS. ANDREWS: They look like they're having so much fun.

JEFFREY: (*Shakes his head and moves closer to his mother's chest.*)

MRS. ANDREWS: (*To* MRS. STALLER) He's not usually like this.

MRS. STALLER: Sometimes they go, sometimes they don't. Mine, it depends on how she feels. If she feels good she'll play over there all morning.

MRS. ANDREWS: All morning?

MRS. STALLER: Oh yes, sometimes it takes that long. We've been here some Mondays 'til one or one-thirty, what with waiting for the blood tests to come up, the results of the bone marrow, the medicines. (*Pause*) Are you going to the parents' meeting?

MRS. ANDREWS: I'm sorry, but I don't know what that is.

MRS. STALLER: It's where the parents get together and talk about what's on their minds. There's a social worker and a psychologist who lead the meetings. Sometimes the doctors come in and talk about different drugs. It lets us get away from the children for a while, too.

MRS. ANDREWS: Does everyone go?

MRS. STALLER: No. Some come every week, some come some weeks, and some never come.

MRS. ANDREWS: Well, I don't know. I'll have to see how Jeffrey's doing.

MRS. STALLER: I understand.

> (*After a period of silence,* DR. ISSACS *enters.*)

DR. ISSACS: (*Walking into the waiting-room area*) There is coffee in the conference room.

> (*Many of the parents rise. Some go over to the tables where the children are playing and then go to the conference room; some go directly to the conference room, waving to their children as they go.*)

DR. ISSACS: (*Walks over to* MRS. ANDREWS.) Hello, Mrs. Andrews?

MRS. ANDREWS: (*Smiles.*)

DR. ISSACS: I'm Dr. Issacs. Do you know about the parents' meetings?

MRS. ANDREWS: Yes, this lady was telling me about them.

DR. ISSACS: Will you come?

MRS. ANDREWS: Well, I don't know. (*Turning to* JEFFREY) Jeffrey, would you like to go play with the children?

JEFFREY: (*Emphatically shakes his head.*)

MRS. ANDREWS: (*Shrugs and looks up at* DR. ISSACS.)

DR. ISSACS: I guess you can bring him with you if you want.

MRS. ANDREWS: (*Looks down at* JEFFREY, *then up at* DR. IS- SACS) Yes, I think I'd like to.

(MRS. STALLER, DR. ISSACS, *and* MRS. ANDREWS, *with* JEFFREY *in her arms, all go to the conference room.*)

SCENE 4: *The conference room in the oncology clinic (used for the parents' meetings) immediately following.*

(MRS. STALLER, DR. ISSACS, MRS. ANDREWS, *and* JEFFREY *take seats. The meeting is already in progress,* MRS. BAXTER *is speaking.*)

DR. ISSACS: (*To those assembled*) Excuse me. I'd like to in- troduce Mrs. Andrews and her son, Jeffrey. This is their first visit to the clinic.

(NURSE GREEN *enters.*)

NURSE GREEN: (*Calls out*) Mrs. Richardson.

(MRS. RICHARDSON, *carrying an infant, rises and follows the nurse out into the hall.*)

MISS KOHNE: Mrs. Baxter, please continue.

MRS. BAXTER: (*With tears in her eyes and crying intermit- tently*) She'll never have a period. She'll never have children. I don't know what I'm going to tell Laura. She's going to ask sooner or later why she doesn't have a period, why she doesn't have breasts. Her sister— they're only ten months apart—has both. She is very precocious. (*Smiles*) I just don't know what to tell Laura, I don't even know. When Laura first went down to surgery we told her she had a mass that might have to come out. She didn't expect "the works" and, well, neither did we. We've told the other kids in two groups. One of the neighbor boys asked my boy if Laura's tu- mor was malignant. All the children know except the one that is closest to Laura. She came back from seeing Laura and said she looked awful. They tell each other everything, so we just wouldn't tell her.

I think she's going to lose her hair now too from that

medicine they give her, but I don't want to tell her. Maybe I should, but—(*voice trails off*). She doesn't look in the mirror anymore, ever since the first day, when she saw how skinny she was. She's been stuffing herself to get fat, but that machine will take her appetite away. Soon too. She's angry (*pause*). And she's depressed. Guess I am too.

I don't know what to do. I've talked to Sister Katherine. She's been real good. Oh (*voice trails off*). I don't know how much of the problem is Laura's and how much is mine. (*Cries.*) Thanks for letting me run on like this.

(*Silence.*)

MRS. HERBERT: Well, I'm having some problems with Marty lately. His teacher called me the other day. Marty's been acting kind of aggressive at school. The teacher says it's like he's real angry about something, but won't say what it is. Is there a personality type that leukemics develop? Maybe I should be sending him to a psychiatrist or something, or maybe *I* should go. (*Giggle.*)

MISS KOHNE: Do you think that Marty might be upset by your pregnancy?

MRS. HERBERT: I don't think so. We're all looking forward to the baby. (*Pause*) No. He seems worse just before he comes to clinic and then for a week or so after.

(*Many mothers nod in agreement.*)

(MRS. RICHARDSON *reenters the conference room and sits down.*)

MRS. MYERS: Steven, my older son, was doing really badly in school when Elliot was sick, and then when Richie died. They [Richie and Elliot] were in the hospital together.

MRS. HANDELMAN: I'm always having trouble with the school about Jennifer. They send her home for the littlest complaint.[1] I'm just not even going to bother send-

---

[1] Schools are informed about the child's condition through the doctor's examination form, which all children in public schools are required to have completed.

ing her back. Friends come around and ask why Jennifer can't go to school. I tell them that the doctors say that she should stay at home. Then they say, "Well, she comes outside and plays," and I say, "Well, that's what the doctors say." I don't tell them what Jenny's got. They don't all have to know. Then they'll start treating her special and I don't need any more of that.

MRS. RICHARDSON: I don't like the way my mother's spoiling the baby. I have a niece the same age and Mom makes the difference. I don't want that. I don't want her to grow up to be a freak or something. She'll be spoiled enough. She's the baby and I have three older boys. After all, she's going to be growing up here, here in the clinic, and she'll know things are different for her.

MRS. BAXTER: Yeah, that's another thing I don't like; the way people were always giving Laura money when she was in the hospital. What's she going to do with it? So I kept it.

(*Mothers join in a nervous laugh.*)

MRS. MYERS: I think people just give them things so that they'll feel better. I don't like them to do it. It's just not good for Elliot or for Steven. I used to tell them so, but I'm tired of telling them. If that's what they have to do, well—. Besides, it stops after awhile, I guess.

(*Brief silence.*)

DR. ISSACS: Dr. Wessley has someone that she would like to introduce to us, and since she has to leave soon, perhaps now would be a good time for her to do so.

DR. WESSLEY: (*Smiles to Dr. Issacs*) I'd like to introduce Miss Bluebond, a graduate student in anthropology at the University of Illinois, who is interested in doing a study of coping behavior with the children in the clinic. She'll explain it in more detail and answer any questions you might have. The doctors approve the study, but she wants to give you an idea of what she wants to do.

48

MYRA: Thank you Dr. Wessley. I am Myra Bluebond and as Dr. Wessley mentioned I am a graduate student in anthropology at the University of Illinois. My primary interest is in child culture, that is the world of the child —how he works, plays, thinks, expresses himself, how he communicates with adults and peers. I am particularly interested in children's concepts of self and view of the world—what anthropologists call world view— for example, concepts of birth, life, death, time, space.

These concepts are expressed in all forms of interaction: play, conversation, and fantasy, with adults and with peers. Expression is not, however, necessarily direct or of singular purpose. A curious statement may have a variety of meanings, of plans and purposes. For example, the statement "Mommy my foot hurts" may be a way of expressing pain, and/or gaining attention, getting more information about the condition that causes it, arousing sympathy, or making an excuse for not playing or for being relieved of a particular chore. Similarly, the child's statement, "Children don't die, do they, Mommy," may be a way of asking if they will die, of asking about his condition, or simply a statement of fact to be tested.

These statements arise out of situations which in turn affect the view that the child has of himself and the world around him.

I want to determine what kinds of expressions children use to express and to cope with what they themselves know and feel about themselves and others that they are in contact with in this clinic and outside in a variety of situations. As such, I will want to observe the children at play, when they are hospitalized, treated, etc.

I will act as an observer. I will talk with the child only when he speaks with me. At no time will I introduce the subject of his illness, or ask questions about his condition. I am interested in what is on the child's mind and what he chooses to express. I am interested in his means of communication and how he chooses to use them with regard to the variety of plans and purposes a child has.

Perhaps with this kind of information we will be able to communicate more effectively with these children.

DR. ISSACS: Thank you. It really sounds like an interesting project. Are there any questions?

MRS. MARTIN: At what age does a child know that he is dying?

MYRA: By the time a child is about two years old he knows about dead worms, animals, etc. He can also distinguish dead things from toys—realizing, at least at some level of consciousness that for the animal to be dead it once had to be alive. Toys were never alive. By the age of three, children can understand that they have a serious illness. All children, sick or well, from ages three on, fantasize and are concerned about dying. Perhaps these children—the leukemics—have even more cause to do so because of what they see happening around them, and because of what they are subjected to. How they come to know worry, and cope, and express these thoughts forms the major thrust of my research.

MRS. HERBERT : Do you think there is such a thing as a leukemic personality?

MYRA: I am really not sure, but answers to that question, or on the road to it, should come through a study such as this, where I will be focusing on their behavior and their thoughts.

DR. ISSACS: Are there any other questions?

(Silence.)

DR. ISSACS: Well then, I guess there are no objections. Since there are no questions and our time is about up, how about if we adjourn for the week?

(As the parents stand up and straggle out into the hall, some of the children come up to greet them. One boy, SETH, clutching a rolled picture in his hand,

*walks briskly toward his father, who is talking to another
parent.*)

SETH: (*Tugging at his father's pant leg*) Come on, you're
wasting time.

MR. WELLER: No, I was just talking to these people.

SETH: Come on, we can't waste time.

SCENE 5: *Waiting room of the oncology clinic, the following Monday,* 10:30 *a.m.*

(JEFFREY *and his mother pass through the double doors
with greater assurance than on the previous Monday.* MRS.
ANDREWS' *smiles are now definite and directed to the people
that she recognizes from the previous week.* JEFFREY *now
looks a little longer at the children gathering about the
table and taking toys from the cart nearby. They go directly
to the receptionist's area, where* MRS. ANDREWS *presents the
card without hesitation or comment. The receptionist
smiles and* JEFFREY *and* MRS. ANDREWS *walk back to the
waiting-room area.* MRS. ANDREWS *takes off her coat and* JEF-
FREY'S, *while he continues to stare at the children playing.*
MRS. ANDREWS *goes and hangs up the coats and returns.* JEF-
FREY, *still engrossed in observation of the other children,
does not seem to notice that she has gone and come back.*)

MRS. ANDREWS: I'm going to the meeting.

JEFFREY: (*Shakes his head and moves toward the children
playing, but remaining on the periphery.*)

O.T.S. 1: Would you like to sit with us and color?

JEFFREY: (*Shakes his head and takes a few steps back. He
sits down on the floor next to two boys—*SCOTT HELLER
and AARON THOMAS—*playing with Lincoln Logs.* MYRA
*is sitting on the floor with them. He plays by himself
watching these two boys play with each other.*)

(DR. WESSLEY *comes from the treat-
ment-room area over to the table in the waiting-room area.
Many children look up.*)

DR. WESSLEY: Scott.

SCOTT: (*Puts down his Lincoln Logs and stands up. Play-*

51

fully but languidly begins to go through DR. WESSLEY'S *lab coat pockets.*)

DR. WESSLEY: Come on, Scott.

(DR. WESSLEY *and* SCOTT *go back to the treatment-room area.*)

JEFFREY: (*Moves over to where* SCOTT *was playing and continues building in silence.*)

(SCOTT *returns from the treatment area and goes over to* MYRA *who is on the floor near* JEFFREY *and* AARON.)

SCOTT: (*Climbs into* MYRA'S *lap.*)

MYRA: What's happening?

SCOTT: Not good.

JEFFREY: (*Looks up.*)

MYRA: What do you mean not good?

SCOTT: (*Buries his head.*)

JEFFREY: (*Goes back to building.*)

(DR. ELLIS *enters the waiting-room area from the treatment-room area.*)

DR. ELLIS: Hi, Jeffrey. Where's your mother?

JEFFREY: She's at the meeting.

DR. ELLIS: How 'bout if you come with me and we'll go get her.

(JEFFREY *and* DR. ELLIS *walk down to the conference room and stand at the entrance.* MRS. ANDREWS *stands up and comes out.*)

DR. ELLIS: How are you?

MRS. ANDREWS: OK (*forces a smile*).

(DR. ELLIS, JEFFREY, *and* MRS. ANDREWS, *who takes* JEFFREY'S *hand, enter the treatment room.*)

SCENE 6: *The treatment room in the oncology clinic, later that morning, 11:20 a.m.*

(DR. ELLIS *riffles through some things on her desk and looks at a piece of paper.* MRS. ANDREWS *helps* JEFFREY *up onto the examination table.*

JEFFREY: (*Lies back as* DR. ELLIS *approaches the table.*)

DR. ELLIS: (*Pulling up* JEFFREY's *shirt and feeling his abdomen*) How are you feeling?

JEFFREY: OK, I guess.

DR. ELLIS: (*Pulling down* JEFFREY's *shirt*) OK, Jeffrey.

DR. ELLIS: (*Walks over to her desk and picks up a piece of paper*) Hemoglobin OK, Platelets OK, White count OK. (*Pause*) Does he complain of any bone pain?

MRS. ANDREWS: No, but he doesn't like to be held or touched much.

DR. ELLIS: I'm going to put the rubberband around now. (*Reaches for the elastic tubing on a table by the examining table and wraps it around* JEFFREY's *arm.*)

JEFFREY: I don't want it.

DR. ELLIS: What is the most important thing to remember?

JEFFREY: (*Whimpers*) To hold still.

DR. ELLIS: (*Takes the syringe from the table and injects it.*)

JEFFREY: (*Whimpers.*)

DR. ELLIS: Just a little bit more. (*Pulls out the syringe.*) Do you want a Band-Aid?

JEFFREY: (*Nods.*)

DR. ELLIS: (*Putting the Band-Aid on him*) There. Has he been any more active lately?

MRS. ANDREWS: Yes, somewhat.

DR. ELLIS: Back in school?

MRS. ANDREWS: Yes. Last Wednesday was his first day back.

DR. ELLIS: Well then, Jeffrey, I'll see you next week. Do you have any other questions, Mrs. Andrews?

MRS. ANDREWS: No. Thank you.

           (JEFFREY *leaves ahead of* MRS. ANDREWS *and waits for her in the hall.*)

MRS. ANDREWS: I'm going to go back to the meeting.

JEFFREY: (*Whimpers.*)

MRS. ANDREWS: All right.

           (JEFFREY *and his mother go down to the waiting-room area.*)

SCENE 7: *Waiting-room area, moments later, Monday, 11:40 a.m.*

(MRS. ANDREWS *sits down in a chair near where* SCOTT, RICHARD, *and* JEFFREY *had been playing.*)

JEFFREY: (*Curls up on the chair beside her and rests his head in her lap.*)
            (*Parents who had attended the parents' meeting file out into the waiting room.*)

MRS. HELLER: (*Walking over to* SCOTT) Scott, would you like to go to lunch?

SCOTT: No, not yet.

MRS. HELLER: It's going to be a while before Dr. Wessley can see us again.

SCOTT: I want to hear what she says first.
            (MRS. ANDREWS *and* JEFFREY *get up, as do many of the other parents and chidlren, and begin to leave. The doctors exit in a group, nodding to the remaining parents and children. All that finally remain are* SCOTT *and his mother.*)

SCOTT: When I get big I'll be able to cross Peter [Scott's younger brother] to school. Won't I, Mommy?

MRS. HELLER: (*With a sigh and a pained expression*) Well, we'll see.

(*Time passes.* SCOTT *fiddles with what is on the cart.*)
            (DR. WESSLEY *returns, goes to her office, and comes back out to the waiting room.*)

DR. WESSLEY: Do you want to come back now?
            (MRS. HELLER *and* SCOTT *follow* DR. WESSLEY *back to the treatment-room area.*)

SCENE 8: *The waiting room of the oncology clinic, the following Monday, 10:00 a.m.*

(JEFFREY *passes through the double doors holding on to* ERICKA, *a little girl who resembles him.* MRS. ANDREWS *follows behind.* JEFFREY *takes* ERICKA *over to the cart and they stand there looking all about while* MRS. ANDREWS *reports to the receptionist.* JEFFREY *leads* ERICKA *over to the table, where other children are coloring, and they sit down next to each other, without a word, and begin to unbutton their coats.* MRS. ANDREWS *returns, smiles, and takes their coats from them.*)

MRS. ANDREWS: You watch out for Ericka now.

(MRS. ANDREWS *walks away from the table, hangs up the coats and goes over to the opposite side of the waiting room. She sits down and begins to read the paper.*)

O.T.S. 1: Hi, Jeffrey. Is this your sister?

JEFFREY: Uh huh.

O.T.S. 1: What's your name?

ERICKA: Ericka.

O.T.S. 1: Would you both like to color? Today we have some chalk to work with.

JEFFREY AND ERICKA: (*Shrug their shoulders.*)

O.T.S. 1: (*Brings them a sheet of paper and places it in front of them. She leans over and places a box of chalk in front of them.*)

JEFFREY: (*Looks about and then picks up a piece of chalk.*)

ERICKA: (*Does the same, and begins to draw.*)

JEFFREY: (*Holds chalk poised and stares.*)

(MRS. MYERS *enters the waiting-room area carrying* ELLIOT *and a diaper bag.*)

MRS. MYERS: (*Setting* ELLIOT *down by the cart*) It's OK to destroy everything.

ELLIOT: Shots! No shots! (*Tries to cling to his mother's legs.*)

DR. ISSACS: (*From the other side of the room*) There is coffee in the conference room.

(MRS. ANDREWS *walks over to* JEFFREY *and* ERICKA.)

MRS. MYERS: Well, I'm going in to the meeting. (*Picks up* ELLIOT *and walks him to where* SHARON *is seated and drops him in her lap.*) Hi (*to* MRS. ANDREWS *who had just walked over*).

MRS. ANDREWS: Hi. Are you two all right here? I'm going over to the meeting. (*Turns and gives each of them a kiss.*)

(MRS. MYERS *and* MRS. ANDREWS *walk down to the conference together.*)

JEFFREY AND ERICKA: (*Color in silence.*)

O.T.S. 1: What did you all have for breakfast today?

LISA: I had some juice and cereal and cytoxin.[2]

MICHAEL: I had juice and eggs and cereal and prednisone.

LISA: That's why you eat so much.[3]

MICHAEL: I know, it's like a tapeworm.

(*Children at the table continue to chalk in silence.*)

(DR. WESSLEY *comes over to the table from the treatment-room area.*)

DR. WESSLEY: OK, Scott, it's your turn.

SCOTT: Oh good, I'm going to get a shot. Shots tickle.

(*Children at the table continue to chalk.*)

(DR. ELLIS *comes over to the table where the children are coloring.*)

DR. ELLIS: Hi, Lisa.

LISA: (*Looks up, glumly*) Hi.

DR. ELLIS: Hi Michael. Hi Elliot.

ELLIOT: (*Whimpers.*)

DR. ELLIS: Hi, Jeffrey. Is that your sister?

ERICKA: (*Looks up.*)

JEFFREY: Uh huh.

DR. ELLIS: What's your name?

ERICKA: Ericka. I'm four.

DR. ELLIS: (*Smiles*) Is your mother at the meeting, Jeff?

JEFFREY: Yeah. (*Stands up.*)

DR. ELLIS: Well, let's go get her first.

(ERICKA *gets up following* JEFFREY *and* DR. ELLIS. *They all go to the conference room and stand*

[2] Cytoxin is one of several antileukemic agents. It is given orally and by injection.

[3] Prednisone, a steriod used in treatment of leukemia, also stimulates appetite.

in the doorway. MRS. ANDREWS *sees them, stands up and comes out of the conference room.*)

MRS. ANDREWS: Hello. (*Bends down.*) Ericka, why don't you go down to the waiting room while we see the doctor. We'll be back soon.

(MRS. ANDREWS, JEFFREY *and* DR. ELLIS *turn and go into the treatment room.* ERICKA *walks back to the waiting room area.*)

O.T.S. 1: (*Noticing* ERICKA *approaching the table*) Do you want to finish your picture?

ERICKA: (*Listlessly*) OK. (*Sits down where she had been, but does not chalk. She picks up a piece of chalk and keeps watching the entryway to the treatment room, where she had seen* JEFFREY *and her mother and the doctor enter.*)

FAITH: (*Has come over to the table and taken a seat across from* ERICKA, *points to one of the doctors' offices where the door is closed.*) The door's closed. That's 'cause the boy's crying. I don't cry no more.

SCOTT: (*Has also returned in the interim*) I don't cry. Shots tickle. I love to get shots.

ELLIOT: Shots! No shots!

ERICKA: (*Stands up and wanders away from the table.*)

O.T.S. 1: Where are you going?

ERICKA: (*Pointing*) Over there. (*Walks as far as where the hallway to the treatment rooms begins and the waiting-room area ends.*)

(*Fifteen minutes later* JEFFREY *comes down that hallway holding on to his mother.*)

ERICKA: (*Looks up at* JEFFREY *with a wide-eyed expression but says nothing.*)

VOICE OF THE RECEPTIONIST: Jeffrey Andrews.

MRS. ANDREWS: I'll go back and get the card. You wait here.

JEFFREY: (*Whimpers and follows his mother back to the receptionist.*)

ERICKA: (*Walks several steps behind them, but stops and waits when they get up to the receptionist's desk.*)

57

(JEFFREY, *lollipop in hand, returns to where* ERICKA *is standing and waiting.*)

ERICKA: I want one too.

(MRS. ANDREWS *catches up to them.*)

JEFFREY: (*Whimpering stopped, states in a clear voice*) You didn't get a shot.

ERICKA: (*Frowns.*)

MRS. ANDREWS: I'll see if I can get you one.

JEFFREY: I want another one.

MRS. ANDREWS: I think that one is enough.

(MRS. ANDREWS *goes back to the receptionist and returns with another lollipop.*)

MRS. ANDREWS: Here, Ericka. I'm going to get our coats and we'll go.

ERICKA: You said we were going to have lunch here.

MRS. ANDREWS: That's why we're going to go now. By the time we finish eating, Grandpa will be here for us.

(MRS. ANDREWS, JEFFREY *and* ERICKA *walk to where the coats are.* MRS. ANDREWS *helps them with their coats.*)

O.T.S. 1: (*Calling from the table*) 'Bye Ericka! 'Bye Jeffrey! Do you want your pictures?

ERICKA AND JEFFREY: (*Walk over silently and take their pictures. They turn and follow their mother out the double doors.*)

SCENE 9: *Waiting room of the oncology clinic, the following Monday, 9:30 a.m.*

JEFFREY *and* MRS. ANDREWS *pass through the double doors. Both appear more tense than they had on previous Mondays. They go directly to the receptionist's desk where* MRS. ANDREWS *turns in the card. They return to the waiting-room area.* MRS. ANDREWS *takes a seat by a woman* [MRS. SMITH] *reading a magazine, whom she does not know;* JEFFREY *sits on his mother's lap.*

MRS. ANDREWS: Do you want to go over there?

JEFFREY: Not now.

MRS. ANDREWS: All right. Are you tired?

JEFFREY: A little.

MRS. ANDREWS: Did you sleep all right last night?

JEFFREY: Not very good.

MRS. SMITH: (*Looking up from her magazine*) Mine's that way too, he never sleeps good on Sunday night before clinic. I guess he's worried about what's going to happen. I don't blame him. I'm the same way myself on Sunday nights when I know we're coming here. He's looking all right, though.

MRS. ANDREWS: His appetite has really picked up.

MRS. SMITH: What's he on? Prednisone?

MRS. ANDREWS: (*Nods.*)

MRS. SMITH: They all eat with that. Funny, it makes you feel good to see them eat. I mean even though you know it's from the medicine for, well, you know—that's doing it. You been coming here long? I don't think I've seen you.

MRS. ANDREWS: No we just started. You?

MRS. SMITH: Two years now. Mark's been doing real well so far. We don't come every week now. Guess that's why I haven't seen you.

MRS. ANDREWS: I hope that will happen for us.

MRS. SMITH: Is he in remission yet?

MRS. ANDREWS: We'll know today for sure.

MRS. SMITH: Oh, I see. No wonder he didn't sleep.

MRS. ANDREWS: Well, yeah. Jeffrey, why don't you go over there and play?

JEFFREY: I don't want to.

(*For some time,* MRS. ANDREWS *and* JEFFREY *sit in silence.* MRS. SMITH *goes back to her magazine.* O.T.S. *walks over to* JEFFREY *and* MRS. ANDREWS.)

O.T.S. 1: Jeffrey would you like to come over and play a game? The children need another person for Candyland.

MRS. ANDREWS: Go on, Jeffrey. You like Candyland (*gives a slight push from·behind*). I'll come over before I go to the meeting.

JEFFREY: (*Grudgingly gets off her lap and follows the* O.T.S. *over to the table.*)

MRS. ANDREWS: I didn't want to say anything in front of Jeffrey, you know, but he's going to have a bone marrow today.

MRS. SMITH: (*Closes the magazine*) I thought so. It's the only way they know if he's in remission or relapse.

MRS. ANDREWS: We haven't told him he was going to have a bone marrow today.

MRS. SMITH: Sometimes they know anyway. It's really pretty hard to keep things from them, no matter how hard you try.

MRS. ANDREWS: Have you told your son?

MRS. SMITH: Mark? No. He knows he has a blood disease (*slight pause*) and, well, I don't know. But they do pick up quick.

(*Miss Kohne comes out to the waiting room and smiles at the mothers and children. Walks over to* MRS. SMITH.)

MISS KOHNE: Well, we haven't seen you for a while.

MRS. SMITH: Yeah, kind of nice for a change.

MISS KOHNE: Are you going to be coming to the meeting?

MRS. SMITH: Yes, uh huh.

MISS KOHNE: Good. (*Looks up. Announcing to the others*) The parents are meeting in the conference room.

(*Some parents rise and follow* MISS KOHNE; *others like* MRS. ANDREWS *go over to where their children are playing and tell them they are going. Some parents remain in the waiting room.*)

MRS. ANDREWS: (*To* JEFFREY) You come and get me when Dr. Ellis comes.

JEFFREY: I know. (*Returns to the game from which he and two of the other players had been temporarily interrupted.*)

60

(MRS. ANDREWS *walks down to the
conference room.* MRS. MEYERS *comes bursting through the
double doors, looking irritated.* ELLIOT *is tossed into Sharon's
lap, crying.*)
(*Various children call out:* "Elliot! Elliot!")
LISA: (*To* ELLIOT) You shouldn't be so crabby already. You
just got here.

(MRS. MYERS *turns and goes to the
meeting.*)
NURSE GREEN: (*Calls from the treatment/waiting-room
"boundary line"*) Smith, Andrews, Phillips, Klemons,
and Weller.

(*Five children rise and go down the
hallway. They return individually and sit back down to what
they were doing as if nothing has happened—merely a brief
interruption.*)[4]
LISA: Guess how much I weigh?
SHARON: Eighty-eight.
LISA: No!
SHARON: Ninety.
LISA: No.
SHARON: Eighty-six.
LISA: No! I weigh the same as I weighed before, eighty-
three pounds.
SHARON: You look like you've gained ten pounds.
SANDY: It's that prednisone. It does things to you.
SHARON: What does it do?
JEFFREY: It makes you eat like a pig and act like a brat.[5]
LISA: It doesn't make me act like a brat.
SHARON: What does it do to you?
LISA: (*Looks down.*)
(*The children resume the game.*)

---

[4] They had been weighed. The children are called in groups of five
to be weighed before they see the doctor.
[5] Common side effects of prednisone include weight gain and mood
swings.

JILL: I'm going to St. Louis next week if the doctor says I can.

LISA: (*Cutting and pasting, apparently not paying attention, does not look up.*) Last time I was there was in November, for my birthday, then I got sick and came up here.

SHARON: I've been to the zoo, have you?

LISA: Yeah, only I was having back trouble so we came up here.

SHARON: Which animals do you like the best?

LISA: We're going to go camping next week.

(ROBERTA *comes through the double doors, tray in hand, and walks directly to the treatment-room area.*)

SETH: (*Looking up from the game*) Uh oh. Somebody's gonna get it.

JEFFREY: (*Stopping in the middle of his move*) Get what?

SETH: A bone marrow.

JEFFREY: How do you know?

SETH: 'Cause Roberta came up with her stuff. She only comes up in the middle of clinic if somebody's going to get a bone marrow.

(DR. ELLIS *comes over to the table, from the treatment-room area.*)

DR. ELLIS: (*Looks about*) There you are, Jeffrey.

JEFFREY: (*Eyes open wide.*)

DR. ELLIS: How about if we go get your mother?

JEFFREY: (*Stands hesitantly.*)

(DR. ELLIS *and* JEFFREY *walk toward the conference room.*)

DR. ELLIS: (*Placing arm around* JEFFREY's *shoulder*) How have you been?

JEFFREY: OK.

(DR. ELLIS *and* JEFFREY *wait at the entrance to the conference room.* MRS. ANDREWS *comes out, looking a bit more serious than she had in previous weeks, when she was called out of the meeting.*)

DR. ELLIS: Hello!

MRS. ANDREWS: Hi. I haven't said anything to him yet.

DR. ELLIS: (*Nods.*)

> (DR. ELLIS, JEFFREY, *and* MRS. ANDREWS *enters the treatment room.*)

SCENE 10: *The treatment room of the oncology clinic, later that morning, Monday, 11:25 a.m.*

(DR. ELLIS *and* MRS. ANDREWS *stand to either side of the examining table.* JEFFREY *gets up onto the table without assistance.*)

DR. ELLIS: Well, you look like you've put on a little weight there.

MRS. ANDREWS: He's gained since his last visit.

DR. ELLIS: How's school? (*Lifts* JEFFREY's *shirt.*)

JEFFREY: (*Lies back.*)

DR. ELLIS: (*Feels* JEFFREY's *stomach.*)

JEFFREY: Fine.

DR. ELLIS: OK. You can sit up now, Jeffrey.

JEFFREY: (*Sits up and adjusts his shirt.*)

DR. ELLIS: His counts look pretty good. I think we'll do the marrow now and after we get the results, talk about the new medication.

JEFFREY: (*Begins to whimper.*)

> (ROBERTA *enters the treatment room and begins to set up at the end of the examination table.*)

DR. ELLIS: We are going to do a bone marrow to see how you are doing.

JEFFREY: (*Lets out a scream.*)

DR. ELLIS: Mrs. Andrews, would you like to go outside?

MRS. ANDREWS: (*Nods.*)

JEFFREY: Mommy, please don't go. Don't leave me.

MRS. ANDREWS: (*Eyes filling up*) I'll be right back when the doctors tell me.

> (MRS. ANDREWS *leaves and stands outside the treatment room by the scales. A nurse approaches her.* JEFFREY's *crying can be heard out in the hall.*)

MRS. ANDREWS: (*To nurse*) I guess I should get used to it, but it's all so new. I'll be all right.

(*The nurse walks back into the treatment room.*)

MRS. ANDREWS: (*Stands against the wall trying to smile and hold back the tears, as other parents and children pass on their way to pick up cards and to see the other doctors in the clinic.*)

(ROBERTA *comes out of the treatment room, walks past* MRS. ANDREWS *and down the corridor.* JEFFREY's *crying stops and* DR. ELLIS *comes out into the hall.* MRS. ANDREWS *follows her back in.*)

JEFFREY: (*As* MRS. ANDREWS *enters and walks over to the examination table*) Mommy! Mommy!

MRS. ANDREWS: (*Hugging* JEFFREY) Were you a good boy?

JEFFREY: (*Sniffling*) I tried.

DR. ELLIS: He did all right. Go and have some lunch now. We won't have the results for an hour or so.

MRS. ANDREWS: (*Nods.*)

(JEFFREY, *clinging to* MRS. ANDREWS, *leaves the treatment room. They walk through the waiting room without looking to either side and pass through the double doors.*)

SCENE 11: *Waiting room of the oncology clinic, that afternoon, 1:00 p.m.*

(*Jeffrey and his mother are seated in the now empty waiting room.* JEFFREY *is swinging his feet and looking about, while* MRS. ANDREWS *is sitting rigidly, looking straight ahead. Soon the waiting room begins to fill with people for the adult oncology clinic [which meets Monday afternoon], who take seats and smile at* JEFFREY.)

(DR. ELLIS *enters.*)

DR. ELLIS: (*To* JEFFREY *and his mother*) Do you want to come with me now?

(MRS. ANDREWS *and* JEFFREY *rise and follow* DR. ELLIS. *They enter the treatment room.*)

64

SCENE 12: *The treatment room, later, Monday, 1:30 p.m.*

(MRS. ANDREWS *and* DR. ELLIS *stand by* DR. ELLIS' *desk, their backs to* JEFFREY. JEFFREY *gets up on the examining table, but does not lie back.*)

DR. ELLIS: We are going to begin giving Jeffrey some new medication and tapering off the prednisone. (*Hands* MRS. ANDREWS *the prescription*) Here's the prescription and the instructions for tapering the prednisone. You can have it filled here or at your own pharmacy. I won't see you now for two weeks. Do you have any questions?

MRS. ANDREWS: How long will this, ah—?

DR. ELLIS: Remission?

MRS. ANDREWS: Yes, last?

DR. ELLIS: That's hard to say right now.

MRS. ANDREWS: Ah (*nods*), I see.

DR. ELLIS: If you or your husband have any questions please call me. (*Turning around to face* JEFFREY) Jeffrey, I'll see you in two weeks.

MRS. ANDREWS: Thank you.

JEFFREY: (*Jumps down from the table.*)

(MRS. ANDREWS *takes* JEFFREY *by the hand and they leave, passing briskly through the waiting room and out the door.*)

ACT III: THE FIRST RELAPSE

It is summer. Fourteen months have passed since JEFFREY *was first diagnosed. He has remained asymptomatic and has had no major side effects or complications from the drugs. He has been coming to the clinic once and sometimes twice a month. He has had a few bone marrows when there was some question, but each turned out to be negative. Except for brief absences for colds and epidemics of*

65

childhood diseases in the school, JEFFREY *has attended school regularly and has been promoted to the second grade.*[6]

SCENE 1: *Nurses' station on the thirteenth floor, Saturday, 10:30 a.m.*

(JEFFREY, *looking pale and uncomfortable, is wheeled off the elevator by his father. His mother walks beside him carrying a shopping bag and a small overnight bag. As they make their way to the nurses' station, they look straight ahead. Their steps are even and regular.*)

NURSE RICHARDS: (*Standing to the left of the receptionist's desk, making notes in a chart. Looks up.*) Hello! I remember you.

JEFFREY: (*Doesn't look up.*)

MRS. ANDREWS: (*Hands the nurse the admission slip.*)

MR. ANDREWS: (*Does not let go of the wheelchair. His hands seem to tighten around the handles.*)

NURSE RICHARDS: Has Jeffrey been exposed to any childhood diseases within the last few days?

MRS. ANDREWS: No.

NURSE RICHARDS: (*Handing* MRS. ANDREWS *a container*) Please see that when Jeffrey has to urinate he does so in this container. (*Looking down at* JEFFREY) Well, Jeffrey, we have a room all ready for you. (*Turning face to* MRS. ANDREWS) He is going to be in reverse isolation. When we get to the room I will explain the procedure.

(NURSE RICHARDS *comes away from the desk and leads the* ANDREWS *family down the hall. She talks to them over her shoulder as they walk.*)

---

[6] The leukemic children are often immunosuppressed as a result of taking the drugs. If they were to become infected they would have a difficult time fighting the infection, therefore they are kept away from other ill children as much as possible.

NURSE RICHARDS: It [reverse isolation] is not so that you don't catch anything from him, it's so that we don't give anything to him, since we don't know what is causing his fever yet, and because his count is so low. It's to protect him from us, not us from him.

(*They reach the entrance to the room and stop.*)

NURSE RICHARDS: (*Pointing to the linen cart near the door*) Jeffrey will not take his linen from the cart, but from the sealed packages down here. (*Bends down and takes a package from the utility table next to the entrance to the room. Hands the package to* MRS. ANDREWS.) On top are the gowns. Parents and visitors must wear gowns, but only visitors and staff need wear the masks. Please make sure that you wash your hands when you come in the room, and especially before touching him. I'll be back to check his temperature in a few minutes.

(NURSE RICHARDS *turns and walks back toward the nurses' station.*)

MR. AND MRS. ANDREWS: (*Unbutton their coats and put them down on the utility table, put on gowns and pick up their coats.*)

(MR. ANDREWS *wheels* JEFFREY *into the room and stands with him by the bed.* MRS. ANDREWS *looks down the hall and enters.*)

SCENE 2: JEFFREY'S *room, some minutes later, Saturday,* 10:45 *a.m.*

(MRS. ANDREWS *undresses* JEFFREY *and puts the gown on him.* MR. ANDREWS *takes* JEFFREY'S *clothes and places them at the end of the unmade bed. He lifts* JEFFREY *into the bed, then goes and stands by the window.*)

MRS. ANDREWS: Are you OK, Jeffrey?
JEFFREY: (*Turns over.*)

(NURSE RICHARDS *enters.*)

NURSE RICHARDS: Well, Jeffrey, you look a little more comfortable. (*Puts a thermometer in his mouth and takes his wrist.*) Would you like some juice?

JEFFREY: (*Shakes his head.*)

MRS. ANDREWS: Jeffrey, I think that you should try to drink some.

NURSE RICHARDS: Well, I'll just bring it in and leave it on the table here for you.

MRS. ANDREWS: Thanks. (*Sits down in a straight chair facing the bed.*)

(NURSE RICHARDS *leaves.*)
(DR. CELLARS *enters and goes over to* JEFFREY's *bed.*)

MRS. ANDREWS: (*Stands.*)

DR. CELLARS: Hello, Jeffrey. I just want to feel your stomach for now. Does this hurt (*presses on stomach*)?

JEFFREY: No.

DR. CELLARS: (*Continues to feel around and checks his legs.*)

MRS. ANDREWS: He's been complaining he has trouble walking.

DR. CELLARS: I see. What's his temperature now?

MRS. ANDREWS: The nurse just took it. It was 103 when I called Dr. Ellis this morning.

DR. CELLARS: OK, Jeffrey. (*Pause*) I see. I've spoken to her. We'll see you in a little while Jeffrey. (*Turns around, raises head.*)

(DR. CELLARS *walks out and* MR. *and* MRS. ANDREWS *follow.*)

JEFFREY: (*Raises his body slightly.*)

DR. CELLARS: (*To* MR. AND MRS. ANDREWS, *outside* JEFFREY's *room*) I think that we should do a bone marrow; from the counts, it looks like Jeffrey may be in relapse and this is the only way we can tell for sure.

MRS. ANDREWS: (*Nods.*)

MR. ANDREWS: (*Shakes his head.*)

68

(DR. CELLARS *turns and walks down the hall.* MR. AND MRS. ANDREWS *go back into the room.*)

JEFFREY: What did he say?

MRS. ANDREWS: (*Walking to the side of his bed*) They want to do a bone marrow.

JEFFREY: (*Cries.*)

MR. ANDREWS: (*Sits down in the lounge chair and stares at* JEFFREY) That's enough, son.

JEFFREY: (*Begins to sniffle.*)

MRS. ANDREWS: (*Sits down in the straight chair and stares at her son.*)

JEFFREY: (*Turns over and falls asleep.*)

SCENE 3: JEFFREY'S *room, that afternoon, 2:45 p.m.*

(JEFFREY *is sitting up watching a baseball game on TV. His parents are not present.*)

MYRA: (*Standing in the doorway*) Hi, Jeffrey. Can I come in for a minute?

JEFFREY: (*Looking away from the TV*) I didn't think I'd ever have to come back here again. I had a bone marrow. It didn't hurt as much as the ones in clinic, though.

MYRA: (*Putting on mask and gown*) How come?

JEFFREY: Because in clinic I cry so much that sometimes they have to stick me twice.

(MYRA *enters and stands at the foot of the bed.*)

JEFFREY: Do you want to watch the baseball game with me?

MYRA: I'd like to, but I promised Lisa that I would see her this afternoon. I just found out that you were here and I thought I'd stop by.

JEFFREY: Oh!

MYRA: I'll stop by tomorrow, though.

JEFFREY: OK.

(MYRA *leaves.*)

69

SCENE 4: LISA's *room, later that afternoon, Saturday,* 3:15 *p.m.*

(LISA *is sitting up in bed staring blankly out the door.*)

MYRA: (*Knocks*) Hi "Lis," can I come in?

LISA: Yeah.

MYRA: (*Puts on mask and gown.*)

LISA: My mom and dad went in town this afternoon.

(MYRA *enters the room, goes over to the sink, and washes her hands.*)

MYRA: (*Walking over to the foot of the bed*) So you're alone for the afternoon.

LISA: Uh huh.

(*Silence.*)

LISA: Once when we were walking through the zoo I began to get back-pains and finally Daddy had to get a wheelchair so I could finish out the day. And then they brought me up here. You see, it was my birthday. On my birthday now I get to pick what I want to do. We go on short trips, like to the Forest Preserve. It's nice. It's a long ride. I don't get sick anymore though. My birthday is November sixth. This year it comes on a Sunday. We had to come to the hospital after the zoo, but first we went back to Essex. (*Silence as she stares at the TV.*) I'm going to get blood. Both times I got a reaction. I don't like it, but it makes me feel better. (*Pause.*) Dr. Cellars is leaving. I don't want to get used to another doctor.

(*In the hallway opposite* LISA's *room,* MRS. ANDREWS *is talking to* MRS. PHILLIPS.)

MRS. PHILLIPS: (*To* MRS. ANDREWS) What are you doing here?

LISA: (*Yelling with great annoyance*) What do you think? Same thing I'm here for—relapse.

MRS. ANDREWS: Things were going so good, too. I just don't understand it.

70

MRS. PHILLIPS: (*Nods.*) I'll talk to you later.

> (MRS. PHILLIPS *enters* LISA'S *room.*
MRS. ANDREWS *goes into* JEFFREY'S *room.*)

LISA: Tom's here, too.

MYRA: Oh?

LISA: Relapse.

> (MR. PHILLIPS *enters.*)

MRS. PHILLIPS: How was your day?

LISA: OK I guess.

MYRA: I think I better go now Lisa. I'll see you tomorrow.

LISA: OK. 'Bye.

MYRA: (*Turning to walk out*) 'Bye.

> (MYRA *leaves.*)

SCENE 5: TOM'S *room, moments later, 4:45 p.m.*

(TOM *is lying listlessly on his bed. The shades are drawn
and the room is dark.*)

MYRA: Hi, Tom. Can I come in?

TOM: Yeah.

MYRA: (*Puts on a gown and mask.*)

> (MYRA *enters and goes over to the sink.*)

MYRA: (*Washes hands with back to* TOM.)

TOM: I had a bone marrow this morning and I don't feel
good.

MYRA: (*Turns around and walks to the bed.*)

> (AIDE THOMAS *stands in the doorway.*)

AIDE THOMAS: How are you doing, Tom?

TOM: I want a pill.

AIDE THOMAS: I'll see if you can have one.

> (AIDE THOMAS *goes down the hall.*)

TOM: Dr. Cellars was here.

MYRA: Yeah.

TOM: (*Silence.*)

> (NURSE LYONS *comes in with a pill.*)

NURSE LYONS: Here you go Tom.

TOM: (*Gets up on an elbow and takes the pill. Lies back down.*)

NURSE LYONS: Tom, do you want anything else?

TOM: (*Shakes his head.*)

(NURSE LYONS *leaves.*)

TOM: Dr. Cellars is leaving. (*Pause.*) Then they are going to have to start the I.V., 'cause the medicine they're using ain't working. (*Pause.*) I want to go to sleep now.

MYRA: OK. I'll see you later.

TOM: But the TV man might come, and if I don't give him the money he'll take it out. It was just left here with time.

MYRA: Do you have the money?

TOM: Yeah. My mom left it before she went home.

MYRA: Well, why don't you give it to me and I'll leave it at the desk for the man when he comes.

TOM: Thanks. (*Reaches over to the night table and hands* MYRA *the money. Turns over and closes his eyes.*)

(MYRA *leaves and runs into* DR. CELLARS *in front of the nurses' station.*)

SCENE 6: *The nurses' station on the thirteenth floor minutes later.*

MYRA: (*To* DR. CELLARS) Why do you think Tom is so upset today?

DR. CELLARS: I told him about the results of the bone marrow.

MYRA: That he was in relapse?

DR. CELLARS: Yes. And I also told him that the medicine we were using wasn't working anymore and that we were going to try another one.

MYRA: I see. How much does Tom know about his condition?

DR. CELLARS: I don't know how much Tom has been told. He does know that he has a blood disease. Really, if

72

you don't have any more questions I'm on my way
home.

> (DR. CELLARS *turns and walks to the*

elevator.)

NURSE RICHARDS: (*Has come up during the conversation
and was writing in a chart*) He's that way.

MYRA: I see. Oh, this is for the TV man from Tom (*hands
her the money*). Could you see that he gets it?

NURSE RICHARDS: Sure. By the way do you know that Jeffrey
is in?

MYRA: Yes, I saw him earlier this afternoon.

NURSE RICHARDS: I don't know. (*Shakes head*) Once the
kids start coming they just come. The mothers know it
and the kids know which ones have had it, how long
and which ones aren't here anymore. They all talk
about it too, except the Costins. They refuse to have
anything to do with the others. They sit separately in
the clinic and they keep the door closed in the hospital.
They deny it. They won't even say the word leukemia.
They think she will outlive the disease like she outlived
the others. (*Turns and picks up a chart.*)

> (NURSE RICHARDS *walks down to the doc-*

tors' conference room.)

SCENE 7: LISA's *room, the next morning, Sunday,* 11:00 *a.m.*

(LISA *is seated in a large lounge chair by the door, facing
the hallway, staring blankly down the hall.*)

MYRA: Hi, Lisa, can I come in?

LISA: (*Listlessly*) Yeah.

MYRA: (*Puts on mask and gown*) What's happening?

> (MYRA *enters the room and sits down*

by the doorway.)

LISA: Nothing. (*Pause.*) Everybody's here that was here
yesterday. (*Pause, tone changes to annoyance.*) Tom's
out of isolation.

MYRA: You saw him go by?

LISA: Yeah, there are kids up and back sometimes, sometimes nurses. (*Pause*) I like this end better 'cause you're
closer to the desk.

(LIZ, a girl about LISA's age, goes by
LISA's *room in a wheelchair.*)

LISA: Hi, Liz.

LIZ: (*Waves back and goes on.*)

LISA: That was Elizabeth. I call her Liz. She was swimming
and she had a small heart attack. She had an operation
and now she is in for rest and observation. She has the
room next door. My mom was talking to her mom. (*Silence*) I'm not sure if Tom will be getting out of the
hospital today; he just got out of isolation. (*Pause*) I'll
be getting out in a while (*voice fades off*). (*Pause.*)
(*Quickly*) If everything goes well I mean.

MYRA: If everything goes well?

LISA: If my things keep and I don't get a temperature.

MYRA: If everything stays the way it is.

LISA: I mean if the medicine works. It's fighting the infection and it helps if I don't have a temperature. It stayed
down and it's staying down.

MYRA: That's good.

(MRS. REEDER *walks by* LISA's *room.*)

LISA: (*Calls to* MRS. REEDER) Tom got out of isolation this
morning.

MRS. REEDER: I know, that's what he wanted. That's what
you want too, isn't it?

LISA: (*Looks down.*)

(MRS. REEDER *walks on down the hall.*)

LISA: It's been a week already. Time does fly when you're
in the hospital.

MYRA: It goes fast.

LISA: It doesn't feel like a week. (*Pause.*) But I do want to
go home.

(*The cart arrives with* LISA's *lunch.
The woman from the kitchen takes off* LISA's *tray, places it
on* LISA's *lap and moves on.*)

74

LISA: (*Looking at the sheet that has her name on it.*) They never spell my name right. (*Looks down at the food and picks at it.*)

MYRA: Well, Lisa, I'll let you eat your lunch now and I'll try to stop by later, if not definitely tomorrow.

LISA: OK. See ya.

SCENE 8: TOM's *room, a half-hour later.*

(TOM *is propped up in bed working on a puzzle with another boy,* MATHEW [*known as* MAT] SPENCER.)

TOM: (*Spotting* MYRA *in the doorway*) See my model.

MYRA: That looks great.

(MYRA *walks over to the bed.*)

TOM: That's Mat, he sleeps next door.

MYRA: Hi, Mat.

MAT: We're working on these (*referring to the puzzles on the bed.*)

(*Silence as they work on the puzzles.*)

MAT: All I want to do is kill myself before this day is over.

MYRA: You want to kill yourself before the day is over.

MAT: I ain't talkin' no more.

MYRA: OK. Don't talk anymore.

MAT: I'll kill myself but I won't talk. (*Pause.*) Tom, do you like to see dead persons?

TOM: (*Curtly*) No.

MAT: You don't like 'em.

TOM: No.

MAT: Do you like to kiss dead persons?

TOM: (*Buries head in pillow*) Aw.

MAT: When you kiss dead persons, what do they taste like?

TOM: I'm sick! Be quiet!

MYRA: You feel sick Tom?

MAT: He ain't sick from nothin'.

MYRA: You sick?

TOM: Uh huh (*begins to whimper*).

MAT: (*Working on the puzzle*). This puzzle's hard.

(*Silence.*)

75

TOM: (*Gets up*) This model's hard. Let's see what *this* model's got. (*Takes another model box off his night table.*) This is a motor for my "zoomer-boomer." My mom brought it this morning.

(NURSE LYONS *enters.*)

NURSE LYONS: (*Walking over to the bed*) Hi, Tom. I can take you downstairs now if you want.

TOM: Yeah. To the gift shop. (TOM *reaches for a comb by the bed and begins to comb his hair.*)

MAT: I want to go too.

NURSE LYONS: (*Nods to* MAT.) What are you doing, Tom?

TOM: Combing my hair.

NURSE LYONS: (*Turning to* MYRA) His hair has really grown since the last time. He was either on cytoxan or had radiation, I forget which; anyway, he's lost it several times.[7]

TOM: (*Puts comb in his pocket.*)

NURSE LYONS: OK. If you're ready to, we'll go.

MYRA: I'll see you tomorrow, Tom.

TOM: OK.

MYRA: 'Bye, Mat.

MAT: 'Bye.

(MYRA *leaves and walks down the hall.* NURSE LYONS, MAT *and* TOM *follow, turning off for the elevator.*)

SCENE 9: JEFFREY'S *room, that evening,* 6:00 *p.m.*

(JEFFREY *is propped up in bed looking about blankly.*)

MYRA: Hi, Jeffrey. Can I come in?

JEFFREY: Yeah, for a little bit, and then I have to go to X-ray.

MYRA: (*Puts on mask and gown.*)

(MYRA *enters, washes hands, then goes over to the bed.*)

[7] Hair loss is a common side effect of radiation and cytoxan.

76

JEFFREY: They did one up here because I couldn't go down, but then it didn't come out so good, so now I have to go down to X-ray. My mom's not here. She went with my dad to eat dinner and they are going to bring something back for me. I'm not hungry though. (*Pause.*) After my X-ray they are going to put an I.V. in me for the medicine, and 'cause I'm not eating real good.

(*A man from the X-ray department enters the room with* NURSE BING.)

NURSE BING: I'll get you ready to go down now.

MAN FROM X-RAY *and* NURSE BING: (*Lift* JEFFREY *into a wheelchair.*)

NURSE BING: (*Wraps* JEFFREY *in several sheets and puts a mask over his face.*) Jeffrey, you hold this (*places his chart in his lap*).

JEFFREY: My mother!

NURSE BING: We'll tell her where you are if she comes back before you.

MYRA: I'll see you later, Jeffrey, if not tomorrow.

JEFFREY: Tomorrow is clinic.

MYRA: I know. I'll be up after clinic.

JEFFREY: (*Nods.*)

(*The* MAN FROM X-RAY *wheels* JEFFREY *down the hall.*)

NURSE BING: (*Straightening out* JEFFREY's *bed*) They really have a hard time of it.

MYRA: (*Nods.*)

(MYRA *leaves the room.*)

SCENE 10: LISA's *room, later that evening,* 7:00 *p.m.*

(LISA *is sitting up in bed fiddling almost unconsciously with a stuffed animal on her tray.*)

MYRA: Hi, Lisa, can I come in?

LISA: Yeah.

MYRA: (*Puts on mask and gown.*)

(MYRA *enters and goes over to the* sink. *Washes hands with back to* LISA.)

MYRA: (*Drying hands and turning around*) How was your day today?

LISA: (*Listlessly*) Well, they changed my I.V.

MYRA: They changed your I.V.

LISA: (*Pouty, but aggressive*) Yeah. I don't know why.

MYRA: When did they do that?

LISA: Well, just a while ago.

MYRA: A few minutes ago?

LISA: No longer than that.

MYRA: While I was at dinner?

LISA: (*Nods.*) Dr. Elwood did it. It hurt when he put it in.

MYRA: (*Referring to the cup over the needle*) It's pretty fancy this time.

LISA: I know. He just put a cup over it.

MYRA: How come?

LISA: So if I roll over. (*Pause.*) I haven't yet rolled over on an I.V. (*Pause.*) I guess it just wasn't working. Mom wasn't here when they changed it.

(*Silence.*)

LISA: I colored today and watched TV and read in the morning.

(NURSE EDWARDS *enters the room and* walks up to the bed.)

NURSE EDWARDS: (*Turning to Myra*) Have you washed your hands?

LISA: (*Indignantly*) Yes, she did.

NURSE EDWARDS: (*Begins to adjust the I.V.*)

LISA: (*To* MYRA) What did you have for dinner?

MYRA: Chicken.

LISA: Ouch! It stings!

NURSE EDWARDS: We have to run it through fast, to get it through in time.

LISA: They started it at 9:00 on Friday. I remember, because I was asleep and they just came in and stuck me.

NURSE EDWARDS: (*Pulls off the Band-Aid near the right of the I.V.*) Will you look at the hair on this Band-Aid.

LISA: (*Flinches and looks away.*)

NURSE EDWARDS: Lisa, do you think that you can stand it for a little while longer so we can get the medicine through in time?

LISA: (*Nods head stoically.*)

NURSE EDWARDS: (*Puts thermometer in Lisa's mouth, waits for a reading, takes it out.*) It's normal. Is the medicine still stinging?

LISA: (*Glares at* NURSE EDWARDS.)

(NURSE EDWARDS *leaves.*)

LISA: They don't use I.V.'s in clinic, just small tubes when they stick you. They use the small tubes of fluid before and after they give the medicine.[8]

(*Silence.*)

LISA: I have to go to the bathroom, but I'm supposed to call the nurse. (*Shouts*) Nurse! Nurse! They'll never hear me, I'm too far from the desk. I have to go!

MYRA: I'll go and get one.

(MYRA *leaves the room and returns with* NURSE EDWARDS, *who closes the door in* MYRA's *face. In a few minutes* NURSE EDWARDS *opens the door and leaves the room.*)

LISA: (*Calls from the bed*) It must be boring to be out of isolation.

(MYRA *enters the room and goes over to the bed.* AIDE LEWIS *walks by the room with the evening treats.*)

AIDE LEWIS: (*From the doorway*) You want a little chocolate milk, or some orange juice? Maybe a little ice cream?

LISA: Some orange juice.

(AIDE LEWIS *enters.*)

---

[8] The fluid being referred to is either dextrose or saline. Which fluid is used depends on the nature of drug being administered.

AIDE LEWIS: (*Brings over orange juice*) We really try to fatten you up here.

LISA: I don't care.

AIDE LEWIS: That's OK, honey, you're not fat.

LISA: Yeah.

(AIDE LEWIS *leaves and walks on down the hall.*)

LISA: (*Sips the orange juice and stares at the I.V.*) I think the lid is coming down.

MYRA: You've been watching your I.V.

LISA: (*Embarrassed*) Uh huh.

MYRA: It's going all right.

LISA: It's not stinging or anything so I think I'll make it. (*Pause.*) It hurts when they take the bandages off, on the hairy parts.

MYRA: It would be nice if they made ouchless bandages that didn't take all your hair with it.

LISA: (*Giggles*) Yeah. Well, you see that one (*points to a large hairless portion on her arm*), I've got spots all over me.[9]

MYRA: All over you?

LISA: Mmm Mmm. See where the hair came out? (*Points to another large hairless spot.*) Spots! See where the hair came out? (*Points to another large hairless part with petechiae*) Spots!

MYRA: I see.

LISA: I've got spots there from when they pulled it out. (*Pause.*) Come over here!

MYRA: (*Walks over to the other side of the bed.*)

LISA: See my tan. I have no tan here. That's where the bandages were. And see down there, that's where, first my legs started hurting. (*Changes to strained tone.*) I could walk and then I could walk until Tuesday and

---

[9] These "spots" in the hairless areas are the petechiae. Petechiae appear as a result of skin "trauma" when platelets are low, as they often are in leukemics in relapse. Some of the children think of them as "baby black-and-blue marks."

then I could walk all day Thursday. Then on Friday I didn't think I could walk, so my mom and dad didn't make me try at first, and so my mom put me in this rocking chair and when she picked me up she bonked me, by accident on the rocking chair, and that's how I got bonked, but when you are in relapse it makes bigger black-and-blue marks quicker. I got this from my father. (*Picks up the tiger on the tray. Puts it down and takes a sip of orange juice.*) Do you like orange juice?

MYRA: Yeah.

LISA: I used to vomit from it, at breakfast. (*Pause.*) Do you know what's wrong with the boy at the other end of the hall? He doesn't go to the clinic.

MYRA: No. All I know is that he plays the guitar.

LISA: I guess there is nothing wrong with his arms then.

MYRA: Well, when he sings he sounds like he has a frog in his throat.

LISA: Maybe he has pneumonia then.

MYRA: Is pneumonia a thing in your throat?

LISA: No, it just sounds that way. It's in your chest. I've had chest pneumonia. A whole lot of phlegm builds up in your chest. It takes a long time, though. Well, not too long a time though. But you know, a while. It's in your chest and your chest hurts when you breathe because you know it isn't used to having so much in it, and then the air has to come through, but there is so much mucous. (*Turns and stares at the I.V.*) It takes two seconds before the next drip.

MYRA: You really keep track of your I.V.

LISA: I have to. When do you have to go?

MYRA: Not for a while yet.

LISA: I don't close my door at night. Then the nurses can hear me. (*Pause.*) Tom got out of isolation and he's real happy about it.

(*Silence for several minutes.*)

LISA: (*Rolls over and closes her eyes. Soon asleep.*)

MYRA: (*Leaves* LISA *a note.*)

(MYRA *leaves.*)

81

SCENE 11: JEFFREY's *room, the following afternoon, Monday,* 3:00 *p.m.*

(JEFFREY *is propped up in bed leafing through a book and his father is pacing around the room.*)

JEFFREY: (*Calls from his bed as* MYRA *walks down the hall*) Who was in clinic today?

MYRA: (*From the doorway*) Tom, Lynn, Jennifer, and Scott. Can I come in?

JEFFREY: (*Excitedly*) Yes.

MYRA: (*Puts on mask and gown.*)

(MYRA *enters the room and goes over to the sink to wash her hands. Her back is to* JEFFREY, *but she can see him in the mirror.*)

JEFFREY: (*Aggravated*) I might have another bone marrow because the one they did on Saturday had too much liquid. (*Now excited*) But I have a plan to blow up the doctors when they try to get me again. I will put dynamite in the bone marrow syringe and when they push down the dynamite in, the syringe will go off.

MR. ANDREWS: Jeffrey!

JEFFREY: I'll have it put that way (*demonstrates with his hands*). And if that doesn't work, I'll wrap myself up in a sheet so they won't find me (*proceeds to wrap himself up, but the I.V. tubing gets in the way*). Damn it!

MR. ANDREWS: Jeffrey!

(*Silence*)

JEFFREY: (*To* MYRA) Do you want to color with me?

MYRA: Well, just for a little while.

JEFFREY: (*Opens the book, takes the box of crayons and offers it to* MYRA.)

MYRA: (*Takes a crayon.*)

JEFFREY: You do that one and I'll do this one.

MYRA: OK.

MYRA AND JEFFREY: (*Begin to color.*)

MR. ANDREWS: Jeffrey, I'm going to get a cigarette. I'll be back soon.

JEFFREY: (*Without looking up*) OK.

(MR. ANDREWS *leaves.*)

MYRA AND JEFFREY: (*Color in silence for several minutes.*)

(MR. ANDREWS *reenters without a word.*)

MYRA: Well, Jeffrey, I think that I will have to be going.

JEFFREY: Are you going to see Lisa?

MYRA: Yes, a little later.

JEFFREY: Well, thanks for coloring. Will you come back?

MYRA: I'll be back tomorrow.

JEFFREY: Good.

MYRA: See you.

JEFFREY: 'Bye.

MR. ANDREWS: 'Bye.

(MYRA *leaves.*)

SCENE 12: TOM's *room, later that afternoon,* 4:30 *p.m.*

(TOM *is dressed and sitting up on the edge of his bed, working on a model.*)

MYRA: (*Outside*) Hi, Tom.

TOM: Wanna see my model?

MYRA: Sure.

(MYRA *enters.*)

MYRA: Hey! That's really neat.

(DR. ELWOOD *enters and walks over to the bed.*)

DR. ELWOOD: Do you know Paul Linden? He goes to the clinic.

TOM: (*Nods, but keeps working on his model.*)

DR. ELWOOD: He says that he's the best model builder.

TOM: He cut my hair once.

DR. ELWOOD: He cut your hair?

TOM: (*Looks up from his model*) Yeah, one night he came in my room and cut it, with a scissors.

DR. ELWOOD: How do you know Paul did it?

TOM: 'Cause he tried to do it again the next night, but the nurse caught him.

83

DR. ELWOOD: Did Paul have hair?

TOM: Yes, he did.

(DR. ELWOOD *leaves.*)

TOM: (*Returns to working on his model.*)

(*Doctors* ABRAMS, WESSLEY, WESSON, ELLIS *and* CELLARS *appear in the doorway. Only* ELLIS *and* CELLARS *enter the room and come up to the bed.*)

TOM: (*Reading the directions to his model, while lying back.*)

DR. CELLARS: (*Grabs the directions away.*) There is nothing like your undivided attention. (*Examines Tom without a word and steps back.*)

DR. ELLIS: (*Steps up to* TOM *and feels around the abdomen.*)

DR. CELLARS: (*Walks to the sink and washes hands.*) Don't start a project that will take you too long, you'll be going home soon. (*Turns around.*)

(DR. CELLARS *and* DR. ELLIS *walk out to the hall.*)

TOM: (*Calls*) When?

DR. CELLARS: (*Without turning around*) Soon. Maybe tomorrow.

TOM: Can I call my mother?

DR. CELLARS: Yes.

(*The five doctors walk down the hall.*)

TOM: (*Turning to* MYRA) Can I borrow a dime?

MYRA: I'll look. (*Digs in her pockets, pulls out a dime and hands it to* TOM.)

TOM: I'll wait a little bit, I don't think she's home yet. Do you want to do some?

MYRA: OK.

TOM: (*Works ever more gingerly on the model.*)

MYRA: (*Assists in silence.*) I have to go now Tom.

TOM: OK. I'll give you back the dime tomorrow when my mom comes.

MYRA: OK. If you want.

(MYRA *leaves.*)

THE WORLD OF JEFFREY ANDREWS

SCENE 13: LISA's *room, that evening,* 6:00 *p.m.*

(LISA *is walking around the room holding on to her I.V. pole.* MRS. PHILLIPS *is sitting and counting out loud.*)

LISA: (*Calls out as* MYRA *passes her room.*) I'm doing my laps.

MYRA: (*Stops in the doorway.*) Well, so you have enough room, I'll just stand here in the doorway.

LISA: It's OK. You can come in.

MYRA: Thanks, I'll stand here.

LISA: You don't have to put a mask and gown on then.

MRS. PHILLIPS: It's as if there is an imaginary line or something. It makes it all so ridiculous, the isolation.

MYRA: I can see what you mean. I guess the germs are supposed to obey the line.

MRS. PHILLIPS: These doctors must think so.

(*Silence.*)

LISA: (*Continues walking*) What am I up to?

MRS. PHILLIPS: You have four more to go.

LISA: Good. (*Continues walking.*)

(*Silence.*)

LISA: (*While walking*) When can I start at the orthodontist?

MRS. PHILLIPS: Why?

LISA: (*Stops walking*) I want to.

MRS. PHILLIPS: Wait until your platelets go up. (*Pause.*) Until you are thirteen or fourteen.

LISA: But I think I should start now.

MRS. PHILLIPS: There's time for now.

LISA: (*Starts walking again, taking slower steps and looking down*) I don't want to do anymore.

MRS. PHILLIPS: You have to. Your feet are getting swollen from laying in bed.

LISA: So what! I don't care! (*Starts to cry.*)

MRS. PHILLIPS: (*Throws* MYRA *a look.*)

MYRA: I'll see you, Lisa.

LISA: (*With tears*) 'Bye.

(MYRA *walks down the hall.*)

SCENE 14: JEFFREY'S *room, later that evening,* 9:00 *p.m.*

(JEFFREY *is hunched over the foot of his bed watching the little remaining activity in the hallway.*)

JEFFREY: (*Calling to* MYRA *as she walks by*) See, they took away my isolation.

MYRA: (*Stops.*)

JEFFREY: I might get to go home tomorrow if the blood test is all right. I just have one blood test to go and then I can see. I mean they can see if I can go home. Then I'll have my I.V. out. Lisa just got her I.V. out and that means she can go home after they watch her. They have to watch my counts, but even then I can go home.

MYRA: That's great.

JEFFREY: Come here.

(MYRA *walks over to the bed.*)

JEFFREY: (*In a very serious and shaky voice*) I hope I don't have to come to the hospital again, I hope this is the last time I have to come. They stick you all the time. (*Tears fall, but he does not vocalize a cry.*) Could you stay 'til I fall asleep? I'll try. (*Lies back.*)

MYRA: (*Nods and takes a seat beside the bed.*)

JEFFREY: Good night! (*Turns over.*)

MYRA: Good night, Jeffrey.

ACT IV: REMISSIONS AND RELAPSES

Seven weeks have passed since JEFFREY *was discharged from the hospital. He has been coming to the clinic every week since then. A remission was attained, but it lasted only about two weeks. Last week he was again found to be in relapse, and has had nosebleeds intermittently for the last two days.*

SCENE 1: *The waiting room of the oncology clinic, Monday,*
   11:00 *a.m.*

(MRS. ANDREWS, *with* ERICKA *holding one hand and* JEFFREY
*the other, quickly passes through the double doors into the
clinic.* MRS. ANDREWS *lets go of their hands and rushes
ahead to the receptionist's desk. From there she goes directly into the meeting, while* JEFFREY *and* ERICKA *go over
to the table in the waiting room, where four other children
are playing with clay.* JEFFREY *and* ERICKA *take seats next to
one another.*)

O.T.S. 2: Hi Jeffrey. Hi Ericka.
JEFFREY AND ERICKA: (*In chorus, rather begrudgingly*) Hi!
O.T.S. 2: Do you know Peter?
JEFFREY: (*Shakes his head no and picks up a piece of clay.*)
ERICKA: (*Picks up a piece of clay and begins to roll it into
   a snake.*)
O.T.S. 2: He was here last week.
JEFFREY: I had a bone marrow.
O.T.S. 2: That's right. He's your age. He just moved here
   and is going to be coming to this clinic.
(*Silence, while the children play with their clay.*)
JEFFREY: (*Sitting and staring at the lump of clay in his
   hand.*) The yellow medicine was supposed to last two
   years, but it only lasted seven weeks. Now I have the
   red medicine, but it won't last as long as the yellow.
PETER: (*Shaping pieces of clay into little balls that resemble
   pills.*) I take ten of these (*pointing to the already finished balls*), each day, but today they are going to
   change my medicine.
JENNIFER: (*Looking up from the animal she is molding.*)
   They have to do a bone marrow first.
PETER: How do you know?
JENNIFER: You'll see. Then they wait four weeks and give
   you another bone marrow and another medicine until
   that one stops working and then they start again.
(*Silence while the children go back to the clay playing.*)

(ROBERTA *enters the waiting room and nods over to the children.*)

JENNIFER: (*Nods back.*)

(DR. ELLIS *comes over to the table from the treatment-room area.*)

DR. ELLIS: Hi, Jeffrey. Hi, Ericka. Peter, I want to see you again.

PETER: (*Cries.*)

DR. ELLIS: We'll go get your mom. I think she went back to the meeting. What's the trouble?

ERICKA: He's scared that he's gonna get a bone needle.

PETER: (*Continues to cry.*)

DR. ELLIS: (*Bends over, puts her arm around Peter and helps him up.*)

(DR. ELLIS *and* PETER *walk back to the conference-room area.*)

(*Silence falls on the group as they continue to play with the clay.*)

ERICKA: (*Wanders away from the table and joins* AARON *on the floor, playing with blocks.*)

(*A half-hour later,* DR. ELLIS *comes over to the table from the treatment-room area.*)

DR. ELLIS: OK, Jeffrey. Let's go back and get your mother.

JEFFREY: (*Puts his clay down and gets up.*)

(DR. ELLIS *and* JEFFREY *walk past* ERICKA.)

ERICKA: (*Stands up.*)

JEFFREY: You can't come. Mommy said.

ERICKA: (*Sits down, and looks up at* DR. ELLIS) I hope he doesn't have to go up to the hospital. (*Looks down at her blocks.*)

(DR. ELLIS *and* JEFFREY *continue down the hall to the conference room. They stand in the entrance.* MRS. ANDREWS *stands up and comes out of the conference room.*)

DR. ELLIS: Hello.

MRS. ANDREWS: Hi! Sorry we're late this morning, but Jeffrey had another nosebleed, and you know it slows things down.

DR. ELLIS: You're my last patient today, Jeffrey.

(DR. ELLIS, MRS. ANDREWS, *and* JEF-FREY *enter the treatment room.*)

SCENE 2. *The treatment room, later that morning,* 11:50 *a.m.*

(JEFFREY *gets up on the examination table.* MRS. ANDREWS *stands to the side of the table and* DR. ELLIS *stands on the opposite side facing* MRS. ANDREWS.)

DR. ELLIS: His platelets are low.

MRS. ANDREWS: (*Nods*) He's had those nosebleeds. And the hemoglobin and white count?

DR. ELLIS: Not really noticeably different from last week.

MRS. ANDREWS: (*Draws a deep breath, purses lips, and nods.*)

DR. ELLIS: Well, we will continue with the medicine we gave him last week.

MRS. ANDREWS: (*Nods.*)

DR. ELLIS: Well, Jeffrey, how are the ol' veins today?

JEFFREY: (*Shrugs*) OK. (*Lies back.*)

DR. ELLIS: Well, where were we lucky before?

JEFFREY: (*Holds out his left arm and indicates a place near the joint.*)

DR. ELLIS: (*Feels around in the place* JEFFREY *indicated.*) OK. (*Picks up the syringe and injects the medicine.*)

JEFFREY: (*Does not even whimper.*)

DR. ELLIS: That's it. (*Pulls out the syringe.*) Do you want a Band-Aid?

JEFFREY: (*Staring down at the sight of the injection*) Yeah. Mommy! (*Sits up.*)

MRS. ANDREWS: What, Jeffrey?

JEFFREY: You know (*points to* MRS. ANDREWS' *purse*).

MRS. ANDREWS: (*Takes a picture of irises, done with a crayon-by-number set, out of her pocketbook and hands it to* JEFFREY.)

JEFFREY: (*Eases his way off the examination table and stands by* DR. ELLIS' *desk.*)

89

DR. ELLIS: (*Looks up*) Yes, Jeffrey?

JEFFREY: (*Hands* DR. ELLIS *the picture.*)

DR. ELLIS: Well, thank you, Jeffrey. It's really very pretty. What kinds of flowers are they?

JEFFREY: (*Looks over to* MRS. ANDREWS.)

MRS. ANDREWS: (*In a stage whisper to* JEFFREY) Irises.

JEFFREY: Oh, yeah, irises.

DR. ELLIS: (*Smiles*) Well, take it a little easy. Have you been in school?

MRS. ANDREWS: (*Nods.*) But he's been coming home a little early, on the days when he gets tired.

DR. ELLIS: That's OK. Do you have any questions?

MRS. ANDREWS: No (*Shrugs and shakes head.*)

DR. ELLIS: OK. Then I'll see you both next week. If there are any problems, please call me.

(MRS. ANDREWS *and* JEFFREY *walk out of the treatment room and stand near the receptionist's desk.*)

JEFFREY: Can we go home now?

MRS. ANDREWS: I don't see why not. Why don't you see if Ericka is ready and I'll wait here for the card.

(JEFFREY *walks down to the now-deserted waiting room.*)

SCENE 3: *The waiting room of the oncology clinic, minutes later, 12:30 p.m.*

(ERICKA *is seated on the floor playing with a truck.*)

ERICKA: (*Stands up when she sees* JEFFREY.) They cleaned up the toys, but they said I could keep this one.

JEFFREY: Well, come on. We're goin' now.

(MRS. ANDREWS *comes down the hall.*)

MRS. ANDREWS: (*Hands each of the children a lollipop.*)

ERICKA: Jeffrey doesn't have to stay, does he?

MRS. ANDREWS: No, not for now.

(MRS. ANDREWS, JEFFREY, *and* ERICKA *pass silently through the double doors.*)

SCENE 4: *The nurses' station on the thirteenth floor, Tuesday,* 12:30 *a.m.*

(JEFFREY, *with his head back, a nose stuffed full of cotton, one hand tightly clutching the finger on the other, is wheeled off the elevator into a darkened corridor. With great definition and a sense of familiarity in their step,* MR. ANDREWS, *pushing the wheelchair, and* MRS. ANDREWS, *carrying a sheet of paper and a shopping bag, walk up to the nurses' station.*)

NURSE SINGLETON: (*Standing in back of the receptionist's desk, puts down the phone.*) Hi, Jeffrey. We've been expecting you.

MRS. ANDREWS: It took us a while in the emergency room. Dr. Ellis called ahead, but there was some confusion.

NURSE SINGLETON: (*Nods knowingly.*)

MRS. ANDREWS: (*Hands her the admission slip.*)

NURSE SINGLETON: Has Jeffrey been exposed to any childhood diseases within the last three days? (*Hands* MRS. ANDREWS *the specimen container.*)

MRS. ANDREWS: No.

NURSE SINGLETON: Well, Jeffrey, your room is all ready.

JEFFREY: Do I have to be in isolation?

NURSE SINGLETON: No, I don't think so. (*Comes from behind the desk.*)

(*The four of them proceed down the hall. They enter the room, without hesitation.*)

SCENE 5: JEFFREY'S *room, moments later, Tuesday,* 12:45 *a.m.*

(NURSE SINGLETON *turns on the light, hands* MRS. ANDREWS *a nightgown from the cart.* MRS. ANDREWS *places the nightgown in* JEFFREY'S *lap and goes over to the unmade bed, takes off her coat, and places it and the shopping bag on the bed.* MR. ANDREWS *lifts* JEFFREY *up onto the bed and goes to sit down in a chair by the window.*)

(NURSE SINGLETON *takes the wheel-chair and leaves.*)

MRS. ANDREWS: (*While undressing* JEFFREY) I think you can let go of your finger now. It's probably stopped bleeding.

JEFFREY: I have to hold on tightly, my platelets are low. (*Continues to hold on to his finger.*)

MRS. ANDREWS: (*Finishes getting* JEFFREY *ready, pulls up the covers and goes to sit in a straight chair by the bed.*) We'll stay with you 'til you fall asleep.

MR. ANDREWS: (*Gets up, turns out the light.*)

SCENE 6: *The nurses' station on the thirteenth floor, later that morning, 10:00 a.m.*

(MYRA *is looking on the wall chart to see who might have come in later in the evening or in the morning. Other personnel bustle about.*)

NURSE STEVENS: Were you here when Jeffrey was admitted?

MYRA: Yes.

NURSE STEVENS: Well he's sleeping now, but do we have a good one for you. Guess who's here?

MYRA: (*Shrugs shoulders.*)

NURSE STEVENS: The one we've all been waiting for—the Costins.

MYRA: Oh!

NURSE STEVENS: Come on, I'll take you down and introduce you.

MYRA: Thanks.

(MYRA *and* NURSE STEVENS *walk down the hall.*)

NURSE STEVENS: She really looks bad. She's so thin and she's lost all of her hair. Her mother says that she doesn't like to wear her wig though, even when she's not in the hospital. You know that she's had leukemia for about six years and has only been hospitalized twice. She's the longest one they have down there. (*Reaches the room.*) The door's shut and I bet the lights are off and the shades are down. They keep the room closed up, as if they want to pretend they're not here or something. But you can't block it out that easily. (*Knocks on the door.*)

MRS. COSTIN: (*Opens the door a crack*) Oh, it's you. (*Opens the door further, but not completely, and stands aside.*)

(NURSE STEVENS *and* MYRA *enter the room.*)

SCENE 7: MARY's *room, immediately following, 10:20 a.m.*

(MARY *is propped up in bed watching TV. The room is dark except for the light from the TV screen.*)

NURSE STEVENS: Mary, I brought a friend with me, Myra. She's an anthropologist and she talks to people.

MRS. COSTIN: (*Walking over to the bed opposite* MARY's *and climbing onto it.*) You a psychologist or something?

MYRA: No!

MRS. COSTIN: (*Straightening up*) Well, what do you want to know?

MYRA: I'm interested in what children talk about and think about.

MRS. COSTIN: I think you'd do better to have some. You married?

MYRA: No.

MRS. COSTIN: (*Laughs*) Well then, I guess you ought to just live with some.

NURSE STEVENS: Well, I have some things to do. See you later, Mary.

(NURSE STEVENS *leaves.*)

MARY: Where did you get your necklace?

MYRA: On an Indian reservation. The same one Tom is from. Do you know him?

MRS. COSTIN: (*To her daughter*) You don't know him. (*Throws* MYRA *an angry glance.*)

MARY: Yes, I do. He gets his hair back real fast. I wish I did. (*Silence.*)

MARY: This is the finger I like to have pricked. It doesn't hurt as much as this one. But my veins aren't so good, so I get pricked lots of places. They can't use the same ones over again too many times.

MRS. COSTIN: Mary, don't talk like that.

(*Silence.*)

MARY: I like to cook. I can make real good Caesar salads. My dad showed me. (*Pause.*) I play the piano too.

MRS. COSTIN: She hasn't practiced since April. She hasn't been feeling too good so I don't make her practice.

MYRA: What other things do you like to do, Mary?

MRS. COSTIN: Go to restaurants. Right, Mary?

MARY: (*Nods unenthusiastically.*)

MRS. COSTIN: I used to be a waitress 'til, you know (*hand gestures forward*). I didn't want to be away from Mary. We were going to do so many things this summer. It's my anniversary on Friday, but I'll be here. I wouldn't leave her. I'm not like some mothers. You know. I sleep here every night.

MYRA: (*Nods*) Mary, are there things you like to do?

MRS. COSTIN: Not if you mean with other children. Mary doesn't play with other kids.

MARY: Girls are mean. Boys are better. I wish I was a boy. Boys play with anybody.

MRS. COSTIN: Mary had this one little girlfriend who we used to take back and forth to school, every day, with this other girl. I didn't want Mary getting tired going to school and, well, coming home she was really dead. Well, one day Mary asked the girl to come over and play and she said no.

MARY: And then she asked if Betty wanted to come over to her house and play.

MRS. COSTIN: Isn't that a sin. Children are that way, though. They're mean. I get Mary for lunch too. She doesn't like to eat in the cafeteria. She likes to come home with me and eat what I make her. Mary doesn't have to do anything she doesn't like to do. She doesn't do anything around the house.

MARY: Joe does, but he hardly ever does it.

MRS. COSTIN: Well, you know how Joe is. I think he feels a little, well—(*voice fades off*). Mary's our "baby." I have two other children, Jack and Cindy. Jack is just a doll. He's so good. He's married now; so is Cindy. She's my oldest. My mother lives with us, too, so don't ask. You know, "Mar," I should call granny and see how she is, she's not really feeling well these days.

MARY: (*Angrily*) She's not the sick one. *I'm* the sick one, you know.

MRS. COSTIN: You know, Mary gets lots of prizes.

MYRA: Prizes?

MRS. COSTIN: You know, presents, like for doing good. Her daddy is always bringing her something. He brings her something every day, and he cooks her special foods. Whatever she has a taste for. Whatever Mary wants Mary gets. Right "Mar"?

MARY: (*Nods.*)

MRS. COSTIN: She's our princess. (*Goes over to the bed and pats Mary's forehead.*)

MARY: (*Flinches away.*)

MRS. COSTIN: I've been a good housewife and a good mother, right "Mar."

(NURSE STEVENS *enters the room.*)

NURSE STEVENS: Myra, there is someone here to see you.

MYRA: Thanks. Mary, I'll try to stop back and see you later.

MARY: (*Nods.*)

MYRA: Goodbye, Mrs. Costin.

MRS. COSTIN: 'Bye, dear.

(MYRA *and* NURSE STEVENS *leave.*)

SCENE 8: *Outside* MARY'S *room, that evening,* 7:00 *p.m.*

(MRS. COSTIN *is standing by the door, tapping her foot.* MYRA *walks by but doesn't notice* MRS. COSTIN *or stop until* MRS. COSTIN *begins to speak.*)

95

MRS. COSTIN: I'm just so mad. Thank goodness Mary is finally asleep now, she wasn't then. Brother. This dumbell, one of those interns I guess, comes in and starts asking me these questions, right in front of Mary. He came in and said, "Can I ask you a few questions?" I said, "Sure." What else could I say? They're always sending these dummies in. Mind you, I make some of them leave right away. I don't want them doing any experimenting on my baby. But this one, well, he wasn't going to do anything, just ask some questions. You have to put up with some of it, I guess. But this was just too much. It's bad enough when they stick them and miss. Anyway, he says, "How long have you known about Mary's disease?" I said, "Look you, step outside with me." I said, "Look, first of all you don't talk that way in front of a child. Mary doesn't know what's wrong with her and she's not going to know. I don't even want to hear the word. Mary knows she has a serious blood disease, anemia—like me—and that's all."

MYRA: Doesn't she notice the other kids in the clinic and ask about them, what's wrong with them, or what happened to them, or when they don't come back to the clinic anymore, why they don't?

MRS. COSTIN: Yeah, sure. But I tell her they went to another clinic.

(NURSE EDWARDS *walks over and* stands next to MRS. COSTIN, *unnoticed at first.*)

MRS. COSTIN: I don't believe in telling my child everything, like some mothers. Look at Jennifer Handelman. You know why that kid always looks so unhappy? I'll tell you—'cause her mother tells her everything. A real kook.

NURSE EDWARDS: There are two theories, you know.

MRS. COSTIN: Yeah, I know, but I don't buy that one. Jennifer's mother goes to those coffee klatches, you know. They used to try get me to go to those things, but I've said everything I'm going to say. It's all on tape if they

96

want to hear it. They try to coax me by saying there's coffee, especially that doctor—what's his name?

MYRA: Issacs?

MRS. COSTIN: Yeah, that's the one. I just send John down to get me some. They all talk about the drugs, the side effects, who died, how, all that stuff. I don't want to know it 'til it happens. Besides, Mary hasn't had most of that stuff happen to her. I know what Mary's got, but I don't have to accept it. Besides, she's different from the others. Like I said she took to the medicines differently from most of them. She's different from the others. Yeah. (*Pause.*) In the beginning we got close with these people and then the kid died and ours didn't; its been that way and it's hard, you know what I mean. So now we just keep to ourselves. It's better that way.

(MARY *is heard calling:* "Mommy!")

MRS. COSTIN: Coming, Mary. (*Runs into the room and closes the door behind her.*)

NURSE EDWARDS: Good luck.

MYRA: (*Smiles and nods.*)

(MYRA *and* NURSE EDWARDS *depart down the hall in opposite directions.*)

SCENE 9: JEFFREY'S *room, later that evening,* 9:00 *p.m.*

(*The room is dark except for the glow from the TV screen.* JEFFREY *is propped up in bed watching the TV and coloring.* MRS. ANDREWS *is sitting in a chair beside the bed, with her hand on the bedside, looking up at the TV.*)

MYRA: Hi. Can I come in?

JEFFREY: Yeah.

(MYRA *enters the room and goes to the foot of the bed.*)

MRS. ANDREWS: How are you?

MYRA: Fine. And you?

MRS. ANDREWS: A little tired now. Jeffrey's been sleeping on and off all day. They gave him some blood, though, and he looks a lot better. Don't you think so? (*Looks to* JEFFREY *and back to* MYRA.) But you know how it gets being around here all day.

JEFFREY: (*Raises his hand to his nose.*)

MRS. ANDREWS: Jeffrey.

JEFFREY: I'm trying not to, but it itches. I'll cover my finger, or I'll get an infection and then an I.V. and then I won't go home.

MRS. ANDREWS: Jeffrey, since Myra's here I think I'm going to go home.

JEFFREY: Oh (*whines*).

MRS. ANDREWS: I really have to, Jeffrey. Daddy is there alone with Ericka and Jason and he's tired. You know, we were here 'til very late last night and then Daddy had to go to work.

JEFFREY: Myra, will you watch this program with me? It's about this guy who needs blood and if he doesn't get it he'll die.

MYRA: If he gets the blood do you think he'll live?

JEFFREY: It helped me.

MRS. ANDREWS: (*Stands up, bends over, and kisses* JEFFREY) Good night, Myra. Thank you.

JEFFREY: Bring me something tomorrow.

MRS. ANDREWS: What do you want?

JEFFREY: A cupcake.

MRS. ANDREWS: OK. I'll stop at the bakery on the way. Good night and thanks again.

MYRA: Good night.

(MRS. ANDREWS *leaves.*)

JEFFREY AND MYRA: (*Watch the TV program in silence.*)[10]

JEFFREY: (*Clicks off the TV*) See, I told you. (*Pause.*) I'm sleepy, but I don't want you to leave.

MYRA: OK. I'll wait until you fall asleep.

JEFFREY: (*Rolls over on his side*) I like to sleep on my side.

[10] The man on the program receives the blood and lives.

SCENE 10: *Nurses' station, the next morning, Wednesday,* 11:00 *a.m.*

(MYRA *is writing at one of the desks.* NURSE RICHARDS *walks over to* MYRA.)

NURSE RICHARDS: You missed all the excitement.

MYRA: What do you mean?

NURSE RICHARDS: Turner was here. I don't know why she was here. She goes around and gives the leukemics presents and talks to some of them. Funny, though, the kids never play with them. They know. Eisen [L.P.N.] went into Jeffrey's room and asked him where he got his mobile. He told her he got it from Sandra and Eisen asked him who Sandra was and he said, "You know the one. She had a son Richard who died. He was very sick." Eisen was a little shocked. Mrs. Costin was furious that she came in and when she didn't recognize Turner and Mary did, Jane [L.P.N.] said she just about flipped because Mary said, "That's Richard's mother. I remember Richard. He, died last summer." Well, you know, Mrs. Costin thinks she keeps it all from Mary. Rhonda says that she tells Mary that the children who don't come anymore go to another clinic.

NURSE WALTON: (*Working on a chart nearby and listening*) Yeah, the great clinic in the sky.

NURSE RICHARDS: By the way, Jeffrey went home this morning. He left this for you. (*Reaches into a cabinet overhead, pulls out a picture and hands it to* MYRA.) He said it was a picture of you and you can tell him if you like it in clinic on Monday.

MYRA: Thanks.

NURSE RICHARDS: Paul's been acting a little strange since Mrs. Turner left. You know, she has sort of "adopted" him. One of the other nurses, I forget who now, said that she heard her talking to him about dying.

MYRA: You don't think she should?

NURSE RICHARDS: Well. (*Pause.*) Oh. I guess I better go and pass out the meds. See you later.

> (NURSE RICHARDS *walks away before* MYRA *has a chance to say more.*)

SCENE 11: *Waiting room in the oncology clinic, Monday (one and a half weeks after* JEFFREY *is discharged),* 11:00 *a.m.*

(JEFFREY *and* ERICKA *pass through the double door, with* MRS. ANDREWS *behind them.* JEFFREY *and* ERICKA *walk over to the table while* MRS. ANDREWS *reports to the receptionist.*)

SHARON: Jeffrey, Ericka. How are you? We missed you last week.

ERICKA: Mommy overslept and Jeffrey didn't wake her.

SHARON: I see. Would you both like to paint today? We can make some room for you. (*Clears a place.*)

JEFFREY: (*Shrugs and walks over to the place* SHARON *clears.*)

SHARON: There, you can sit next to Lisa, and you can sit next to Ian, Ericka. (*Turning head toward* ERICKA) Ian is Scott's brother. He comes to the clinic like Jeffrey does.

ERICKA: (*Sits down and looks around the table.*) I don't have a paint brush.

LISA: You can use mine. I don't feel like painting. (*Hands Ericka the brush.*)

JEFFREY: (*Picks up the brush in front of him and begins to paint.*)

ERICKA: (*Looks at what* JEFFREY *is doing, then begins to paint.*)

> (MYRA *enters the waiting room.*)

MYRA: Hi, Jeffrey. Hi, Ericka. Hi, Ian; hi, Lisa.

JEFFREY: (*Looks up*) Did you get my picture?

MYRA: Yes, thank you very much. I hung it up in my kitchen. (MYRA *pulls a chair over to the table, next to* LISA.)

100

LISA: (*Begins to play with* MYRA's *hair.*)

MRS. ANDREWS: (*From the other side of the waiting room*) I'm over here.

JEFFREY AND ERICKA: (*Continue painting. They do not look up.*)

JEFFREY: (*Looks up to* MYRA.) It's a picture of you.

LISA: (*To* MYRA) Did you ever read the *Secret Garden?*

MYRA: No, tell me about it.

LISA: Well, it starts out in India. This girl's mother dies, of cholera I think, and she goes to live with her uncle in England. His wife fell off a branch in the garden and no one can go in there any more. He keeps his son locked up in one of the hundred rooms.

MYRA: Uh huh.

LISA: And his wife is buried in the garden and no one is allowed in there, but the girl found the key under the bird's eggs.

SCOTT: (*From the other end of the table*) When we lived in Detroit there used to be a lot of dead birds in our yard.

MYRA: A lot of dead birds?

SCOTT: Yeah, the cat killed them.

(*Silence.*)

(DR. WESSLEY *enters the waiting-room area, from the treatment-room area. She stands on the side opposite the children's table, playing with* ELLIOT.)

DR. WESSLEY: (*Calls*) Lisa Phillips.

LISA: (*Gets up from the table and walks over to* DR. WESSLEY.)

(DR. WESSLEY *and* LISA *go down the hall to the treatment rooms.*)

(MRS. HELLER *enters the waiting room and comes over to the table where the children are painting.*)

MRS. HELLER: Hi, Ericka. Hi, Jeffrey. Scott, Ian, I'm going over there to sit by Mrs. Andrews until the meeting.

SCOTT: Did you get the medicine?

101

MRS. HELLER: Yes, I did. They finally got to me. (*Walks over to the opposite side of the waiting room, where* MRS. ANDREWS *is sitting.*)

MRS. HELLER: Hi. (*Sits down.*)

MRS. ANDREWS: Hi. How are you? I saw Scott and Ian, but I didn't see you.

MRS. HELLER: I was waiting in line for the medicine and I sent the children up ahead. I didn't know what to say. Mrs. Manello was there waiting with Esther for the medicine. She really looks bad. I said, "How's Esther," and she said, "I think she's dying." And then, wouldn't you know it, Ian said, "What did she say?" I think I said she was doing fairly or something like that. And then I told them that they may as well go upstairs. I just don't know what to tell him anymore, but I think I'm going to have to tell him something soon. You know, Scott was in last week.

MRS. ANDREWS: No I didn't. We missed clinic last week, and the week before Jeffrey had been in, and this week's been hard, because Jeffrey's been in and out.

MRS. HELLER: Same with Scott. He was having some bleeding, so Wessley said to bring him in and she'd take a look. Well, that night when we went home . . .

DR. ISAACS: (*Calls from the edge of the waiting-room area* There is coffee in the conference room.

MRS. HELLER: Ian said that he liked to be with me because I say what I mean. "You never lie, Mommy." You know I think he was trying to ask me something or else he was getting around to it. (*Stands up.*)

MRS. ANDREWS: (*Stands up.*)

(MRS. ANDREWS *and* MRS. HELLER *leave the waiting-room area and go to the conference-room area.*)

SHARON: Scott, do you want to tell us about your picture?

SCOTT: (*Shakes his head.*)

SHARON: What's that building in the center?

SCOTT: The Sedgwick building. My daddy took us to the top last weekend.

(DR. WESSLEY *comes over to the table from the treatment-room area.*)

JEFFREY: My daddy's gonna take me fishing this summer. (*Pause, looks to* ERICKA.) But I always get sick and then we can't go. (*Looks down at his picture.*)

ERICKA: (*Without looking up from her painting*) Yeah. He messes up all the plans.

SHARON: What are these, Scott (*pointing to thick diagonal lines coming out of the building*).

SCOTT: They are the fire escapes.

SHARON: Hi, Dr. Wessley.

DR. WESSLEY: Hello. Well, Scott. I'm ready for you.

SCOTT: Good. I've been waiting here real long and we got here early.

DR. WESSLEY: I know, it took a while for the medicine.

SCOTT: My mom just came back. She's over there (*looks over to where she was sitting*). I guess she went to the meeting.

DR. WESSLEY: OK. We'll go get her.

(SCOTT *and* DR. WESSLEY *walk back to the treatment-room area.*)

IAN: (*Looking over at* DR. WESSLEY *and* SCOTT *passing* EL-LIOT) Did Elliot have vincristine too?

MYRA: Yes, why?

IAN: I thought so. He lost his hair like Scott did. The kids at school called him baldy. I hope Scott doesn't lose his hair again from the cytoxan, but my mother said he might.

(DR. ELLIS *comes over to the table from the treatment-room area and takes* JEFFREY *back with her.*)

ERICKA: (*Gets up from the table and goes over to the Bozo doll and proceeds to pummel it.*)

IAN: (*Turns and looks over to* ERICKA.)

103

MYRA: That makes you feel bad, doesn't it.

IAN: (*Turning back around to* MYRA) Yeah, I don't like it when they call Scott names and when he goes in the hospital. (*Pause.*) I don't want to talk about it.

MYRA: OK.

IAN: Will you play catch with me? Just 'til Scott gets back?

MYRA: All right. (*Stands up and walks over to the aisle with* IAN.)

IAN: (*Picks up the ball from the cart and throws.*)

MYRA AND IAN: (*Continue to play in silence.*)

(SCOTT *comes out of the treatment-room area and over to* IAN.)

IAN: (*Stops and holds the ball.*) Do you have to go in the hospital?

SCOTT: (*Shakes his head.*)

IAN: (*To* MYRA) You almost made me forget. Scott, do you want to play?

SCOTT: No, I'm just gonna wait for Mom. She went back to the meeting.

IAN: I don't want to play any more. (*Puts down the ball and goes over to the table with* SCOTT. *They sit down.*)

(JEFFREY *comes out of the treatment-room area and goes over to the table.*)

ERICKA: (*Sees* JEFFREY, *lets go of the Bozo doll, and follows him over to the table.*)

JEFFREY: Where's Jennifer?

SHARON: She just got here. She was late and I think she went to the bathroom. She'll be out soon. Why?

JEFFREY: I have to ask her what a relapse is. (*Walks over to the bathroom.*)

(JENNIFER *comes out of the bathroom followed by* LISA, JILL, *and* LAURA.)

JEFFREY: What's a relapse?

JENNIFER: That's a bad time. There are good times and bad times. It's usually when the medicines aren't working and your body is sick again.

JEFFREY: Oh, I guess I'm in a bad time still.

JENNIFER: How do you know? Did you get a bone marrow?

JEFFREY: No, I just had one.

JENNIFER: But not this week?

JEFFREY: No.

JENNIFER: Are they going to give you another one?

JEFFREY: No. It's not even three weeks.

JENNIFER: Do you have the same medicine? I mean did they give you the same stuff as last time?

JEFFREY: Yeah, I'm pretty sure.

JENNIFER: Well, that means you haven't gotten a remission yet from what they are giving you. The medicine isn't working yet. So you're still in relapse.

JEFFREY: My mother's coming (*sees her on her way over to the bathroom.*) I have to go now.

JENNIFER: See ya.

(JEFFREY *walks over to his mother, who is now standing with* ERICKA.)

MRS. ANDREWS: Are you ready?

JEFFREY: (*Nods.*)

(MRS. ANDREWS, JEFFREY, *and* ERICKA *pass through the double doors.*)

SCENE 12: *Waiting room of the oncology clinic, the following Monday, 9:00 a.m.*

(MRS. ANDREWS *wheels* JEFFREY, *head hung low, tears in his eyes, through the double doors.* ERICKA *walks beside them carrying a grocery bag in one hand, and holding the door with the other.* MRS. ANDREWS *wheels* JEFFREY *over to an empty area in the waiting room.* ERICKA *drops the sack and runs over to the Bozo doll and begins punching.*)

MRS. ANDREWS: Jeffrey, I'll go back and give in our card so we get taken right away.

JEFFREY: (*Whimpers.*)

MRS. ANDREWS: Look Jeffrey, I have to so we get taken right away.

105

JEFFREY: When?

MRS. ANDREWS: I'm sure when Dr. Ellis comes in she'll take us first.

JEFFREY: And then we'll go upstairs?

MRS. ANDREWS: (*Voice showing greater and greater annoyance*) Yes, probably.

(MRS. ANDREWS *walks back to the receptionist's desk.*)

(SHARON *comes into the waiting room and walks over to* ERICKA.)

SHARON: You're early this week.

ERICKA: Yeah. (*Takes a good punch at the doll and stops.*) Jeffrey didn't sleep. He's going in the hospital again. See, there's his stuff (*points to the shopping bag beside the wheelchair.*)

SHARON: Did the doctor say so?

ERICKA: No.

SHARON: Then how do you know?

ERICKA: Leave me alone (*resumes punching.*)

(SHARON walks over to JEFFREY *as* MRS. ANDREWS *returns from the receptionist's desk.*)

SHARON: Hello, Mrs. Andrews. Hi, Jeffrey.

JEFFREY: (*Listlessly*) Hi.

MRS. ANDREWS: (*Grimaces and looks at Sharon.*)

SHARON: How are you?

JEFFREY: I have fever and my legs hurt.

MRS. ANDREWS: Jeffrey, do you want a pill?

JEFFREY: No.

MRS. ANDREWS: Why don't you take one now, before it starts to hurt more?

JEFFREY: I don't want one.

MRS. ANDREWS: (*Grinding her teeth*) Jeffrey.

JEFFREY: Leave me alone. (*Begins to cry.*)

MRS. ANDREWS: (*Looks up to* SHARON) He doesn't like to say he has a lot of pain. He's afraid they'll do a marrow. I don't know, he seems to know when they are going to do one anyway.

(DR. ELLIS *passes through the double doors and goes directly to* JEFFREY.)

DR. ELLIS: Hi, Jeffrey. Mrs. Andrews, how 'bout if you bring him back now?

(MRS. ANDREWS, JEFFREY, *and* DR. ELLIS *go back to the treatment rooms.*)

SCENE 13: *Nurses' station on the thirteenth floor, some minutes later, 9:55 a.m.*

(*Many people are milling about the nurses' station. Morning rounds are over and personnel are off to their various tasks.* MYRA *walks by the station on her way to the elevator.*)

NURSE STEVENS: (*Calls out*) Myra.

MYRA: (*Walks over.*)

NURSE STEVENS: Jeffrey Andrews is on his way up from the clinic.

NURSE DICKERSON: I saw him this morning sitting outside 101. He really looks grim.

MYRA: What's he being admitted for?

NURSE STEVENS: The usual: fever, bone pain. He's probably in relapse.

MYRA: Well, I'm on my way down to clinic now. I'll see him when I get back.

NURSE STEVENS: Yeah, and probably a few more by then too.

MYRA: (*Nods.*)

(MYRA *walks toward the elevators.*)

SCENE 14: *Near the elevators on the thirteenth floor, that afternoon, 2:30 p.m.*

(MRS. ANDREWS *is sitting by the elevator looking alternately at other children playing and at the window.* MYRA *steps off the elevator.*)

MYRA: Oh! Hello, Mrs. Andrews. How is Jeffrey doing?

MRS. ANDREWS: Oh, I don't know anymore. The same. He's

107

been sleeping almost all day from the medicine they gave him, and he didn't get any sleep last night. Neither did I for that matter.

MYRA: How are you doing?

MRS. ANDREWS: OK, I guess. My parents just left. They came and got Ericka. They were watching Jason all day, so I kept Ericka here for a while. It's been hard for my mother. She's not so well either. We just found out that she has diabetes. And with Jeffrey getting sick on and off, and it doesn't seem like there will be much of a let-up. She's taken off a lot to be with Jason, and Ericka has been home all summer, but she started back to school last week. I brought her here today because I knew something like this would happen and I thought maybe she should be with me. (*Pause*) You know when I told her her grandparents were going to come and take her home she asked me if Jeffrey was going to die. I mean I didn't, well, we just held each other. She's only five and a half. I told her that he would come home this time.

MYRA: So you think she knows, but you wanted her to know that it wouldn't be this time.

MRS. ANDREWS: Yes. (*Shaking her head*) We haven't said anything to her, but I think she knows.

MYRA: What do you think Jeffrey knows?

MRS. ANDREWS: I'm not sure anymore. He doesn't ask as many questions as he used to, but I think he knows a lot more than he says he does or lets on.

MYRA: Where do you think he gets his information from then?

MRS. ANDREWS: Well it's not from us, I know that. We just don't talk about it and he doesn't ask. Probably from the other kids in clinic. I think children ask each other because they know they'll get a straight answer, and besides, maybe they see it makes us uncomfortable. We really have a hard time talking lately, and I think he knows it and just doesn't talk to me.

108

MYRA: Do you think he knows that he will die from this?

MRS. ANDREWS: I don't think he knows that yet. Only one child has died since Jeffrey was diagnosed, and it was really so soon after Jeffrey was diagnosed, and Jeffrey didn't know him. He hadn't relapsed yet and was only coming to clinic every few weeks. But I don't know. There are a lot of other children now who are sort of at the end of the line. I know there are at least six in the clinic. Ellis said. Four of them are here now.[11] The other two must be Phillips and Handelman.[12] Dr. Ellis told the Wellers that when the drugs run out here they could go to Bethesda. They have the drugs three or four years before here. It's terrible the way there is so much more involved—politics and all. Donna said that there is a form of asparaginase for children who are allergic, but Ellis said that we were lucky even to have asparaginase.[13] They just started getting it here and they have been using it at N.I.H. for three years now.[14]

But I don't know if I'd take Jeffrey there now. This place is so familiar. I'd have to be pretty sure that they could do something.

MYRA: More than prolong his life.

MRS. ANDREWS: No, just prolong it for a reasonable amount of time. (*Looks at watch*) I better go back now and see how Jeffrey's doing.

(MRS. ANDREWS *and* MYRA *walk toward the nurses' station, then go in opposite directions down the hall.*)

[11] At that time the four leukemics included Jeffrey.

[12] Dr. Ellis did not give Mrs. Andrews any names, but all of her guesses were correct except for Handelman.

[13] L-asparaginase is another antileukemic drug. In conversation it is simply referred to as asparaginase.

[14] Abbreviations used by parents and physicians to refer to the National Institute of Health, Cancer Research Hospital, Bethesda, Maryland.

SCENE 15: MARY'S *room, later that afternoon, 5:00 p.m.*

(MARY *is propped up in bed.* MRS. COSTIN *is leaning on the edge of the bed and looking out the door.*)

MYRA: Hi, Mary.

MARY: I got some prize today from my Uncle Fred.

MRS. COSTIN: She got a doll and . . .

MARY: Shut up.

MRS. COSTIN: We haven't been doing well at all lately. I never say the right thing. I never do the right thing. She won't talk to me, like I'm bad news or something.

MARY: (*Sighs.*)

(DR. WESSON *comes to the door.*)

DR. WESSON: (*From the doorway*) Well, Mary, how are you doing?

MARY: OK.

DR. WESSON: Have you been coughing like you're supposed to?

MRS. COSTIN: Yeah, but only a little. She says it hurts her.

DR. WESSON: Look, Mary, I know it hurts a little maybe, but you have to do it. You want to go home, don't you?

MRS. COSTIN: Yeah, Mary, I want to take you home. I've got so much planned for us to do.

MARY: (*Turns away from the doctor and pretends to sleep.*)

DR. WESSON: Mrs. Costin.

MRS. COSTIN: (*Follows* DR. WESSON *out the door and they begin to talk just outside* MARY'S *room. The conversation is definitely within* MARY'S *hearing.*)

MYRA: Mary.

MARY: Shut up. I have to listen.

DR. WESSON'S VOICE: I think we should continue the inhalation therapy, maybe even increase it a little, to make her cough. She's got to cough. That stuff's not good sitting in her chest like that.

MARY: (*Whimpers.*)

110

MRS. COSTIN'S VOICE: Do you think I should still go tomorrow?

DR. WESSON'S VOICE: I don't see why not. By all means. You
don't have to stay here every minute with Mary. Mary
will probably be able to go home soon.

MRS. COSTIN'S VOICE: Well, thank you.

(DR. WESSON *walks on down the hall;*
MRS. COSTIN *comes back into the room and goes back to*
where she was standing when DR. WESSON *was in the room.*)

MARY: Well, what did he say?

MRS. COSTIN: That he wants you to cough more.

MARY: Is that lady going to come anymore?

MRS. COSTIN: Yes, she is.

MARY: (*Whimpers.*)

MRS. COSTIN: Oh, come on Mary. You never used to be this
way. Now you cry about every little finger stick. You
used to even be good for the bone marrows.

MARY: I'm tired.

MYRA: Well, Mary. I'll see you tomorrow when your mom
leaves.

MARY: All right.

MRS. COSTIN: Thank you, Myra. You know, I wouldn't leave
her unless you were going to stay with her all day and
not see anyone else.

MYRA: I understand. I'll see you tomorrow Mary.

MARY: 'Bye.

(MYRA *leaves the room.*)

SCENE 16: JEFFREY's *room, the next morning, Tuesday,*
10:30 *a.m.*

(JEFFREY *is propped up in bed, playing with some cards on*
his tray. There are several tubes running into his I.V. and
he watches them almost as much as he plays with the
cards.)

MYRA: Hi, Jeffrey, can I come in?

111

JEFFREY: Yeah.

(MYRA *enters.*)

MYRA: I missed you yesterday, you were asleep.

JEFFREY: Yeah, I had fever and my legs hurt, from relapse, so Dr. Ellis said I should come in.

MYRA: Well, I didn't expect to see you.

JEFFREY: I knew I was coming in. (*Pause.*) I just keep coming back, I guess I'll never really get better. (*Looks up at I.V. and then down at the I.V. board.*) Do you know what medicine that is? (*points to stains on the I.V. board*).

MYRA: No. Is it one of the antibiotics?

JEFFREY: No. That's in *that* bottle (*pointing to one of the three hanging on the pole*). They might change it after the cultures come back.

MYRA: Do you know what a culture is?

JEFFREY: Yes. They watch the germs grow on it, and then they give you an antibiotic to fight the germs. Today they cultured my pee pee. They tried to culture my stink, but I didn't do it. (*Pause*) Well, guess.

MYRA: Is it gentomycin?

JEFFREY: I said it wasn't an antibiotic. Do you give up?

MYRA: Yes.

JEFFREY: It's methotrexate. It makes the sick blood go out and the good blood grow in. (*Pause*) The methotrexate burns. I hope it burns the doctors.

(*Silence.*)

JEFFREY: Do you want to play cards with me?

MYRA: Well, OK. For a little bit.

JEFFREY AND MYRA: (*Play "fish" for fifteen minutes.*)

JEFFREY: Did you see Tom?

MYRA: No, not yet.

JEFFREY: He must still be in X-ray then. I saw him go by and Eisen said that was where he was going.

JEFFREY AND MYRA: (*Play "fish" for about ten minutes more.*)

MYRA: Well, Jeffrey, I think I should be going now.

112

JEFFREY: I know. OK.
MYRA: I'll see you tomorrow.
JEFFREY: Good. 'Bye.
MYRA: 'Bye.

(MYRA *leaves.*)

SCENE 17: MARY's *room, that afternoon,* 3:00 *p.m.*

(MARY *is sitting in bed.* NURSE DICKERSON *is sitting beside her.* MRS. COSTIN *has left for her banquet.*)

(MYRA *enters carrying a box of crayons and some paper.*)
MARY: What took you so long?
MYRA: I was detained.
MARY: (*To* NURSE DICKERSON) You can go now. Myra's here.
NURSE DICKERSON: Thank you, your highness. (*Smiles.*)

(NURSE DICKERSON *leaves.*)
MARY: This is my mommy's robe. I'm holding it 'til she gets back. (*Pause.*) Are those crayons for me?
MYRA: They are for you to use if you want to draw.
MARY: Are they new?
MYRA: Yes.
MARY: OK. Then I'll do a picture for my mother.
MYRA: (*Places the box of crayons and a sheet of paper on the tray before her.*)
MARY: (*Struggles to get a crayon out.*)
MYRA: Do you want some help?
MARY: It's hard to do with an I.V. in your hand.
MYRA: (*Spills out the crayons.*)
MARY: (*Works silently. Picks up the crayons with one hand and holds the paper down with the hand the I.V. is in. She draws a vase with some flowers in it and a watering can beside it.*)
MYRA: (*When the picture is completed*) I think your mother will like the picture.
MARY: I'm tired now.

113

MYRA: Would you like to make some paper dolls?

MARY: No, I want you to make them.

MYRA: I'll tell you what—I'll cut them out and you tell me how to color them.

MARY: Well, OK.

MYRA: (*Cuts out four paper dolls with pigtails*) What color do you want the hair?

MARY: (*Shrugs.*)

MYRA: Should they all have the same color or different colored hair?

MARY: Same color.

MYRA: Which color?

MARY: (*Hands* MYRA *the black crayon.*)

MYRA: (*Colors the hair on the four dolls black.*)

MYRA: What color do you want the blouses?

MARY: I don't know. I'm tired. Don't ask me.

MYRA: OK. Do you want me to finish them?

MARY: Yes.

MYRA: (*Finishes coloring all the dolls.*)

MARY: (*As* MYRA *puts down the last crayon*) They look the way I used to look.

MYRA: Oh.

MARY: Yeah, when I had hair. (*Turns over and buries head in the pillow. Begins to doze.*)

(*At 4:45 p.m. the aide from the kitchen brings* MARY's *dinner in and sets it down by the bed.*)

MARY: (*Awakens*) Where's my mommy?

MYRA: She's not here yet.

MARY: (*Starts to cry*) I'm not going to eat 'til she gets here. I'll wait 'til Mommy comes.

MYRA: OK.

MARY: She promised she'd come after the beauty shop and I hope she didn't lie. (*Continues to whimper, then suddenly changes to a clear voice*) Call my mommy and ask her to bring some shrimp from the Chinamen.

MYRA: OK, Mary, I'll see what I can do.

(MYRA *leaves the room and goes down to the nurses' station.*)

114

SCENE 18: *The nurses' station, moments later.*

(*The station is empty except for* NURSE LYONS, *who is seated at the desk.* MYRA *arrives.*)

NURSE LYONS: I was hoping you would come out for a minute. Mrs. Costin keeps calling and she wants to talk to you. Mary giving you a hard time?

MYRA: No. It's just for some reason she thinks her mother is coming back soon and Mrs. Costin told me she was going to the banquet.

NURSE LYONS: I thought that might happen. "Days" [day shift] told us that Mary carried on so when her mother left that Mrs. Costin told her that she would just go and have her hair done and then come back. I just can't understand it. When she's here Mary's always yelling at her and when she leaves she cries. (*Phone rings.*) Excuse me (*picks up the phone.*) Hello, thirteen east, Miss Lyons speaking. Yes. Hold on. (*Handing* MYRA *the receiver*) It's for you. Guess who?

MYRA: (*Puts phone to her ear*) Hello, Mrs. Costin.

MRS. COSTIN'S VOICE: Is Mary crying for me? Tell me the truth now.

MYRA: She is acting like most kids would.

MRS. COSTIN'S VOICE: Does she miss me?

MYRA: Yes, but she'll be all right.

MRS. COSTIN'S VOICE: Did she eat her dinner?

MYRA: No, not yet.

MRS. COSTIN'S VOICE: Well, tell her to tell Jack what she wants and he'll go out and get it for her when they get there. He'll be there soon.

MYRA: OK.

MRS. COSTIN'S VOICE: Have Jack and Judy call me as soon as they get there, I want to make sure that you are telling me everything.

MYRA: Yes, I will.

MRS. COSTIN'S VOICE: 'Bye.

MYRA: 'Bye. (*Hangs up.*)

115

NURSE LYONS: (*Nods knowingly, smirks.*) Have fun!

MYRA: Yeah, sure.

    (MYRA *leaves the nurses' station and goes back to the room.*)

SCENE 19: MARY'S *room, moments later.*

MARY: (*In a clear voice*) Well, did my mother say she was coming?

    (MYRA *enters the room and goes over to the bed.*)

MYRA: Jack and Judy are on their way over.

MARY: (*Becomes hysterical*) Didn't she know I wanted her? I only said the shrimp to get her to come. Doesn't she love me? She lied to me. Doesn't she know I need her? (*Sobs more and more bitterly and begins to have trouble breathing.*)

MYRA: Mary. Stop it. She was in the shower and when Jack gets here he'll go and get the shrimp.

MARY: (*Still sobbing somewhat*) I don't want Jack, I want Mommy. Myra, please call her and tell her. Please call her (*sobs more loudly, then catches her breath and stops, voice changes to a clear tone*). Tell her I'm sick or something. I'm really bad. Please call her, Myra.

MYRA: I'll see what I can do.

    (MYRA *leaves the room and goes to see* DR. WESSON. *He agrees with* MYRA *that* MRS. COSTIN *should not be called.*)

SCENE 20: MARY'S *room, immediately after* MYRA'S *conversation with* DR. WESSON.

(MARY *is sitting up in bed looking out the door and crying bitterly.* MYRA *comes to the door and she stops crying.*)

MARY: Did you talk to my mother?

    (MYRA *enters the room.*)

MYRA: She knows that you miss her and . . .

MARY: (*Interrupts*) Did you tell her how upset I was, how

I cry? She knows I get a pain (*points to her chest*) right here when I cry. She knows I get a pain and it's not good for me. She doesn't love me. The banquet is more important to her than I am.

MYRA: Now come on, Mary.

MARY: (*Continues to cry, until she finally falls asleep.*)

MYRA: (*Sits down in the chair beside her bed.*)

(*At* 7:00 *p.m.* JACK COSTIN *arrives and* MYRA *leaves the room.*)

SCENE 21: MARY's *room, the next morning, Wednesday,* 10:45 *a.m.*

(MARY *is all dressed and sitting in a chair by the bed.* MRS. COSTIN *and an* O.T.S. *are putting things in paper bags.*)

MYRA: (*From the doorway*) Hi, Mary.

MRS. COSTIN: We're going home today. I was so surprised. Excuse me but I want to finish before they change their minds or something. Poor Mary's so nervous she bit off all her nails.

MARY: Hi, Myra.

O.T.S. 3: (*Holding up the paper dolls that* MARY *and* MYRA *had worked on*) What should I do with these?

MARY: Put them in their graves, in the Kleenex box. Let me do it. Bring it over here.

O.T.S. 3: (*Brings the Kleenex box and the dolls over to* MARY *and puts them on her lap.*)

MRS. COSTIN: Well, that's the first thing you've offered to do since the doctors said we could go.

MARY: I'm burying them (*carefully arranges each doll between two sheets of Kleenex*).

O.T.S. 3: Is there anything else you want to pack or want help with? (*Takes the box away.*)

MARY: Be careful.

(*Silence.*)

MYRA: Well, Mary, I think I better go now. You're just about packed.

117

MARY: Will you come to my house and visit me?

MYRA: Well, we'll see.

MRS. COSTIN: Of course Myra will come to the house, if that's what you want. We'll call her tonight from home.

MYRA: OK. See you Mary.

> (MYRA *turns and walks down the hall.*)

SCENE 22: JEFFREY's *room, that afternoon,* 5:30 *p.m.*

(JEFFREY *is propped up in bed eating his dinner and looking out the door.* MYRA *passes by the doorway.*)

JEFFREY: My mom went for dinner. Please come in my room.

> (MYRA *enters the room.*)

MYRA: Hi, Jeffrey. What you up to?

JEFFREY: I want to play a game. You be Jeffrey (*silence*) and I'll be Myra.

MYRA: OK. What do I have to do to be Jeffrey?

JEFFREY: You have to be in the hospital all the time. You have to get shots all the time. You have to have I.V.s all the time and you have to be sick all the time.

> (NURSE EDWARDS *enters the room.*)

MYRA: Is that all you have to do?

JEFFREY: Uh huh.

NURSE EDWARDS: Excuse me, Myra, could I see you now?

MYRA: Yes. Jeffrey, I'll try to stop back later.

JEFFREY: OK. And then we can finish.

MYRA: Sure thing.

> (MYRA *leaves the room with* NURSE EDWARDS *and they walk down the hall.*)

SCENE 23: *Just down the hall from Jeffrey's room, immediately following.*

NURSE EDWARDS: Myra, it's Jenny. She's not responding. They sent for the priest and they want you to go in.

MYRA: OK.

(MYRA *and* NURSE EDWARDS *walk over to* JENNIFER's *room.*)

NURSE EDWARDS: (*Passing the linen cart and taking a towel*) I think we should put something on the door. I mean, well, Jeffrey's right across the way and Tom's been going back and forth.

MYRA: Well.

NURSE EDWARDS: (*Holds the door open.*)

(MYRA *enters* JENNIFER'S *room and the door is closed behind her.*)

(*Sometime later, at 9:10 p.m., the hospital loudspeaker sounds.*)

HOSPITAL LOUDSPEAKER: Number one on thirteen east. Number one on thirteen east.

(*Minutes later, 9:15 p.m., a variety of hospital personnel begin arriving on the floor and rush to* JENNIFER'S *room.*)

HOSPITAL LOUDSPEAKER: All children in their rooms.

SCENE 24: *The nurses' station, later that evening, 11:30 p.m.*

(MYRA *is seated alone at the receptionist's desk making some notes. A man carrying a black briefcase marked "Eye Bank" approaches the desk.*)

MAN FROM EYE BANK: I'm here for the eyes.

MYRA: To your right. The third door on your left.

(*The* MAN FROM THE EYE BANK *turns and walks down the darkened corridor.*)

ACT V: THE TERMINAL STAGE

SCENE 1: JEFFREY'S *room, the next morning, Thursday, 10:00 a.m.*

(JEFFREY *is out of bed and seated on a chair. His back is to the door and he is watching TV.* MYRA *knocks on the door, but* JEFFREY *doesn't turn around.*)

119

MYRA: Jeffrey. Can I come in?

JEFFREY: (*Nods without looking back.*)

(MYRA *enters and pulls up a chair next to* JEFFREY.)

MYRA: Jeffrey.

JEFFREY: (*Staring at TV, in a rather loud voice*) There's nothing wrong with me. Nothing's bothering me. I'm not upset.

MYRA: OK.

JEFFREY: (*Eyes on the TV*) I'm not upset.

MYRA: Well, can I sit here for a while then?

JEFFREY: Yeah.

MYRA AND JEFFREY: (*Sit and watch the TV in silence. While there is a great deal of activity in the hall,* JEFFREY *never takes his eyes off the TV screen.*)

MYRA: Well, Jeffrey, I think I better go now.

JEFFREY: OK.

(MYRA *leaves.*)

JEFFREY: (*Continues to stare at the TV, does not even turn when other children call to him.*)

SCENE 2: TOM'S *room, moments later.*

(TOM *is lying on his side, his back to the door. The room is dark.*)

(NURSE BARTON *enters the room.*)

NURSE BARTON: Tom, would you like to go down to the play-room?

TOM: (*Turns over*) Uh huh. (*Pause.*) Jennifer died last night. I have the same thing, don't I?

NURSE BARTON: But they are giving you different medicines.

TOM: What happens when they run out?

NURSE BARTON: Well, maybe they will find more by then.

TOM: Oh (*turns over and buries head in the pillow*).

(NURSE BARTON *comes out of the room.*)

NURSE BARTON: Myra. I just couldn't.

MYRA: Do you want to talk about it?

NURSE BARTON: (*Tears coming to eyes*) Oh, I don't know!

(MYRA *and* NURSE BARTON *walk down the hall and turn off into the medicine room.* NURSE BARTON *closes the door.*)

SCENE 3: *Near the telephone booths on the thirteenth floor, east wing, that afternoon,* 1:00 *p.m.*

(MRS. ANDREWS *is standing by the phone booth.* MYRA *walks up to her.*)

MYRA: Hi. How are you doing?

MRS. ANDREWS: OK I guess. I just called to see if Joe left yet. He stayed overnight last night with Jeffrey and then I came this morning. He said he'd be back tonight. Wow, I don't know.

MYRA: Don't know what?

MRS. ANDREWS: Well, you know. Jenny seemed so fine and all and then all of a sudden. At least she didn't suffer too much. They brought her in and she died that day. I want to call Alice but it's sort of hard to know what to say. Mindy called and the funeral is Saturday. She's having a viewing; I don't know if I want that. My mother-in-law I think expects us to have a wake and all that, but I don't know, somehow, for a child. But it's funny, she acts like it's never really going to happen. And whenever she comes she cries and all. I just didn't want her around and all (*voice fades off*). (*Pause.*) He just won't talk to me. He didn't say anything to his father all evening. They just sat and watched a night game on TV and then later, you know, they come around and shut all the doors. I guess just in case anyone's up.

Did he say anything to you? (*Without waiting for an answer*) It's funny, though, I know he knows. He's really on edge today. I asked him if he wanted to do

121

some schoolwork. He's really good in school. With all his absences he's still at the top of his class. Ericka just started school. She's bright and all, but the teacher, she has the same one Jeffrey had, even said, "She's no Jeffrey." He always does his work. This is the first day he hasn't wanted to, and he's been a lot sicker. I asked him if he wanted to do some the teacher sent home, and he yelled, "I'm not going to school anymore." And I said, "You'll be going home soon." He hasn't had a fever and the cultures are negative. And he yelled again, "You know I won't be going to school anymore." And then he turned over and refused to talk. That's why I think it was more than him just being ornery. He likes school and is the smartest in his class. He knows.

The nurse saw me in the hall and she went in. She told me that he really wouldn't talk and then she asked him what he'd been doing and he told her about every day and every night this time except last night. He didn't even say that his father stayed with him, and that was the first time too.

We just can't seem to talk about it; I guess in some ways I'm really the one that can't talk about it and he knows it. (*Phone rings.*) Maybe that's for me. (*Picks up the phone*) Hello, Mindy (*gives a sign*).

(MYRA *walks on down the hall.*)

SCENE 4: *Nurses' station, Thanksgiving Day, 4:30 p.m.*

JEFFREY *was discharged early Friday morning. He returned to the hospital a few weeks later with CNS involvement and fever. Between September 3rd and Thanksgiving Day,* JEFFREY *was admitted six more times. He has not had a remission since late August and has continually complained of bone pain. He has recently lost his hair from radiation therapy and is quite thin. He is now being admitted for severe bladder and urinary tract bleeding. He had just been discharged, two days before, to be home for the holiday.* JEFFREY, *looking pale and exceptionally thin and frail, perhaps because of his lack of hair, is wheeled off the elevator. His father looks down as he walks with definition and familiarity to the desk.* MRS. ANDREWS *looks forlorn, but walks close beside the wheelchair, carrying only a large pocketbook and a piece of paper in her hand. The halls are strangely empty. Most of the children were given holiday passes.*

NURSE WALTON: (*Standing beside a large picture of a turkey at the receptionist's desk*) Hi. Happy Thanksgiving.

MRS. ANDREWS: (*Hands her the slip*) Yeah, some Thanksgiving.

NURSE WALTON: (*Hands* MRS. ANDREWS *the container.*) Well, Jeffrey, I'll go to your room with you and help you get settled. (*Comes around the desk and walks slightly ahead of them.*)

(*The four proceed to* JEFFREY'S *room.*)

MRS. ANDREWS: (*As they walk*) You really don't have to come back. We didn't bring that much, you know. (*Reaching the room*) Well, at least you're not in isolation, Jeffrey.

NURSE WALTON: I'm afraid he is. The gowns just haven't come up yet. There isn't much of a staff on the holidays.

MRS. ANDREWS: Figures. Usual great organization.

MR. ANDREWS: (*Gives* MRS. ANDREWS *a glance.*)

NURSE WALTON: Jeffrey, I'll go get you a sterile gown and underpants.

MRS. ANDREWS: You don't have to bother with the underpants.

NURSE WALTON: OK.

(NURSE WALTON *goes down to the* nurses' *station.* MRS. ANDREWS, MR. ANDREWS *and* JEFFREY *enter the room.*)

NURSE WALTON: (*Walking in to the nurses' station*) Are there any more sterile gowns around?

NURSE RICHARDS: Did you check the closet in 1312?

NURSE WALTON: Yeah. There are only large size children's gowns and linen.

NURSE RICHARDS: OK. I'll order some. How does he look?

NURSE WALTON: I don't know. I've never seen him this bad. I'd be surprised.

NURSE RICHARDS: Yeah, I know.

(NURSE RICHARDS *walks out of the nurses' station to the doctors' conference room and* NURSE WALTON *walks toward the stairwell.*)

SCENE 5: JEFFREY'S *room, that evening, Thanksgiving Day,* 7:30 *p.m.*

(JEFFREY *is lying in bed, listless.* MRS. ANDREWS *is seated in the lounge chair beside the bed, reading aloud.*)

MYRA: Can I come in?

JEFFREY: (*Nods.*)

MYRA: (*Puts on a mask and gown. Washes hands outside the room.*)

(MYRA *enters the room and stands silently by the bed until the story is over.*)

MRS. ANDREWS: (*When the story is finished, stands up*) While Myra's here, Jeffrey, I'm going to go have a cigarette.

JEFFREY: I want some more of the peppermints.

MRS. ANDREWS: I'll call Daddy.

JEFFREY: I want them now.

MRS. ANDREWS: But honey, there aren't anymore now. One of the day nurses gave him some peppermints. Richards did.

(MRS. ANDREWS *leaves the room.*)

JEFFREY: Turn up the TV.

MYRA: (*Goes over and turns up the TV.*)[15]

---

[15] This is the floor TV, which has no remote control. It was donated by a family whose son died of leukemia, and leukemics are given first priority on the use of this TV.

JEFFREY: Sit down.

MYRA: (*Sits down in a straight chair by the bed.*)

JEFFREY: (*Begins to doze.*)

MYRA: (*Gets up.*)

JEFFREY: Sit down. Please, Myra.

MYRA: OK. I'll stay 'til your mom gets back. (*Sits back down.*)

　　　　　　　　(*Two older people,* MRS. ANDREWS' *parents, enter the room.*)

JEFFREY: (*Closes his eyes.*)

GRANDMOTHER ANDREWS: (*Adjusts the sheets*) Poor kid. (*Looks up at* MYRA) Who are you?

JEFFREY: (*Opening eyes*) That's Myra from clinic.

MRS. ANDREWS: We've heard so much about you.

MYRA: Thanks. Jeffrey, I'll stop back and see you tomorrow since you have company.

JEFFREY: 'Bye.

MYRA: 'Bye.

　　　　　　　　(MYRA *leaves the room.*)

SCENE 6: *By the elevators on the thirteenth floor, the next morning, Friday, 11:00 a.m.*

(MRS. ANDREWS *is sitting, with her back to the children at play, smoking a cigarette.* MYRA *steps off the elevator.*)

MYRA: Hi.

MRS. ANDREWS: He's been sleeping on and off all day. He doesn't seem to have much strength. I had to keep checking to see if he was still breathing. He's up now, though. I guess I should be in there, but I stay there when he's sleeping. If you're going to see him anyway today, why don't you go now.

MYRA: OK.

　　　　　　　　(MYRA *walks down the hall to* JEF-FREY'S *room.*)

125

THE WORLD OF JEFFREY ANDREWS

SCENE 7: JEFFREY'S *room, moments later.*

(JEFFREY *is propped up in bed looking through a coloring book and watching TV.*)

MYRA: Hi, Jeffrey. Can I come in?
JEFFREY: Yeah.
MYRA: (*Puts on a mask and gown. Washes hands.*)
(MYRA *enters.*)
MYRA: I saw your mother at the elevator. She'll be in soon.
JEFFREY: (*Angrily*) I told her she could only have one cigarette.
MYRA: Jeffrey, why do you always yell at your mother?
JEFFREY: Then she won't miss me when I'm gone.
(NURSE WALTON *enters the room.*)
NURSE WALTON: Jeffrey, I think we have to get a new I.V. started. It looks like this one has infiltrated.
JEFFREY: (*Starts to cry.*)
NURSE WALTON: Now, Jeffrey, come on. This isn't like you. Do you want me to get your mother?
JEFFREY: Yes.
(NURSE WALTON *leaves the room.*)
JEFFREY: I want to finish this picture and then I'm going to give the book to Ericka. The cookie is for my dad. I don't want it.
(NURSE WALTON *reenters.*)
NURSE WALTON: Myra, you're wanted down the hall. Jeffrey, your mother is—there she is.
(MRS. ANDREWS *enters.*)
MYRA: 'Bye, Jeffrey.
(MYRA *leaves the room. As she walks down the hall, she hears* JEFFREY, *in a loud voice, yell,* "I told you you could only have one.")

SCENE 8: *Outside* JEFFREY'S *room, the next evening, Saturday, 9:00 p.m.*

(MR. *and* MRS. ANDREWS *are standing outside* JEFFREY'S *room.* MYRA *walks up to them.*)

126

MR. ANDREWS: He's still sleeping.

MRS. ANDREWS: He slept most of the day.

MYRA: I see.

MRS. ANDREWS: He's been pretty drugged. His pain seems to be worse. I don't know about this time. He's been in partial relapse for months now.

MR. ANDREWS: Partial remission.

MRS. ANDREWS: I call it relapse. You have to face reality.

MR. ANDREWS: You call that (*nodding toward the room*) living?

(*Silence.*)

MYRA: How are Ericka and Jason taking it?

MRS. ANDREWS: Ericka's been saying some really weird things lately, like, "You know, Jeffrey, me and Jason are going to live the longest." Jeffrey looked like he was going to cry and, well, I just walked out of the room. That was too much. Ericka was practically hysterical the other night when we told her that Jeffrey would have to go in. Her grandmother said that she cried herself to sleep.

MR. ANDREWS: Jason is at the age where he is beginning to feel shifted around, but it's Ericka who really feels it. He's better when he's at home. Ericka likes to do things for him, but he thinks she's incompetent and yells at her a lot.

JEFFREY: (*Calls from the room*) Mommy.

MRS. ANDREWS: (*Goes into the room.*)

MR. ANDREWS: Would you like to see some pictures of Jeffrey? (*Pulls out his wallet.*) This one is before he got sick. You know, Dr. Ellis doesn't expect him to make it to Christmas. I think he knows it, because he keeps asking us for his presents now.

MRS. ANDREWS: (*Comes out the door*) Joe, could you come in here for a minute?

MR. ANDREWS: Excuse me.

MYRA: I'll see you later.

(MR. ANDREWS *enters the room and* MYRA *walks down the hall.*)

127

SCENE 9: *The nurses' station, the following morning, Sunday, 9:00 a.m.*

(NURSE RICHARDS *is seated at the receptionist's desk.* MYRA *walks up to the desk.*)

MYRA: Hi. How's Jeffrey?

NURSE RICHARDS: He really looks bad and the bleeding is worse. They've ordered some platelets, but it really seems . . . well. He's been asking for you. I think you should go down now. Mrs. Andrews just went for some coffee and to call her mother.

MYRA: OK. I'll see you later.

(MYRA *walks down to* JEFFREY'S *room.*)

SCENE 10: JEFFREY'S *room, moments later.*

(JEFFREY *is lying in bed. The TV is on, without the sound, but he is not even looking at the picture.*)

MYRA: Hi, Jeffrey. Can I come in?

JEFFREY: (*Nods almost imperceptibly from the bed.*)

MYRA: (*Puts on a mask and gown and washes her hands.*)

(MYRA *enters the room.*)

MYRA: Are you comfortable, Jeffrey?

JEFFREY: (*In a slow whisper*) Yeah. Will you read me the part in *Charlotte's Web*, where Charlotte dies. The book is over there.

MYRA: Sure (*goes over to the night table and gets the book and sits down. Shows* JEFFREY *the chapter entitled "Last Day."*)

JEFFREY: (*Nods.*)

MYRA: Can you see OK?

JEFFREY: (*Nods.*)

MYRA: (*Begins to read aloud.*)[16]

---

[16] The following reading is from E. B. White, *Charlotte's Web*, 1952:163-171.

"Charlotte and Wilbur were alone. The families had gone to look for Fern. Templeton was asleep. Wilbur lay resting after the excitement and strain of the ceremony. His medal still hung from his neck; by looking out of the corner of his eye he could see it.

'Charlotte,' said Wilbur after awhile, 'Why are you so quiet?'

'I like to sit still,' she said. 'I've always been rather quiet.'

'Yes, but you seem especially so today. Do you feel all right?'

'A little tired, perhaps. But I feel peaceful. Your success in the ring this morning was, to a small degree, *my* success. Your future is assured. You will live, secure and safe, Wilbur. Nothing can harm you now. These autumn days will shorten and grow cold. The leaves will shake loose from the trees and fall. Christmas will come, then the snows of winter. You will live to enjoy the beauty of the frozen world, for you mean a great deal to Zuckerman and he will not harm you, ever. Winter will pass, the days will lengthen, the ice will melt in the pasture pond. The song sparrow will return and sing, the frogs will awake, the warm wind will blow again. All these sights and sounds and smells will be yours to enjoy, Wilbur—this lovely world, these precious days . . .'

Charlotte stopped. A moment later a tear came to Wilbur's eye. 'Oh Charlotte,' he said. 'To think that when I first met you I thought you were cruel and blood thirsty!'

When he recovered from his emotion, he spoke again.

'Why did you do all this for me?' he asked. 'I don't deserve it. I've never done anything for you.'

'You have been my friend,' replied Charlotte. 'That in itself is a tremendous thing. I wove my webs for you because I liked you. After all, what's a life, anyway? We're born, we live a little while, we die. A spider's life

129

can't help being something of a mess, with all this trap- ping and eating flies. By helping you perhaps I was trying to lift up my life a trifle. Heaven knows anyone's life can stand a little of that.'

'Well,' said Wilbur, 'I'm no good at making speeches. I haven't got your gift for words. But you have saved me, Charlotte, and I would gladly give my life for you —I really would.'

'I'm sure you would. And I thank you for your gen- erous sentiments.'

'Charlotte,' said Wilbur. 'We're all going home today. The fair is almost over. Won't it be wonderful to be back home in the barn cellar again with the sheep and the geese? Aren't you anxious to get home?'

For a moment Charlotte said nothing, then she spoke in a voice so low Wilbur could hardly hear the words.

'I will not be going back to the barn,' she said.
Wilbur leapt to his feet. 'Not going back?' he cried. 'Charlotte, what are you talking about?'

'I'm done for,' she replied. 'In a day or two I'll be dead. I haven't even strength enough to climb down into the crate. I doubt if I have enough silk in my spinnerets to lower me to the ground.'

Hearing this Wilbur threw himself down in an agony of pain and sorrow. Great sobs racked his body. He heaved and grunted with desolation. 'Charlotte,' he moaned. 'Charlotte! My true friend!'

'Come now, let's not make a scene,' said the spider. 'Be quiet, Wilbur. Stop thrashing about!'

'But I can't *stand* it,' shouted Wilbur. 'I won't leave you here alone to die. If you're going to stay here I shall stay, too.'

'Don't be ridiculous,' said Charlotte. 'You can't stay here. Zuckerman and Lurvy and John Arable and the others will be back any minute now, and they'll shove you into that crate and away you'll go. Besides, it wouldn't make any sense for you to stay. There would be no one to feed you. The Fair Grounds will soon be empty and deserted.'

Wilbur was in a panic. He raced round and round the pen. Suddenly he had an idea—he thought of the egg sac and the 514 little spiders that would hatch in the spring. If Charlotte herself was unable to go home to the barn, at least he must take her children along.

Wilbur rushed to the front of his pen. He put his front feet up on the top board and gazed around. In the distance he saw the Arables and the Zuckermans approaching. He knew he would have to act quickly.

'Where's Templeton?' he demanded.

'He's in that corner, under the straw, asleep,' said Charlotte.

Wilbur rushed over, pushed his strong snout under the rat and tossed him into the air.

'Templeton!' screamed Wilbur. 'Pay attention!'

The rat, surprised out of a sound sleep, looked first dazed then disgusted.

'What kind of monkeyshine is this?' he growled. 'Can't a rat catch a wink of sleep without being rudely popped into the air?'

'Listen to me!' cried Wilbur. 'Charlotte is very ill. She has only a short time to live. She cannot accompany us home because of her condition. Therefore, it is absolutely necessary that I take her egg sac with me. I can't reach it, and I can't climb. You are the only one that can get it. There's not a second to be lost. The people are coming—they'll be here in no time. Please, please, *please*, Templeton, climb up and get the egg sac.'

The rat yawned. He straightened his whiskers. Then he looked up at the egg sac.

'So!' he said in disgust. 'So it's old Templeton to the rescue, again is it? Templeton do this, Templeton do

131

that, Templeton. please run down to the dump and get me a magazine clipping. Templeton please lend a piece of string so I can spin a web.'

'Oh hurry!' said Wilbur, 'Hurry up Templeton.'

But the rat was in no hurry, he began imitating Wilbur's voice.

'So it's "Hurry up Templeton," is it?' he said. 'Ho, ho. And what thanks do I ever get for these services, I would like to know? Never a kind word for old Templeton, only abuse and wisecracks and side remarks. Never a kind word for a rat.'

'Templeton,' said Wilbur in desperation, 'if you don't stop talking and get busy, all will be lost, and I will die of a broken heart. Please climb up!'

Templeton lay back in the straw. Lazily he placed his forepaws behind his head and crossed his knees, in an attitude of complete relaxation.

'Die of a broken heart,' he mimicked. 'How touching! My, My! I notice that it's always me you come to when in trouble. But I've never heard of anyone's heartbreaking on *my* account. Oh, no. Who cares anything about old Templeton?'

'Get up!' screamed Wilbur. 'Stop acting like a spoiled child!'

Templeton grinned and lay still. 'Who made trip after trip to the dump?' he asked. 'Why, it was old Templeton. Who saved Charlotte's life by scaring that Arable boy away with a rotten goose egg? Bless my soul, I believe it was old Templeton. Who bit your tail and got you back on your feet this morning after you had fainted in front of the crowd? Old Templeton. Has it even occurred to you that I'm sick of running errands and doing favors? What do you think I am, anyway, a rat-of-all-work?'

Wilbur was desperate. The people were coming. And the rat was failing him. Suddenly he remembered Templeton's fondness for food.

132

'Templeton,' he said, 'I will make you a solemn promise. Get Charlotte's egg sac for me, and from now on I will let you eat first, when Lurvy slops me. I will let you have your choice of everything in the trough and I won't touch a thing until you're through.'

The rat sat up. 'You mean that?' he said.

'I promise. I cross my heart.'

'All right, it's a deal,' said the rat. He walked to the wall and started to climb. His stomach was still swollen from last night's gorge. Groaning and complaining, he pulled himself slowly to the ceiling. He crept along 'til he reached the egg sac. Charlotte moved aside for him. She was dying but she still had strength enough to move a little. Then Templeton bared his long ugly teeth and began snipping the threads that fastened the sac to the ceiling. Wilbur watched from below.

'Use extreme care!' he said. 'I don't want a single one of those eggs harmed.'

'Thith thtuff thticks in my mouth,' complained the rat. 'It'th worth than caramel candy.'

But Templeton worked away at the job, and managed to cut the sac adrift and carry it to the ground, where he dropped it in front of Wilbur. Wilbur heaved a great sigh of relief.

'Thank you, Templeton,' he said. 'I will never forget this as long as I live.'

'Neither will I,' said the rat, picking his teeth. 'I feel as though I'd eaten a spool of thread. Well, home we go.'

Templeton crept into the crate and buried himself in the straw. He got out of sight just in time. Lurvy and John Arable and Mr. Zuckerman came along at that moment, followed by Mrs. Arable and Mrs. Zuckerman and Avery and Fern. Wilbur had already decided how he would carry the egg sac—there was only one way possible. He carefully took the little bundle in his

133

mouth and held it there on top of his tongue. He remembered what Charlotte had told him—that the sac was waterproof and strong. It felt funny on his tongue and made him drool a bit. And of course he couldn't say anything. But as he was being shoved into the crate, he looked up at Charlotte and gave her a wink. She knew he was saying good-bye in the only way he could. And she knew her children were safe.

'Good-bye!' she whispered. Then she summoned all her strength and waved one of her front legs at him.

She never moved again. Next day, as the Ferris wheel was being taken apart and the race horses were being loaded into vans and the entertainers were packing up their belongings and driving away in their trailers, Charlotte died. The Fair Grounds were soon deserted. The sheds and buildings were empty and forlorn. The infield was littered with bottles and trash. Nobody, of the hundreds of people that had visited the Fair knew that a gray spider had played the most important part of all. No one was with her when she died." (*Closes the book.*)

JEFFREY: (*Dozes off*).

MYRA: (*Places the book by his bed, leaves him a note on the end of the bed.*)

(MYRA *leaves the room.*)

Later that afternoon, at 5:15 p.m., JEFFREY ANDREWS *died.*

CHAPTER THREE

What Terminally Ill Children
Know about Their World

All of the leukemic children whom I studied faced death with a great deal of understanding about the world of the seriously ill and their place in it. They knew the institution and the disease as well as any lay adult. This chapter delineates the range of the children's knowledge of the hospital structure, personnel, disease treatment, process, and prognosis at the time of death. Particular attention is given to areas of knowledge that had been foreign to the children before they were diagnosed. How this knowledge was acquired, its role in shaping behavior, world-view, and self-concept is discussed in the following chapters.

1. THE HOSPITAL'S PHYSICAL PLANT

None of the children involved in the study had ever been hospitalized for a serious illness or injury prior to their hospitalization for diagnosis. A few had been hospitalized for minor surgery (e.g., tonsilectomies, hernia repairs) before they were three years old. Although many of the children lived in the city where the hospital was located, none had visited it; the majority had not even heard of it. It was also virtually unknown to the children from the surrounding tristate area. One twelve-year-old boy from the southern part of the state did remark that he thought he had heard "people back home" talk about it as "the place where you go to die."

For the most part, the leukemic children lived in relative isolation from the rest of the ward. At times this was for medical reasons (e.g., reverse isolation or wound isolation), and at other times it was for personal reasons (e.g., their parents did not want them to leave their rooms or be visited by other patients). But this isolation did not seem to be a barrier to the children's rapid acquisition of information about the hospital order. What follows is an account of the children's knowledge of the covert and overt functions of various rooms, of written and unwritten rules, and of hospital regulations and procedures.

Pediatric Department

All the children knew that the pediatric department was one of several departments in the hospital. Commonly referred to as "peds," the department utilized the top three floors of the hospital. One floor was for the pediatricians' research activities; they did not normally see patients here. Two floors were for in-patient care. Of these two in-patient floors, one was for children aged five and above, and the other for newborns and children less than five years old. The children differentiated the two groups in terms of "kids who don't wet the bed" or "don't wear diapers" as opposed to "kids who do." Most of the children I studied had never stayed on the fourteenth floor, reserved for the younger children. Those who had, when describing the fourteenth floor, said that when there was not enough room on thirteen, older children were sent to fourteen. None spoke of thirteen as also serving for the overflow from fourteen. During the period in which I conducted my study, thirteen had never served for the overflow.

The layout of a hospital floor is easy to understand. By observing the equipment, one can discern the probable function of any room; however, such observations may not indicate what the room is really used for, or its other functions.

The children were well aware of the multiple purposes hospital rooms served in addition to their designated functions as: treatment room, lab, conference or doctors' room, kitchen, supply room, medicine room, "O.T." (the occupational therapist's office and adjoining playroom), schoolroom or playroom, nurses' station or "desk" (as the nurses' station was often called).

The treatment room, next to the nurses' station, served not only for diagnostic procedures, but also as a medical supply and examining room. The children did not expect to be taken to the treatment room for routine procedures like cultures and blood tests (CBCs), or for major surgery. It was for things somewhere in between, like bone marrows, spinal taps, or lumbar punctures, which were carried out in the treatment room, unless the patient was in reverse isolation. If one of these procedures was done in their own rooms, the children knew that the supplies came from the treatment room. Although leukemic children were examined, even on first admission, in their own rooms, they knew that other patients were usually first examined in the treatment room. Some of the children mentioned that the treatment room was also used by doctors from other floors (e.g., surgeons) when they had a patient on thirteen and "they wanted to look at him" or "to change the bandage or something." Such occasions usually involved "a lot of people."

Many of the children commented on how it seemed that "if the doctor doesn't want your mother around, he takes you in the treatment room." Some doctors did remark that they preferred carrying out procedures in the treatment room, because it was easier to keep the parents out and the children were easier to manage. Or, as one intern remarked, "If you take them in there you don't have to ask the parents to leave. It's a lot easier without them."

The results of diagnostic procedures on hematology patients were analyzed in the lab on the thirteenth floor. The only lab on thirteen, it technically belonged to pediatric hematology, and was not used by other services. The children, all hematology patients, did not make this distinction. Instead, they often spoke of the lab as "Roberta's lab." Roberta was the laboratory technologist assigned to pediatric hematology, and was there all day. The children knew that the hematologists often gathered in the lab after lunch to discuss the results of various tests. Often the children would be seen milling about the area "waiting for their doctor."[1]

The conference room or doctors' room, or office, as it was often called, was the scene of formal and informal meetings among the physicians. Rounds were held there, doctors from other services reported there when they came on the floor, cases were charted, and doctors relaxed there. The children's awareness of the kinds of information discussed in the doctors' room was revealed by the lengths to which they would go to glean the information. One child went so far as to plant a tape recorder in the conference room.

The children and their parents did not enter the doctors' room without being asked, but they would often call to a doctor from the doorway. On weekends and in the late evenings, this unwritten rule was relaxed. Interestingly, the children observed this rule when I was in the doctors' office and they wanted to speak with me. Usually, if children wanted my attention, even when I was in the middle of a conversation, they would walk right up to me and start talking. When in bed, they would call to me or send someone to get me. But when I was in the doctors' office, writing up my notes or talking to one of the physicians, the children acted towards me as they did towards the physicians present. At such times, I believe, the children were observing the rules of the room, rather than treating me as a physician. On other occasions, even when I was in the company of the physicians, children treated me differently than they did the latter.

The children also commented that the nurses "can't just go in there." While there was no such written rule, nurses did not enter the conference room without a specific reason. Generally they stopped by only to consult a doctor or to look

[1] "Their doctor" was always one of the hematologists. They never referred to a resident or an intern as "their doctor."

for charts. They never went in on a break to socialize among themselves, and rarely to socialize with the physicians. Such fraternization as did take place occurred only in the evening and involved residents, interns, and medical students, not attending staff. Fraternization with the attending staff was rare.

The kitchen was to the nursing staff what the conference or doctors' room was to the physicians. It was the place where the nurses made rounds (passing information on to the next shift, also known as "report"), held case conferences, met with the staff psychiatrist, and took their breaks. On the evening shift, many nurses ate their dinner in the kitchen. At one time, the kitchen was used to prepare food for the pediatric service; its only current food-related function is to serve as a storage area for snacks sent up from the kitchen and for food children want to save. To the children, the conversations that took place in the kitchen were more important than any food-related activity. In their descriptions of the kitchen, food aspects were relatively minor.

The children knew that the kitchen was "off limits," and they followed the same procedure as in the doctors' room, calling to the nurses from the doorway. As with the doctors' room, rules were relaxed in the evening. At report time, the children often listened in around the kitchen doorway. They were especially interested in "who was on" and who would be "their nurse." Being invited into the kitchen during the slow evening hours and on weekends was one of their particular pleasures. The kitchen was a good place to talk to the nurses, the children thought. Many held lengthy conversations with the nurses in the kitchen and from the hallway.

The supply room was another room whose name did not suggest its major function. During the day shift, it was used as a lounge by the nurses' aides, the woman in charge of supplies, and the housekeeping staff. The R.N.s, however, never took breaks in the supply room, and the L.P.N.s rarely did. The children revealed their awareness of the utilization of this area when discussing the whereabouts of a particular person at any given moment.

The medicine room was also a nurses' area. The children agreed that it was where the nurses went to get the medicines ready. They were dispensed in small cups with water, or in an injection into the I.V. tubing, the I.V. bottle, etc., from larger bottles kept in the medicine room. The medicines either came up in the shoot from the pharmacy or were already in inventory on the floor. Some children also mentioned that "the nurses go in there [the medicine room] to talk private . . . to other nurses and to doctors they like." While this was not necessarily the case, many of the conversations held in the medicine room were not drug-related. The doctors rarely walked into the medicine room.

"O.T." was the children's name for the office and room next to it used by the occupational therapy staff and students assigned to pediatrics. The office was used by the pediatric occupational therapist and her students, and later in the year by one assistant, for conferences, storage, and socializing. Even though many of the leukemic children had never been to the playroom next to the office, they knew that it was used for group occupational therapy sessions and for testing. They were also aware that many of the things that came down on "the cart" to clinic on Monday morning came from that room and from the O.T. office.

Whenever the occupational therapist or her students were there, the children were allowed to go to O.T. They could also go to O.T. for scheduled play periods, or to borrow games and arts-and-crafts materials. Realizing that no other hospital personnel had access to the room, they usually just walked away if they found it closed. When they did ask staff for games, or crayons and paper, they did not expect them to go to the O.T. room, but thought they would get them from the "desk."

Across the hall from O.T. was the schoolroom, set aside by the hospital for use by the teacher sent by the city board of education. The room had a blackboard, a piano, and a locked floor-to-ceiling cabinet for storing books and other instructional materials. During school hours, the teacher met with the ambulatory children in small groups according to age. Other patients were seen in their rooms.

Many of the children referred to the schoolroom as "the playroom." They would often wander down to the schoolroom in the evening to play the piano and just "mess around." This was especially true when a group of veteran patients of about the same age were hospitalized together. They knew that they were not supposed to be there unsupervised, but if there was a nurse available to check on them and they did not cause too much trouble, they would be allowed to stay.

Many of the nonleukemic children mentioned that the schoolroom was used by parents "to cry in" when their child died. If a class was in session, word would be sent ahead to the teacher and the class would be dismissed. If class had not already started, it would be canceled or postponed. During these times, the schoolroom was strictly off limits and the children knew it.

The parents would wait in the schoolroom for the nurses to collect the child's belongings and prepare the child to be seen by the parents before being wrapped for the morgue. The hematologist or the resident met with the parents there to answer any questions and to ask for permission to do an autopsy. Sometimes a chaplain was present. Nurses often went in and out to dispense medication to the parents and to offer sympathy.

The schoolroom served several other functions. It was used as a dining room twice a day for the ambulatory patients, as an entertainment room where civic and military groups came to perform for the children, and as a nursing-staff party room for the staff Christmas party, and nurses' baby showers, special birthdays, and farewell parties. On rare occasions, it was used by parents staying overnight. The children, ambulatory and nonambulatory, knew when the room was being used for any of the above purposes.

141

The centrally located nurses' station, or as it was more commonly known, "the desk," was the hub of all activity, as the children were well aware. All doctors and other hospital personnel stopped there when they arrived on the floor. It was the first place the children had to go when they arrived and the last place they had to stop before they could go home. Calls came in and out constantly; announcements over the floor loudspeaker were made there; charts were kept at the desk. To the children, the desk was the place where they could always find someone. They knew that if certain individuals were there and it was not too hectic, they could wander about the area and even sit on the desks. They often said that it was not permitted, but "they let us." They quickly scattered when those who might object entered the area.

There were also two definable areas that served important functions: the area around the two pay-phones and the area near the elevator. Each area was named after its central object. The open telephone booths, where patients and their relatives made and received calls, were located opposite the desk. There were no phones in the rooms, and the phones at the nurses' station were for hospital business only, although the children were sometimes permitted to use these during off-hours to call home. During the day, they knew they had to use the pay-phones, and nonleukemic children would often "hang around" and share each other's calls. For the majority of the leukemic children, this was a rare activity and their knowledge of it was mostly hearsay. They knew that their parents spent most of their time out of the room around the phones and at the elevators. When children wanted their mothers, they would often ask someone to check at the phones and the elevator. They described the elevators as the place "where the parents go to smoke." Nonleukemic children often lingered near the elevator pretending to wait for O.T. to open. When I asked one nine-year-old hematology patient, who knew that O.T. was closed,

142

why she was standing around the elevators, she said, "I know what I'm doing." Later she told a leukemic child whose mother she had seen seated at the elevator that the mother would have to leave the hospital earlier than she had promised.

Clinic

None of the children involved in the study had ever been to the pediatric oncology clinic prior to their first visit following discharge from the hospital after diagnosis. Many of the children had never been in any clinic situation. On Monday mornings, the children went to clinic. If a holiday occurred on Monday, they reported on Wednesday afternoon to the pediatric hematology clinic.

The children referred to the pediatric oncology clinic simply as "clinic." Only some of the children knew the full name. Two children who had been patients for more than five years used an older designation, tumor clinic.

The children differentiated between the pediatric oncology clinic, the pediatric clinic, the pediatric hematology clinic, and the adult oncology clinic. The pediatric oncology clinic was for "other children like us, who have the same thing," and it met on the third floor. The "regular children's clinic" met on the first floor. The "Wednesday afternoon clinic is for kids with different blood diseases." The adult oncology clinic was for "adults with the same thing." It met on Monday afternoons in the tumor clinic. The children, waiting for the results of their bone marrows, sat with the adult oncology patients who were waiting for that clinic to open.

Although the children knew that the clinic was part of the hospital, they tended to describe it separately. In part, this was because going to the hospital as an in-patient was very different from being a clinic out-patient (see chapters one and four). The clinic included a waiting-room area, with a women's bathroom and reception desk for patients scheduled to see the radiologist; treatment and examination room area; a reception desk for patients scheduled to see the hematologists; and a conference room.

A reception desk was located in the waiting room to the right as one entered the clinic. All the children knew that this was not the desk to which they were to report, but very few knew that it was for radiology patients or individuals receiving radiation therapy. This latter group had to report first to the hematology reception desk, at the opposite end of the clinic.

The waiting room was divided in half by a wooden latticework divider. On one side of the divider, tables were set up for children in the playgroup to use. This was not a formal group. Children came and went, participating in activities as they chose. The small furniture marked this as a gathering place for children; on the opposite side of the divider, full-size chairs set up in rows within a "U" of chairs along three walls marked that side as a gathering place for adults.

The "O.T. cart" that was brought down by the occupational therapist was placed at the end of the divider. The children knew that they could take the games, toys, and art supplies from the cart and play with them anywhere in the clinic. They knew that things usually had to be put back on the cart by noon, but that they could retain one thing to play with if it was returned before they left the clinic for the day.

The children were well aware of the various activities besides toileting that went on in the women's bathroom, located on the "adult" side of the waiting room. Older girls held meetings there about the disease, various drugs, and what was happening to other children. When adults entered the bathroom, the girls ceased conversation and often left. Boys revealed their awareness of what happened in the bathroom by their tendency to gather, clutching a toy, near the bathroom entryway.[2]

[2] See Act IV, Scene 11, of "The World of Jeffrey Andrews."

144

The children also knew what kind of information was exchanged by parents in treatment rooms and in the conference room when children were not there. The children's awareness was evident in the lengths to which they would go to obtain such information. They would often hide behind office doors and try to listen. Andy (a six-year-old boy) for example, became quite fidgety when his parents went to talk to the doctor without him. He stopped playing and said, "I think I better go get weighed [the scales were located across from the treatment rooms]." I responded, "You already got weighed." Getting up from his chair, Andy replied, "Well, I'll go check again." He went down the hall, creeping against the wall so as not to be seen, and stepped to the side of the scale to listen.

The children would also wander in and out of parents' meetings in the conference room. When I heard one five-year-old girl call the meeting "the P.T.A.," I asked her what the P.T.A. was, thinking that perhaps she did not know the subject of these meetings. She told me that it was "where the parents go to talk about what's wrong with you." Children knew they were talked about over coffee, and they would eavesdrop on conversations in the waiting room; this was almost as much a reason to delay separating as was emotional anxiety.

The children did not describe the reception desk where they checked in and out as a hub of activity, as they did the desk on the floor. The reception desk was simply where one handed in the card, retrieved the card, and received a Tootsie Pop. In the clinic, the most active area was between the treatment rooms and the hallway where medicines were drawn up.

Other places in the hospital that, although part of the clinic process, were not located there, were no mystery either. The children knew that no matter how sick they were, they had to stop and get a blood test on the first floor before going up to the clinic. They also knew that they could not see the doctor until he or she had received the results of the blood test. They knew that the medicines

145

came either from the first-floor pharmacy or from the doctors' refrigerator on the twelfth floor. If medicines were to come from the pharmacy, the parent had to wait for them.

X-rays for the clinic and X-rays for the hospital were taken in the same place. The difference was, children in clinic waited with their mothers, children in the hospital waited with the nurse, or an X-ray technician came up to the room.

Most children could tell how to get from the clinic to the cafeteria to the phone booth, and to other floors. This was no easy matter, as the halls were a maze with many dead-ends, and not all the elevators went to all floors.

Other Places in the Hospital

The children also knew the location of the gift shop, vending room, blood bank and emergency room. They would often ask permission to go to the gift shop or vending room, but rarely asked to be taken any other place. They never mentioned the blood bank unless asked about it. Conversation about the emergency room was infrequent, except in regard to admission, or transfusion as an out-patient.

2. HOSPITAL PERSONNEL

The children were in basic agreement that the staff ranked from top to bottom as follows: hematologists, residents, interns, nurses, and medical students. Some children put medical students above nurses. Children who made distinctions among various types of nurses put the medical students below the R.N.s, but above the L.P.N.s, nurses' aides, and housekeepers. But the children were quick to perceive that placement was not always so clear-cut. For example, nurses who technically ranked below doctors could sometimes talk doctors out of things. Sometimes the residents went against the hematologists' decisions.

The children differentiated among the allied professions —occupational therapists, lab technologists, and teachers—

but judged them equal to the nurses. Some children also mentioned a certain social worker when discussing this category of personnel, but those who had had no contact with her did not mention her. A very few children mentioned the dietician, who was also included in this equivalent, but different from nursing, category.

The children did not place the TV man, the ward clerk, leaders of the parents' group, or me, anywhere in the hierarchical structure. Unlike any of the above, we never wore uniforms or even lab coats, nor did we perform any medical services. Hospital personnel who were never mentioned by the children included the chaplains, secretarial help, and physical therapists.

The children pointed out to me that each group was identifiable by its duties and time and modes of appearance. None of the children were incorrect in their accounts of the social organization. What varied was the completeness of their descriptions, the degree of detailed information that they gave me.

Pediatric Hematologists

The pediatric hematologists, known as the "heme team," were identifiable by the long white coats they wore over their street clothes. They made rounds every morning. On Monday afternoons, however, they were led about by the head of pediatrics, also a hematologist. I often asked the children how they knew the man who came on rounds on Monday afternoon was a hematologist. After all, he did not treat any of them in clinic. He was not one of their own or their peers' doctors. Several said that their family physician had sent them to this hospital because of this man. Others said as much or that he did not go on the other rounds. Some children commented that on Tuesday mornings he occasionally went to a few rooms with the residents, interns, and medical students.

Only a few children were aware of the ranking within the heme team. They knew that Dr. Ellis and Dr. Cellars were

147

not as high as Dr. Wesson or Dr. Wessley, but they did not know why. Many did not know where to place Dr. Wesson, probably because he had so few patients, only one of whom was hospitalized during the study. Many of the children were aware of research projects that the doctors were involved in, as well as the other types of blood diseases that they treated.

The children identified the hematologists as "their doctors." Everyone saw "their doctor" in the clinic as well as in the hospital, and usually had the same doctor throughout the course of the illness. Hematologists "make all the decisions. Everybody has to do what they say." When a resident or an intern came in to do a procedure and the children had not been told about it in advance, they would often ask if the hematologist told the resident that he could do it. When it came to asking about going home, the children asked the hematologists first.

The residents and the interns were well aware of the children's feelings and would often refuse to do a bone marrow on them. "Why should I do the scut work? Let one of them." The children often heard the residents saying such things, or arguing with the parents about a particular procedure. They could often succeed at stalling a procedure by putting up a fuss in front of the resident.

This attitude toward residents, as opposed to attending staff, was not as prevalent among inexperienced non-leukemic patients. It was even less prevalent among inexperienced nonhematology patients. They were more willing to put the resident at the top. Also, nonleukemic patients generally knew more about the ranks and role of residents, interns, and medical students than leukemic patients. In part, this was because they had more dealings with them over a longer period of time than the leukemics did; they were seen by the residents more than by the "attending men" (which included the hematologists). Much of the non-leukemics' knowledge of residents was based on observation of behavior, and the residents and interns did more for these children than they did for the leukemics.

Residents

The children were quick to point out that the residents were younger than the hematologists and some mentioned that they were older than the interns. But that was not the only thing that distinguished them from the hematologists and interns. Like the "attendings," the residents wore lab coats over their street clothes most of the time. But sometimes, when they were on duty all night, they wore what the interns did—scrub suits, or as one child described them, "white pajamas." Female residents who worked in the nursery or who were on at night wore scrub dresses and lab coats. But no matter how old they looked or what they wore, the residents had blue name tags and the interns had green name tags. One resident continued to wear his green name tag from internship days. When this was pointed out, many of the children just said, "He didn't get his new one yet." In many cases the children had seen him "move up." "Move-up day" (July 1) was noticed by many of the more experienced patients.

According to the children, the residents could do "almost anything" the hematologists could do. The qualification stemmed from the fact, previously mentioned, that the children often heard the hematologists tell the residents what to do.

The children knew that the residents ran the floor and that if they wanted medicine at night for pain, they were dependent on them. When they were admitted to the hospital, the resident did the history and physical before the hematologist did. The residents made rounds with the interns, medical students and, on some mornings, with an attending physician. When they made these rounds, the charts clanked along on a metal structure that looked like a laundry-basket frame. In the afternoon, they made rounds without looking at patients. A few children noted correctly which residents ranked higher than others.

Interns

The younger children did not consistently distinguish interns from residents, as the older or more experienced patients did. For that matter, neither did many of the parents. The male interns wore white scrub pants, shirts, ties, and short white jackets. The female interns wore white skirts, blouses and short white jackets. The "whites" were provided by the hospital.

None of the children knew that the interns were assigned to particular residents. While some noticed that their blood cultures were always taken by the same intern, and that that intern accompanied the resident who came in to do the bone marrows and spinal taps, and even mentioned the coincidence, none of them ever spoke of interns being assigned to residents.

Some of the children remarked that the interns started I.V.s more often than did residents and medical students. All the children knew who would probably come in to restart their I.V.s, but only the more experienced knew that the intern was sent only if the veins were hard to find. Otherwise a medical student would be sent. The hematologists often left word that no medical students were to try to start I.V.s. A few of the children would tell the medical student who came in start an I.V. that they wanted a certain intern to do it. When the medical student would ask why, the children would usually tell him that the intern was better, even though they had no way of knowing whether this was really so. The intern was, however, a "real doctor"; medical students were not.

Medical Students

Although the children referred to residents and interns as "Dr." So-and-So, they referred to medical students by their first names. They would often laugh when a medical

150

student was paged with the title "doctor," saying, "He's not a real doctor yet." When I asked one eight-year-old girl why they called him doctor, she replied, "So the patients don't get shook."[3] I believe she was right, especially about some of the other floors, where the medical students did a great deal of the routine work.

To the children, the only differences between the medical students and the nurses were their dress and their ability to start I.V.s. The medical students wore street clothes and short white jackets. There was one male medical student who worked part time as a nurses' aide and wore a scrub suit. The children did not consider him a nurse. All the nurses were female. The children never confused female medical students with nurses, nor did they, like many adults, confuse female doctors with nurses. They acknowledged the mixing of sexes.

Nursing Staff

Few nurses wore caps, but most wore colored uniforms, the idea being to appear less imposing to children, especially the younger ones. This was never the case. Even a newly admitted child could tell the difference between a woman in a yellow dress and a woman in a yellow uniform. The child reacted to the uniform, regardless of its color. It was not simply a reaction to strangers; when a stranger in street clothes appeared, the child did not cry.

Many of the children were aware of the conflicts that existed between the nursing staff and the physicians. A few called my attention to the fact that the nurses always addressed the doctors, and sometimes the medical students, as "doctor"; yet the doctors addressed the nurses by their first or last names. The children also liked to tell stories of romances between staff members. Their accuracy was often uncanny. Much of this behavior came out only in the eve-

[3] Duff and Hollingshead (1968:478) found this kind of reasoning on the part of some of the hospital administrators where they did their research.

151

ning, when the hospital was left to the residents, interns, and medical students.

All the children knew that the nurses worked in shifts, and that they were the only staff members to do so. As discussed earlier, they knew when and where the shifts reported to each other, and would often be around to listen.

Children who could distinguish R.N.s from L.P.N.s from nurses' aides did so on the basis of the nurses' responsibilities. Most frequently, the distinction made was that all the R.N.s, but only some of the L.P.N.s, and none of the nurses' aides, could "pass meds." The children who did not make these distinctions abstractly could, however, tell which individuals did what. All nursing personnel could take temperatures; however, the L.P.N.s usually took temperatures at the same time as blood pressures. The nurses' aides helped bathe the children, passed out snacks, and often kept the children company.

When the children mentioned nurses' aides, they often mentioned the housekeeping staff too. The one housekeeping person that they singled out was the "supply lady." "She's in charge of the linen and gives you stuff like old syringes to play with." This woman kept the floor stocked and often gave the children bits and pieces of medical supplies to play with. They often talked about her distinctive dress. She wore a scrub suit or dress with a hospital gown on backwards. Some of the children also singled out the man who washed the rooms. They talked about how he did not seem to like to clean the isolation rooms and grudgingly put on a mask and gown. Very few of the children mentioned the woman who cleaned the beds. In the context of describing the housekeeping staff and nurses' aides, some of the children mentioned the kitchen help. "They come up with the trays." The children talked about how they failed to get the food up to the rooms hot and did not remove trays promptly.

The student nurses performed many of the same tasks as

the nurses' aides and L.P.N.s. Although the children could not necessarily distinguish licensed R.N.s from licensed L.P.N.s, they could distinguish student R.N.s from student L.P.N.s, probably due to the difference in uniforms; also, they got to know the student R.N.s better than the student L.P.N.s. The student L.P.N.s came on the floor as a group accompanied by their instructor, and stayed for only part of the morning, perhaps for only one day. The student R.N.s came up for longer periods of time, without an instructor, and often worked on the floors on weekends and in the evening to earn extra money.

Other Hospital Personnel

As noted earlier, the children distinguished between non-nursing personnel, but classified such members with the nursing staff—the schoolteacher, the "O.T. (occupational therapist)," the lab technician, and the social workers.

The children under five did not mention the schoolteacher, as they had no contact with her. The older children did and knew when and where she worked. They felt that she could not really make them do anything. Since the leukemic children were often in reverse isolation, she would usually come to their rooms to give them a lesson. They often refused to let her come in, sometimes rejecting school and school work as a way of saying "I'm dying."

All the children were quite familiar with the role of the O.T. and her students on the thirteenth floor and in the clinic. They were not as aware of her activities off the floor and outside the clinic, including lecturing to occupational therapy students, testing children, and participating in FATIS (Family Adaption to Terminal Illness) meetings. And they did not know that, like the doctors, she wrote reports in the charts after play sessions.

All the children spoke about Roberta, the lab technician. Although they knew that she did all the hematology patients' bone marrows in the hospital and in the clinic, they

153

did not know that she did not do other patients'. The children knew that when Roberta came to the clinic, it was for a bone marrow. CBCs (blood tests) were always done before clinic by her or reported through her to the hematologists.

The social worker on the floor was unknown to the majority of the leukemic children. She was not involved with any of the hematology patients. She did see two of the parents, however, and tried to become involved with one of the children. The child, however, wanted no part of her, feeling that she asked too many questions, smiled too often, and stayed in the room too long. The children did not know that the woman had been a nurse. She was addressed as "Sister," which they mentioned more than the fact that she was a social worker. The children noted she wore a lab coat over street clothes, not a habit.

Another social worker, Miss Green, was mentioned only by the children she served. They said that she sometimes gave them toys and came to talk to them. Only one child added that she helped to get his parents transportation money.

While the TV man was not spoken of as part of the structure, he was a very important person to the children. They knew when he came and how much money they had to give him for daily or weekly TV service. Children over six knew that the TV man did not give credit. If a child did not have the money when he came to collect, the TV was taken out. Recall that in the play, Tom was quite concerned that Myra get the money to the TV man before he left for the day.

The ward clerk was more familiar to the ambulatory patients, especially those whose mothers did not stay at the hospital all day. These children would often go to her and ask for things to do. She would let them paste things in the charts, staple forms, count materials, etc. For the child of nine who could read, this was a sought-after position. They also went to the ward clerk for permission to use the ward phones during the day if they did not have money, "dimes."

3. OTHER PATIENTS

While the leukemic children lived in relative isolation from the rest of the patients on the floor, they did know something about them. What they knew, however, was limited to what "the regulars" (this included the "sicklers" and the "hemophiliacs") would tell them about these other children, since the leukemics were for the most part confined to their rooms. The "regulars" were the major carriers of ward news and gossip.

The leukemics knew the most, of course, about the other leukemic children. Even on the rare occasions when they were placed in rooms with nonleukemic children, they still tended to know more about the other leukemic children on the floor than about their own nonleukemic roommates.

All the children could distinguish between leukemic and nonleukemic patients. "They [the leukemic patients] come to Monday clinic." "We [leukemic patients] all have the same blood disease. You know Greta, she comes [to the hospital] all the time. Well, she has a blood disease [sickle cell disease] too, but she goes to another clinic."

They constantly called attention to what was happening to other children, drawing parallels or distinctions.

CHILD: Is Gene getting vincristine again?

MYRA: Yes, I think so.

CHILD: When I had vincristine the second time I lost my hair. (*Pause.*) Gene gets his hair back real fast, I wish I did.

CHILD: Jeffrey can't walk. I bet he's in relapse.

MYRA: You think it's relapse.

CHILD: Well, it could be he's weak, but he's weak because he's in relapse.

The children always knew who else was in the hospital from the clinic, why they were there, and the protocol that they were on: "Jeffrey's in his first relapse"; "Tom has a lot

155

of relapses"; "Esther's in isolation"; "Jeffrey's getting plate-lets to stop his bleeding" (further examples are in the play).

Most striking, in light of what others have said (Rich-mond and Waisman 1955:43, Natterson and Knudson 1960:20), is that the children did know who was alive and who was dead.

> TOM: Jennifer died last night. I have the same thing, don't I?
> NURSE: But they are giving you different medicines.
> TOM: What happens when they run out?
> NURSE: Well, maybe they will find more before then.

> MARIA: I'm going to play with Luis [a child who died six months earlier] in heaven.

> ANDY: I knew Maria died. I saw the cart come for her. They told everyone to go in their rooms.

Even the children who were isolated tended to know a great deal about other children's conditions, often more than the respective parents knew. Mary Costin was not per-mitted to play with or speak to other children in the clinic or in the hospital. Her door was kept closed and her mother kept a watchful eye over her and those who spoke to her. Her statements, however, revealed that she was well aware of what was happening to other children and was contin-ually trying to gather more information: "Gene gets his hair back real fast, I wish I did"; "You know Ellen, she's the one with the scars on her legs"; "Is Rachel going to be coming here? I was like her when I started coming"; "Did Alan get blood for his anemia part? He looked pale"; "Did Jeffrey go up? I thought so. He brought his stuff."

One day when several of the leukemic children were hospitalized, Mrs. Turner, who had recently lost her own son, came to visit them and brought gifts. When she came into Mary's room she greeted Mary and Mrs. Costin by name. Mrs. Costin said that she was sorry, but that she did not remember Mrs. Turner's name. At that point Mary chimed in, "That's Richard's mother. I remember Richard. He died last summer."

In general, though, the leukemic children knew very little about other leukemics beyond their experiences as fellow sufferers. They knew almost nothing about each other's lives outside the hospital or clinic, except through disease-related conversations. A child might know that another had been to Disney World or to the zoo, but also that the child got sick there; or that another child liked to go fishing, but also knew that the child could not go any more.

Knowledge about other children's personal lives was also affected by the parents' relationship to each other. At one point during my study, a great deal of visiting was going on between several leukemic families. The children got to know one another and the siblings of the other children. They spoke relatively little, however, about the knowledge they acquired from these outside contacts, unless it was disease-related.

4. THE DISEASE: TREATMENT, PROCESS, AND PROGNOSIS

Not all the children knew the name of their disease, acute lymphocytic leukemia. Of those who did, very few ever referred to it by name. Not knowing the name of the disease was no barrier to learning as much as any lay adult about it, and its treatment, process, and prognosis.

All the children knew that chemotherapy was the common mode of treatment. "They give you medicines to make you better." The children had a great deal of technical information about the drugs used in treatment—the purposes for which the drugs were given, their side effects, when and how the drugs should be given, their efficacy at various points in the illness, and how long the drugs' effects lasted. The children divided the drugs into two categories according to purpose. One category consisted of the maintenance and induction drugs (e.g., vincristine, methotrexate, and

157

cytoxan), the drugs used to treat the disease, or in the words of one child, "that made the sick blood go out and good blood grow in." The other major category consisted of antibiotics and pain medications, the drugs used to treat the problems resulting from the disease or in reaction to drug treatment. The children never confused these two categories by ever supposing that the antibiotics helped their leukemia or that the antileukemic agents cured an infection.

ANDY: (*Pointing to red stain on I.V. board*) Do you know what this is?

MYRA: No.

ANDY: Guess.

MYRA: Is it gentomycin? [*an antibiotic*].

ANDY: No. It's not an antibiotic.

MYRA: Is it keflin? [*an antibiotic*].

ANDY: I said it's not an antibiotic.

MYRA: I give up.

LISA: It's for my blood.

MYRA: Is it vincristine?

LISA: No. I had that already. It's daunomycin.

This certainty about the uses of different drugs was true even of children who could not rattle off all their names. They would distinguish blood medicines from pain medicines when asked what a particular drug was for.

The children were well aware of the extremely toxic side effects of many of the drugs and were especially concerned with those that altered their physical appearance. They knew, for example, that prednisone created mood swings and weight gain: "Prednisone makes me eat like a pig and act like a brat"; "It's [*prednisone*] like a tapeworm."

They were conscious of the alopecia that resulted from cytoxan.

CHILD: Don't! [*in response to someone stroking his hair*]. I'm getting cytoxan.

158

CHILD: (*When other children were discussing what they needed for their Halloween costumes*) I needed a wig for Halloween.

O.T.: What were you?

CHILD: No! I was getting cytoxan.

Stomach and mouth ulcers that they got from methotrexate were another frequent topic. Many children also remarked that the drugs themselves sometimes created problems requiring as much treatment as the disease: "There's blood in my pee from the cytoxan and they can't stop it. Maybe the platelets will help." Some even knew that some drugs were so toxic that one could die from the drugs as easily as from the disease: "I'm going to die soon. They are trying to help my blood, but it's [*the medicine*] making my liver bad."

The children realized that before any drug could be administered, a procedure had to be performed to determine the type and the amount of the drug to be given. Before a new antileukemic drug (e.g., induction drug) could be administered, for example, there would have to be a bone marrow. At the end of four weeks, there would be another bone marrow, and in most cases another new drug (e.g., maintenance drug) would be started.

PETER: (*Shaping pieces of clay into balls that resembled pills*) I take ten of these (*pointing to the already finished balls*) each day, but today they are going to change my medicine.

JENNIFER: (*Looking up from the animal she was molding*) They have to do a bone marrow first.

PETER: How do you know?

JENNIFER: You'll see. Then they wait four weeks and give you another bone marrow and another medicine until that one stops working and then they start again.

The children often spoke about what was involved in a bone-marrow aspiration, and were very anxious in the face of it. It was not uncommon to see children pulling out their hair, running from the clinic (legs riddled with pain), pretending to be in great shape, or to hear children making inappropriate jokes about how bone marrows tickled, and then screaming wildly before, during, and after being injected, on hearing that they were scheduled for a bone marrow. But it was also clear that the procedure itself did not bother them, as the anxiety continued (often to an even greater degree) after the procedure was completed; the children were more anxious about the results. This could only be if the children had some grasp of the significance of the procedures. In fact, the children knew not only the bearing these had on their hospitalization, but also the meaning of the laboratory results. Children would, for example, refuse to go to lunch until they had heard the results of the bone marrow.[4]

NURSE: Does it bother you to have a bone marrow?
TED:[5] No. It's waiting for the results.
NURSE: Does it hurt?
TED: No! All you feel is the press. They make it red and use a needle to take it out. Oh, yeah, they numb it first.

MYRA: What's happening?
SCOTT:[6] Not good.
MYRA: What do you mean not good?
SCOTT: (*Putting head in* MYRA's *lap*) I have to have a bone marrow. Dr. Wessley said it's not good. I think Mommy's in there crying.

[4] When bone marrows were given in the clinic, the results were not ready until after 1 p.m. The doctors always suggested that patients and their parents go to lunch in the interim, rather than remain in the waiting room.

[5] This eight-year-old boy ran out of the clinic whenever he was told he was going to have a bone marrow.

[6] This five-and-a-half-year-old boy claimed shots and bone marrows "tickled." He cried more after the procedure, while waiting for the results, than before and during it.

The children knew not only that an unexpected bone marrow was not a good sign, but also why it was not a good sign. First, it was an indication of a change in their condition, and changes were not usually for the better. More often than not, it was an indication that the drug they were on was no longer working and a new drug would have to be started. And of course, that drug might not work as well as the one they already failed on: "The yellow medicine was supposed to last two years, but it only lasted seven weeks. Now I have the red medicine, but it won't last as long as the yellow was supposed to." Second, the results usually indicated relapse or the onset of "bad times." It would be four weeks before the doctors could tell if a remission had been attained, at which point a new medicine would be started and with it the hope of a more lasting remission—"a good time."

JEFFREY: What's a relapse?

JENNIFER: That's a bad time. There are good times and bad times. It's usually when the medicines aren't working and your body is sick again.

JEFFREY: Oh, I guess I'm in a bad time still.

JENNIFER: How do you know? Did you get a bone marrow?

JEFFREY: No, I just had one.

JENNIFER: But not this week.

JEFFREY: No.

JENNIFER: Are they going to give you another one?

JEFFREY: No. It's not even three weeks.

JENNIFER: Do you have the same medicine? I mean did they give you the same stuff as last time?

JEFFREY: Yeah. I'm pretty sure.

JENNIFER: Well, that means you haven't gotten a remission yet from what they are giving you. The medicine isn't working yet. So you're still in relapse.

The children knew that the disease was a series of relapses and remissions, of "good times and bad times,"

161

against a backdrop of bone pain, headaches that did not go away with aspirin, hemorrhaging that never seemed to stop, constant weakness, anemia, and infections that required hospitalization. Just as the treatment of the disease was determined by a bone marrow, the treatment of any of these related sicknesses was determined by special tests and procedures. When they complained of bone pain, they had X-rays as well as bone marrows.[7] When they complained of headaches, they had spinal taps or lumbar punctures.[8] When they were exhausted and pale, they were given blood. When they were infected, they came into the hospital, were placed in reverse isolation, had cultures taken, and were given their antibiotics intravenously. And whether they complained of anything specific or not, when they felt well and when they did not feel well, they were given "CBCs" (blood tests), to assess changes in the disease.

All the children knew that a low platelet count indicated bleeding or the onset of relapse. Many knew that a low hemoglobin was often an indicator of secondary anemia. Many also knew that a high white count or the presence of immature white cells or leukemic cells indicated that the disease was going out of control. There was, however, only one child who could recognize all of these blood factors under a microscope.

The CBC was necessary not only for establishing the status of the disease, but also for determining the course of treatment. For example, transfusions were indicated for low platelet counts as well as for secondary anemia. The children knew, however, that there were two different types of transfusions, platelet and whole blood; which one was used depended on a variety of factors determined through exam-

[7] The X-rays were used to identify possible disease infiltrate to the bone or to palliate pain.

[8] Through these tests the doctor could discern whether or not there was leukemic infiltrate to the brain (referred to as C.N.S. involvement). If there was, the child received skull irradiation and/or a course of intrathecal methotrexate (an antileukemic drug injected in the spine).

162

ination of the CBC. Platelet transfusions were indicated when the platelet count was low. "They are going to give me platelets today to try to stop the bleeding." Whole blood transfusions were given for secondary anemia, indicated by a low hemoglobin: "I got blood for my anemia part." Even when a blood transfusion was for both anemia and the hemorrhaging that resulted from low platelets, the children distinguished one purpose from another. A five-year-old Spanish-American child put a hand puppet up to the I.V. tube, which had the blood flowing through it.

MARIA: (*Makes drinking sound for puppet*).

MYRA: Is he going to drink the blood?

MARIA: Oh, damn blood. I cannot drink the blood.[9]

MYRA: You cannot drink it?

MARIA: No. (*Pause*) I want to eat this (*points to potato chip*).

MYRA: You want to eat this? (*Holds potato chip up to puppet's mouth.*)

MARIA: Mmm. Mmm. (*Puppet and child shake head no*) I want the other blood.

MYRA: Which?

MARIA: The one that's over there. (*Points to the blood in the bag, as opposed to blood in mouth.*)

MYRA: This one?

MARIA: Yeah. (*Puts cookie in the puppet's mouth.*) A blood cookie. I want a blood cookie.

MYRA: The puppet wants a blood cookie.

MARIA: Yeah. He's not bleeding no more.

MYRA: All better.

MARIA: No, he tired. Needs more cookie.

MYRA: Here.

[9] The child identifies herself with the puppet, and speaks through the puppet. In the first part of the conversation she reiterates the doctor's instruction not to swallow the blood clots that formed in her mouth as a result of the low platelet count. In the second part of the conversation she shows her awareness of the need for blood transfusions for relief of the "tired feeling" that results from the anemia.

The transfusions, like the bone marrows, created anxiety unrelated to the pain of the procedure.[10] The children often worried about getting allergic reactions to transfusions, because then the blood would have to be stopped, and they felt that they needed it fast. For example, when a character was dying on TV, a few children suggested giving him a transfusion; "It made me well." Many felt that getting new blood was the key to making them better, and that since transfused blood was new, it should make them better. After all, they invariably felt better and people told them that they looked better after a transfusion.

Not only did the drugs and the disease impede platelet function and production, they also hampered immuno function. The children were often immuno-suppressed and, as a result, easy targets for infection. They talked about how easily they became infected and what they had to go through to be treated. In most cases, they had to be hospitalized, placed in reverse isolation, and cultured, before treatment could even begin.

> JEFFREY: They took cultures today from my I.V.
> NURSE: Do you know what a culture is?
> JEFFREY: Yeah. Germs grow on it and then they give you antibiotics to fight the germs.
> NURSE: Do they culture other things?
> JEFFREY: Yeah. My throat. They tried to culture my stink, but I didn't let them do it.

Once treatment had been started, however, they still were not free to leave, even if the leukemia was under control or their blood had improved. Going home hinged on the infection being cured: "I cover my finger or I'll get an infection, then a fever and then an I.V. and then I don't go home."

> CHILD: I'll be getting out in a while.
> MYRA: That's good.

[10] Transfusions are relatively painless.

164

CHILD: If everything goes well I mean. (*Pause.*) If my things keep and I don't get a temperature. I mean if the medicine works. It's fighting the infection so it helps if I don't have a temperature. It stayed and it's staying down, that's good.

The series of relapses and remissions, of good times and bad times, of periods at home and periods in the hospital for transfusions, infections, and hemorrhaging, did come to an end—in death. All of the leukemics that I studied knew their prognosis. All knew that they were dying before death was imminent. They did not, however, all express their awareness in the same way. Some children said directly, "I am going to die," or "I'm going to die soon. They are trying to help my blood, but it's (the medications) making my liver bad." Other children were less direct. They talked about never going back to school, of not being around for someone's birthday, or of burying dolls that they said looked the way they used to look. All of these forms of expression are indications that the children knew they were dying.

The leukemic children acquired a great deal of information about the hospital, staff, rules and procedures; about the disease, its treatment, process and prognosis, before they died. The fact that they managed to acquire so much information was even more remarkable because they learned in a situation in which the parents and the staff unconsciously conspired to keep them in painless ignorance. In the next chapter, I explain how the children managed to acquire various kinds of information, the differences in children's knowledge, and the effects particular kinds of information had on self-concept and behavior.

CHAPTER FOUR

How Terminally Ill Children
Come to Know Themselves
and Their World

Leukemic children's acquisition of information about the hospital order, the disease process, treatment and prognosis, other leukemic children, their own parents and themselves, is part of a complex learning process in which social rules and roles are learned as well. This larger process is a socialization process.

1. BECOMING AWARE AS
A SOCIALIZATION PROCESS

Acquisition of Factual Information About the Disease

The leukemic children acquired factual information about their disease in five stages, as follows:[1]

	1	2	3	4	5
gnosis	"it" is serious illness	names of drugs and side effects	purposes of treatments and procedures	disease as a series of relapses and remissions (− death)	disease as a series of relapses and remissions (+ death)

[1] Neither these stages nor the stages in changes in self-concept are ironclad. Human behavior is a rule-governed activity, not subject to the lawlike regularity of the natural world. Behavior in situations can be governed by rules without always being in accord with them. Therefore, stages are not "disproved" by single or even several "counter examples." Also, as the nature of the institution, education of hospital personnel, and approaches to the care and treatment of terminally ill children change, so might these stages. Particular experi-

166

Each stage was marked by the acquisition of significant disease-related information.[2, 3] The children first learned that "it" (not all the children knew the name of the disease) was a serious illness. At this time, they also accumulated information about the names of the drugs and their side effects. By the time the children reached stage 2, they knew which drugs were used when, how, and with what consequences. The third stage was marked by an understanding of the special procedures needed to administer the drugs and additional treatments that might be required as a result of the drugs' side effects. The children knew which symptoms indicated which procedures, and the relationship between a particular symptom and procedure. But they saw each procedure, each treatment, as a unique event. Not until they reached stage 4 were they able to put treatments, procedures, and symptoms into a larger perspective. By then, the children had an idea of the overall disease process —that the disease was a series of relapses and remissions, that one could get sick over and over again in the same way, and that the medicines did not always last as long as they were supposed to, if at all. But it was not until the fifth stage that the children learned the cycle ended in death. They realized that there was a finite number of drugs and that when these drugs were no longer effective, death became imminent.

What the children learned at any one stage was necessary for interpreting information in the next stage. For example, the children needed to know all the names of the drugs and side effects, and the purposes of various treatments and

---

ences are critical to passage through these stages, to the socialization process.

[2] This chapter is on a more theoretical level, therefore there are very few examples in the body of the text. Instead, I refer the reader to other places in the book for illustration of specific points.

[3] Examples of statements and conversations reflecting each of these stages of awareness can be found in chapter three, section 4, and in the corresponding subsections of the next section of this chapter. Subsections are titled according to the five stages.

procedures (stage 3), before they could put them in perspective and see the disease as a series of relapses and remissions (stage 4). They had to have certain concrete information before they could move to a higher level of abstraction. Information was cumulative; without the requisite information, the children could not integrate new information to come to a new conclusion. For example, if a child knew the names of all the drugs and their side effects, as well as the purposes of various treatments and procedures (stage 3), but did not know the disease was chronic (stage 4), the news of another's death did not lead the child to conclude that the disease had a terminal prognosis.

Neither learning all the disease-related information possible at a particular stage, nor accumulating information that was necessary for passage to another stage, insured such passage. A child could be saturated with information about drug names and side effects (stage 2), without moving to stage 3. Or a child could know all about various treatments and procedures—their purposes and effects (stage 3) —and have heard about relapses and remissions, yet not move to stage 4. In order for children to pass to another stage, they had to have certain experiences.

Experience

For two major reasons, experience was critical to passage through the stages. First, the children needed the disease experiences (e.g., nosebleeds, relapses, bone pain) to gather significant disease-related information. At any sign of illness, the children were taken to the clinic, where they could again meet their peers and discuss what was happening to them. Second, the disease experience enabled them to assimilate this information by relating what they saw and heard to their own experience. The children did not ask about things that were not happening to them. Although a child might have heard the doctor talk about spinal taps, for example, when he suspected CNS (Central Nervous System) involvement, the child did not participate in the conversations about CNS involvement unless he had him-

168

self experienced the major symptom—headaches. Furthermore, often children having such discussions would not allow others who had not experienced headaches to participate in conversations about CNS involvement, spinal taps, and dosages of interthecal methotrexate they themselves required.

The place of experience in the socialization process helps illuminate why a child could remain at a given stage without passing to the next for what seemed an unusual length of time. Tom, for example, remained at stage 4 for a year, whereas Jeffrey remained at stage 4 for only a week. Since passage to stage 5 depended on the news of another child's death, and none had died after Tom reached stage 4, he could not pass to stage 5. When Jennifer died, the first child to die that year, all the children in stage 4, regardless of how long they had been there, passed to stage 5.

The role of experience in developing awareness also explains why age and intellectual ability were not related to the speed or completeness with which the children passed through the stages. Some three- and four-year-olds of average intelligence knew more about their prognosis than some very intelligent nine-year-olds, who were still in their first remission, had had fewer clinic visits, and hence less experience. They were only aware of the fact that they had a serious illness.

Changes in Self-Concept

As the children passed through the five stages in the acquisition of information, they also passed through five different definitions of themselves. These different self-concepts can be represented as follows:[4]

dx	1	2	3	4	5
well	seriously ill	seriously ill and will get better	always ill and will get better	always ill and will never get better	dying (terminally ill)

[4] Examples of statements and conversations reflecting each of these changes in self-concept can be found in the corresponding subsections

169

It becomes evident that the children's views of themselves were the result of various kinds of information that they had acquired in interaction with others, as well as through personal experiences. It also becomes clear that the children could not proceed to the next level of awareness without the requisite view of themselves. If, for example, a child knew all about the relapse and remission cycle, was aware that the disease was chronic, and heard that another child had died, she would not come to the conclusion that she too would die, unless she saw herself as never getting better.

2. THE STAGES OF AWARENESS

Passage to Stage 1

Leukemic children and their families were suddenly thrust into a bewildering world.[5] The family pediatrician had told them only that they should go to the research hospital for further testing. When they arrived at the hospital, they felt confused and lost.[6] The hospital ambience, with all its forms, protocol, procedures, and strange faces, is overwhelming enough; but for these people, filled with fear and dread, it was paralyzing.[7] One of the memories parents

---

of the next section of this chapter. Subsections are titled according to the five stages.

[5] For a complete description of the thoughts, feelings, and reactions of parents and children during the first hospitalization, see Act I of "The World of Jeffrey Andrews," particularly Scenes 1-5, and 12.

[6] Not knowing what to expect is symbolized in the play by the suitcase. The parents packed very little, not even toys. By the second hospitalization, they knew what to expect and packed not only a suitcase, but also a bag full of toys. As the disease progressed and there were more "emergencies," the parents, and finally the children, packed in haste—filling shopping bags. By the final hospitalization, however, they once again brought very little, because there was nothing the child seemed interested in doing, and because his condition required isolation and/or many changes (e.g., owing to heavy bleeding). The hospital provided pajamas.

[7] In the play, note the reaction of the parents when they enter the room (Act I, Scene 2).

most frequently described was the first time the "heme team" entered their child's room. They remembered how the doctors spoke to them and asked them if they had any questions, and of not knowing what to say.

They recalled answering questions but not being able to "put things together," of "feeling out of it," "in a fog," even before they were told the diagnosis: "I was so totally in the dark"; "I had no idea, and everyone smiled so nicely." But they soon realized that these people, these strangers, were rapidly becoming some of the most important people in their lives. Soon they would be hanging on their every word, probing their looks, actions, and moods.

This was often the children's first hospital visit, and they were as much in the dark as their parents, if not more so. They started to assess the situation from the moment they stepped off the elevator,[8] and quickly made the distinction between "them" and "us," or those in uniform and those not.[9] The "us" were the patients and their families,[10] who took orders and spoke only when spoken to. The "them" came and went when they pleased, with or without explanation, which was usually only offered to adults. At this point "them's" major characteristic was that they inflicted pain or brought news of something that caused pain. While children might be unsure of their own criteria for subdividing "them," they were aware of differences in personnel beyond the obvious distinction of doctor and nurse. These finer distinctions were not based on uniform. For example, although Roberta dressed like a doctor, often came with doctors during rounds, and was present during bone marrows (when nurses often were not), the children knew that she was not a doctor.

[8] For details of the assessment process, see the play, Act I. The assessments made by Faith and Jeffrey typify those made by all the children.

[9] "Uniform" included white or colored nursing uniforms, lab coats over street clothes, and white jackets over street clothes.

[10] Later, after the child's world had become more hospital-centered, "us" included only other leukemic children. Parents were either seen as members of "them," or as not part of the scheme at all.

JEFFREY: That lady stuck me today.
MYRA: The one with the white coat and the tray?
JEFFREY: Yeah. But she's not a doctor.
MYRA: How do you know?
JEFFREY: I don't know, but I know she's not a doctor.

By the second day of hospitalization, the children began asking about what was happening to them. The questions were limited to very concrete matters, such as whether a particular procedure would hurt or not—much like those a normal child would ask on visiting a hospital for the first time. The more probing "why" questions only came after the children had reached stage 1, and these continued until stage 5, when the children stopped asking questions altogether.

Until the diagnosis was made (about the second or third day after admission), the children were, in their own eyes and in the eyes of their parents, no different from other children. Parents required the children to behave as they had before the hospitalization. Children should understand when parents had to leave, they felt, and not make a fuss, should eat whatever was put before them, and in general "act properly," as they had been taught. Children still were treated as "normal," and they responded as such, even using "normal" child routines to get what they wanted and to manipulate their parents. To get out of eating, a child like Jeffrey would often say something like, "I have to go to the bathroom." Later in the disease process, a child would be more inclined to use phrases similar to Mary's, "Don't make me eat that. It'll make me sicker. I'll get a worse pain."

Once the diagnosis was made, however, everything changed. People, especially the family, started to treat the children differently, who then noticed the change. The children remarked on the sudden deluge of gifts: "I get more presents than my sister"; "Look at all my stuff"; "It's like Christmas!" They talked about what they received, things they did not even ask for, how they did not have to do

certain things anymore, and how their fathers often would
not go to work. They spoke in hushed tones about the conversations they had tried to listen in on, but could not hear.
They announced how people cried and looked sad when
seeing them: "Mommy cries when she sees me"; "Nanny
stares and shakes her head at me."

Astute observers, as time went on the children became
more astute, more capable of drawing conclusions from people's behavior. They knew the indices for various types of
behavior and what they meant. These skills were sharpened
as people began telling them less, acting out more, and
slipping with greater regularity.

The children put people's behavior together with the tests
and treatments they were receiving and concluded that they
were really sick, "seriously ill," "very, very sick." "This is not
like when I had my tonsils out"; or even "when I cut my
head open." "This" was somehow worse, as were they.

Stage 1

The children tried out their newly acquired self-concept
on everyone they saw. Children at stage 1 would often ex-
claim, "I'm really pretty sick, you know," and then offer as
evidence the changes in people's behavior towards them or
the physical changes in themselves, especially the "wounds"
suffered from procedures. The strategy they used for announcing this new view of self I refer to as "exhibition of
wounds." The children would begin by counting their
needle pricks and pointing to them.

> One, two, three, four (*pointing to finger*); five, six
> (*pointing to hip*); seven, eight (*pointing to forearm*).
> I've had three blood tests and one marrow. They drew
> blood for cultures and gave me my I.V.—it came out.

> I had five sticks and they still couldn't get a vein (*for
> I.V.*).

The exhibition of wounds occurred either as one entered
the room, or, if the visitor spoke first, just after the visitor

had spoken. For example, when I entered Jeffrey's room for the first time I quickly told him my name (as I did with all the children), that I was an anthropologist and studied children, particularly what they thought about and what they did. He responded, as did the other children, by exhibiting his wounds. "One, two, three, four (*pointing to two fingers and his right hip*). Two were for bone marrows and two were for blood tests."

At stage 1, the exhibition of wounds would open every encounter; at stage 2, 3, 4, or 5, it would be used only on the first encounter, simply as a way to inform the newcomer of the child's identity. For children at stage 1, who needed to test their newly acquired view of themselves, repetition was extremely important. The children found confirmed in people's reaction to their pronouncement the fact that they differed from other children. Interestingly, even the children who were not permitted to talk about how they were different, how they had changed, would, even in their parents' presence, "exhibit their wounds." Because of the timing of the exhibition-of-wounds strategy and the way it was used, I argue that observation of exhibition of wounds can be used as an indicator in assessing whether children are at stage 1 or beyond.

The children held to a view of themselves as very ill or seriously ill until they saw evidence that they were getting better. This evidence did not appear until the children had made at least four consecutive clinic visits, had spoken with other children, and had been told by their mothers that they were in remission.

Passage to Stage 2

Children first visited the pediatric oncology clinic the Monday after their discharge from the hospital. Despite the fact that they were feeling and doing better than they had in the hospital, they still saw themselves as seriously ill, in part because other people were still acting as they had been when the children were hospitalized for diagnosis.

Relatives were still crying and bringing presents whenever they came. The children were still receiving special attention at home. The painful procedures continued. Furthermore, the people that they saw in the clinic did not look very well. In the play, when Jeffrey and Mrs. Andrews entered the clinic for the first time, they focused on the bald, bloated, pale, frail, and bruised children, many of whom were crying in wheelchairs.

As in the hospital, when the mothers and children came to the clinic for the first time, they clung to one another, suffering a real fear of separation, but for different reasons. The parents feared separation in ultimate terms. They wanted to be with the children as much as possible, because they did not know when they might lose them.[11] The parents did not force separations, even when they wanted to be alone.

MOTHER: Jeffrey, wouldn't you like to go over there and play with those children?

JEFFREY: Un Un (*shaking his head at the same time*).

MOTHER: They look like they are having fun.

JEFFREY: (*Shakes his head and draws closer.*)

---

[11] As the disease wore on, however, the parents felt a greater need for separation. This often occurred when the mother's anticipatory mourning had ended, but the child had not died; or when the child was suffering a great deal and parents felt conflicts about wanting it to be over. The clinic provided an excellent opportunity for separation for two reasons. First, if the child was coming to the clinic, not hospitalized, he was not on the verge of death. Second, separating to attend the parents' meeting was socially acceptable. But in spite of needs to separate and rationalizations for separation, the parents still felt conflicts about separating. These conflicts were greatest at their own child's first relapse, and when another child died. While these incidents reawakened the fear that their child would die, they also kindled a desire to begin to separate, so that it would not be as painful when the time came. Thus the parents were always in a bind about separation—a bind that was often communicated to the child, and which he acted upon. These actions are described and discussed in the subsection on stage 5, below, and in chapters five and six.

The children were no longer told that they had to go out and play, and in some cases, they were not even sent to school.[12] The children observed this behavior and often manipulated their parents. Even when they were in remission, children would sometimes say to their mothers, "I don't wanna go to school." Rather than say, "You don't look sick" or "But nothing hurts you," the mothers would reply, "OK, stay home."

Children at stage 1 did have real fears of separation, but in contrast to their parents, these were not due to awareness of the prognosis. They were more afraid of the unknown, the unfamiliar. In the clinic they were once again in a strange and threatening environment. The children held on to their mothers, the one thing that was familiar to them. Hence, as the children became more familiar with the clinic and the other children there, separation was much easier for them.

They began to participate in the children's groups. They went to the playgroup either immediately after entering the clinic or when their mothers went to the parents' meeting. Even children who were forbidden to participate in the playgroup managed to make contact with the other children, if only briefly—while the other children played, they watched and listened. The proximity of the main play area to the waiting-room chairs, where some adults and children sat, made this possible. Also, the children often spread out from the center area, right in front of or beside children who, not being permitted to join the others, sat by themselves. Each child then had an opportunity to observe and to question other children.

During their first clinic visits, the children, like their parents, watched more than they talked. When they finally did talk, the subjects were drugs and their side effects. The side effects were what they were experiencing and what they

[12] See Futterman and Hoffman's (1970:477-494) discussion of the mothers' fear of separation as a major contributor to transient school phobia in leukemic children who are in remission.

176

thought it meant to have the disease. They heard about other things (e.g., drug protocol, death of other children), but did not yet participate in discussions of them, for they had not had the experiences to relate them to.

Through these peer-group conversations, children could learn a great deal about various drugs and their side effects, the information required for passage to stage 2. But even when children knew the names of all the drugs and their side effects, they did not pass into stage 2 until they had experienced a remission as well as a few rapid recoveries from minor disease-related incidents (e.g., nosebleeds, headaches). Without these experiences, the children did not relate the drugs to getting better. Once they saw the relationship of the drugs to recovery from the disease, as well as from minor disease-related incidents, they came to a view of themselves as "seriously ill, but will get better." This self-concept was expressed in terms such as, "I'm very sick but the medicines are going to make me all better," or "Mom says I'm fine now, 'cause the medicine really worked. See, all my hair came out."[13]

Stage 2

Children at stage 2, like their parents, spent much time accumulating more information about various antileukemic drugs and all of their possible side effects. They carried on long and detailed conversations about them in much the same way as they had exhibited their wounds. But, whereas the exhibition of wounds took place in the presence of adults, these conversations were generally conducted only with other leukemic children. The children sought support for their beliefs that the drugs would make them better.

As time passed without further incidents, this hope seemed to become more real. After all, there were fewer

[13] Many of the parents and children thought that the worse the side effects, the harder the drug was working and the more effective it was. If it killed the hair cells, in their view, it must certainly have killed all the leukemic cells.

trips to the clinic, less pain and discomfort, and a return to normal activities: "See, the medicine did make me better"; "The medicines really work good. I'm all better now. I can ride my bike and everything." People began to treat the children normally again, to share their hopes and delusions. Past experience, the diagnosis itself, were all pushed aside. "You'll see, he's going to be different."

The longer the first remission lasted, the stronger hope became, and the less emphasis was placed on the illness. Through the mutual reinforcement of being treated as "fine" and acting "fine," children could retain a definition of themselves as "sick" but now better. They could remain at stage 2 until the incident occurred that would cause them to think otherwise—the first relapse.

Passage to Stage 3

Until the children experienced the first relapse, they had no reason to suspect that this disease was something from which they could not recover. The chronic aspects had not presented themselves, that is to say, the relapse-remission cycle had not repeated itself. There was nothing familiar about the minor episodes; each was different from the others, and from the time of diagnosis. But with the first relapse, all became too familiar. The same symptoms returned and the same procedures followed. The relapse-remission cycle was now underway. People began reacting as they had when the children were first diagnosed.

The first relapse was a shock of recognition that called for a reorganization of thoughts and feelings on the part of parents, staff and children. During the months of remission, the parents had had the opportunity to forget that their children were truly sick with an incurable disease. They had time, except for a few brief interruptions, to live "normal" lives again. Mrs. Andrews' comments in the play are a common refrain, "Everything was going so good. We thought maybe he'd be different." But a relapse changed all that. Everyone was well aware of the larger significance of a relapse. "Once they start coming they just come and then they . . ." The question of how long it would be before the staff saw them again was now answered.[14] The children were now like all other leukemics, and the staff acted accordingly.[15]

The staff began to speak less openly with the children, answering as few of their questions as possible, and answered those only because they were aware of the "long haul to come." Only brief explanations were given for what they were doing, and then only at a very concrete and descriptive level. They never went into the larger implications of a given procedure or why they had to do it. Going quickly in and out of the room, they avoided extended interaction.[16] Contact was kept at a level that would prevent intense involvement, which would make treating the children (e.g., carrying on painful procedures) difficult in the face of the inevitable terminus.

The children, however, were now anxious to build up relationships with people they encountered. They wanted people around them, to talk to and question; Mother alone would not suffice.[17] In fact, the children were less desirous of Mother's company than of others'. In an effort to enjoin people to stay, the children would offer things, invite them to watch TV or play with toys. Then they would begin firing the questions.

The children soon realized, however, that adults were reluctant to answer questions, no less volunteer information, so they asked their parents less and less about the treat-

[14] So important is this first relapse that Act III of the play does not include the remission. Remissions now lose significance—for once the child relapses for the first time, the "game" is over.

[15] This is symbolized in the structure of the play. In Act III, Jeffrey is less central. Attention is drawn to other children, whom he now resembles.

[16] This reaches a height in stage 5. It is shown in the play, in Act III, by the extensive number of exits and entrances by the staff into the child's room with little going on. The reasons for this behavior, especially in stage 5, are developed in chapter six.

[17] This is in contrast to stage 5, when they desire people around, but do not want to talk to them.

179

ments and their condition. The parents were well aware of this: "I think he knows it upsets me"; "He knows I hedge because it makes me uncomfortable." The children began to recognize and observe the taboos on speaking about their disease, their condition, and later, about the prognosis. They continued, however, to take clues from their parents' behavior. Alan, for example, knew that things were not going well when, in spite of how good he felt, his mother would cry. "In my house, crying and bad things go together." Frank knew that he was going into the hospital from his mother's behavior.

> I knew I was going to wind up here today. My mother talked to the doctor and she took some plant that the medicine man gave her last summer and she boiled it on the stove. That's what she does to make these smaller (*pointing to abscess scars*). I breathe it.

The children started to rely more heavily on overheard conversations between their parents and the doctors, between other parents, and between the doctors. To obtain information, children would often pretend to be asleep, or turn down the TV volume, or ask people to be quiet when the doctors congregated by the door to speak with parents. In the clinic, they would hide near offices when parents spoke with the doctor.

The children knew that the adults told one another things that they did not tell children; this added significance to the information gleaned from eavesdropping. After awhile, the only information that took precedence over information from other children was information overheard among adults. The children considered information *volunteered* by adults to be the least reliable.

The staff was increasingly seen in the same light as parents; their behavior earned such a position: "They don't smile either when they see me." The staff's refusal to answer questions directly, and parries such as "Well, we'll see" or "I don't know," eroded their credibility. "I asked three times when I could go home and they said, 'I don't know.' They saw the tests. They told me that's why [to see when I could go] I had to have them." If the staff did not know, who would? In the children's eyes, the staff had no excuses for not knowing.

The children realized that in many ways neither they themselves nor people's reactions were any different than they had been at the time of diagnosis. In fact, reactions were more extreme: "They cry more now"; "They ain't tellin' me nothin' this time. [At least] last time she told me the medicines I was gettin' and when I was havin' a bone marrow." They also noticed that they were getting the same drugs that they had when diagnosed—not the same drugs they had when they complained of headache or bone pain during the first remission. Finally, they believed that the drugs made them well again. Unless the children integrated all of this information at once, they did not enter stage 3. If they did integrate it, they concluded that they would always be sick, but would ultimately get better. This self-concept was often expressed in hopeful expressions like, "I hope I don't have to come here [the hospital] again. I hope this is the last time I have to come. They stick you all the time. (*Tears fell, but the child did not vocalize a cry.*)"

Stage 3

After the first relapse, the children were left more and more to their own devices. They sought out peers for information on the purposes of various treatments and procedures. They formulated hypotheses about the relationship between various symptoms and the drugs, procedures, or treatments employed, and checked them out with peers.[18] As one parent said, ". . . they know they'll get a straight answer [from their peers]."

After the second remission was obtained and the children's condition appeared stable, the parents attempted to go back at least to the time of the first remission. Their behavior reinforced the children's conclusion that although

[18] For examples, see the quoted conversation on pages 157ff., chapter three, above.

one could get sick many times, one would always recover. And, as when the first remission was attained, the children held this view until they had another relapse.

Passage to Stage 4

With the onset of other relapses, coupled with complications from the drugs, the children's sense of well-being began to fade. There seemed to be no freedom from pain. They could do less and less for themselves. People stopped planning things because the plans could be cancelled at any time. There were not even breaks from the illness for holidays and birthdays. The children were increasingly aware of being different from other children, not only physically, but also culturally: "I can't go to school."[19] Their world was rapidly being transformed by the disease, becoming more hospital-centered and less home-centered, until this transformation peaked at stage 5.[20]

Each new disease experience increased their doubts that they would ever get better, as the pattern of relapses and remissions was now apparent: "There are good times and bad times, but you're always sick"; "It'll never stop." Information and experiences were assimilated until the children came to view themselves as always sick and never really getting better. "I'll always be sick over and over again."[21]

Stage 4

Even though a world like other children's (the world that was once theirs too) was becoming increasingly closed

---

[19] School attendance could have this kind of impact because of what it represents in American society. School is what children do. Going to school marks one as a child.

[20] This is represented in the play structure. As going home lost significance for the child, going-home scenes in the play were deemphasized and finally omitted.

[21] This is symbolized in Act IV of the play by turning attention away from Jeffrey and toward the other children. But whereas in Act III this was to show how Jeffrey was like the other children, in Act IV it is to show how nothing special was happening to him any longer—just more of the same.

to the leukemics, they still tried to make contact with it. They did not want to be in reverse isolation, because they feared people would not come to see them. "It's too much trouble [to put on a gown and mask, wash, etc.]." They anxiously awaited the arrivals of various people: "When will Odessa [the R.N.] be here? She's real funny and talks to me"; "I think I made Dr. Richards feel bad. He doesn't come in anymore. I ask too many questions."

Children at stage 4 were aware of who no longer came in to see them, and they wanted to know why. Not least among these were fellow leukemics. As long as there was a valid reason (e.g., he really did go home) why a peer suddenly stopped coming by the room or sending a message, the children remained at stage 4. Only on hearing of the death of a peer did the children realize that the cycle of relapses and remissions did not continue indefinitely. It had a definite end—death.

Passage to Stage 5

A child, after hearing of another child's death, passed from stage 4 to stage 5 in a matter of sentences.[22]

TOM: Jennifer died last night. I have the same thing. Don't I?

NURSE: But they are going to give you different medicines.

TOM: What happens when they run out?

NURSE: Well, maybe they will find more before then.[23]

This synthesis was not possible unless the children were at stage 4. Recall that prior to stage 4 the children saw their

[22] Karon and Vernick (1968:78) also found that the death of another child affirmed to a child that he too would die. Even people who did not believe that children did or could know their prognosis went to great lengths to keep the news of another child's death from advanced-stage leukemics. So, at some level, these adults must have entertained the notion that the news of another's death could make children aware of their own prognosis.

[23] For other examples and further discussion of these types of conversations, see the final subsection of this chapter, below.

relapses and remissions as unique events, with no lasting consequences or long-range significance. The hospital and disease episodes would pass. They were not part of an inescapable pattern. They were sick, but would get better; hence, the death of another child seemed to have no connection to their own lives.

Once children reached stage 4, however, they had fitted all of their acquired information into a pattern of relapses and remissions, of never getting well. And just as all other events could be fitted into the scheme, so too could the death of another child. It could not be seen in isolation, but was part of the same chain of events that they were. They realized that they shared with peers not only the same experiences, but also the same prognosis.[24]

Children at stage 5 expressed awareness of their prognosis in a variety of ways—in their choice of topics of conversation and reading, art work, play, view of time and behavior toward others. Some children at stage 5 also made direct statements about their prognosis: "You see, I'm dying." Other children made less-direct statements: "I'm not going to be here for your birthday"; "I'm not going back to school."

Stage 5

After a child died and his death had been discussed, the other children rarely mentioned him again. Children who identified with the dead child never mentioned him at all. Names of dead children, who did not return to the clinic, became taboo. The surviving children would often walk away (or if bedridden, turn over) whenever the deceased

[24] Karon and Vernick (1968) found, as I did, that children aware of their prognosis (at stage 5) would often try to go back, to act as they had before this awareness. But since these actions were usually confined to discussing things like drugs (stage 2 or 3), and only with certain people, and since the rest of their behavior was typical of stage 5, not stage 2, it was possible to determine that they were in fact at stage 5. Why some children put up such a pretense is explained in the following chapter.

was mentioned. Although they might accept a toy from the deceased child's mother, they never played with it. They would usually ask that the toy be put away or be taken out of their room.

Children facing death did not play with their toys very often, but when they did, play usually involved references to death and disease. They would put dolls, toy animals, and coloring books in graves. Mary, for example, made only one thing in the entire two months she was hospitalized, before she died—"turtles for people's graves." She also took paper dolls that, on an earlier occasion, she had remarked looked like her, and buried them in a Kleenex box.

> o.t.s.: Mary, what should I do with these? Mary? (*holding up the paper dolls that* MARY *and* MYRA *had worked on*).
>
> MARY: Put them in their grave, in the Kleenex box. Let me do it. Bring it over here.
>
> o.t.s.: (*Brings the Kleenex box and the dolls over to* MARY *and puts them on her lap.*)
>
> MRS. COSTIN: Well, that's the first thing you've offered to do since the doctors said we could go.
>
> MARY: I'm burying them. (*Carefully arranges each doll between two sheets of Kleenex.*)

In stage 5, sedentary activity, especially coloring, increased, but the number of themes decreased. Most pictures dealt with destruction, storms, fires, and other disasters. One seven-year-old boy, noted for his art work, abruptly started to draw only pictures of graveyards. "Give him a crayon, a pencil, anything, he draws graves." A seven-year-old girl whose pictures of birds and flowers decorated the offices of many staff members suddenly changed her style. Although she was not a religious child, she would often draw pictures of crucifixions. One crucifixion scene she often repeated was a picture of a blond girl, like herself, on a blood-red cross in the same position as Jesus. The sun shone brightly in the upper right-hand corner. In the lower right-hand corner, at the foot of the cross, was a church. In the lower left-hand corner, further from the cross, was a Bible.

Not only was the children's art work affected, but also their choice and discussion of literature. The most popular book among these children was *Charlotte's Web*.[25] When Mary and Jeffrey reached stage 5, it was the only book they would read. Several children at stage 5 asked for chapters of it to be read to them when they were dying. But as one parent stated, "They never choose the happy chapters." They always chose the chapter in which Charlotte dies. After any child died, the book had a resurgence of popularity among the others.

Although not every child at stage 5 limited his reading to *Charlotte's Web*, each one would, when reading or retelling a story, focus on those aspects of the story that dealt with death, disease, or violence—regardless of whether or not it was the main thrust of the story. For example, in the following conversation, an eight-year-old girl speaking about *The Secret Garden* discusses the disease and deaths of the mother, aunt, and boy. She does not mention the girl, the main character, except in terms of her relation to the disease and death of these other characters. The main character is merely a vehicle for discussing the other elements.

LISA: Did you ever read *The Secret Garden*?

MYRA: No, tell me about it.

LISA: Well, it starts out in India. This girl's mother dies, of cholera I think, and goes to live with her uncle in England. His wife fell off a branch in the garden and no one can go in there anymore. He keeps his son locked up in one of the hundred rooms.

MYRA: Uh huh.

[25] At the time this research was conducted, *Charlotte's Web* was not as popular as it is now; the movie had not yet been released. The first children to have *Charlotte's Web*, and who spoke about it to other children, received it before they became ill.

LISA: And his wife is buried in the garden and no one is allowed in there, but the girl found the key under the bird's eggs.

The child also seems quite concerned with establishing the cause of death.

This was true in all the children's conversations involving death or disease. Although more common in conversations about the death of a peer (see examples 1, 2, and 3, below), it also occurred in more fantasy-oriented discussions of death (see example 4 below and the burial of Mary's paper dolls, Act IV, Scene 21, in the play).

1. SCOTT: You know Lisa.
   MYRA: (*Nods.*)
   SCOTT: The one I played ball with. (*Pause*) How did she die?
   MYRA: She was sick, sicker than you.
   SCOTT: I know that. What happened?
   MYRA: Her heart stopped beating.
   SCOTT: (*Hugged* MYRA *and cried*) I hope that never happens to me, but . . .

2. TOM: Jennifer died last night. I have the same thing. Don't I?
   NURSE: But they are going to give you different medicines.
   TOM: What happens when they run out?
   NURSE: Well, maybe they will find more before then.

3. BENJAMIN: Dr. Richards told me to ask you what happened to Maria.[26]
   MYRA: What do you think happened to Maria?
   BENJAMIN: Well, she didn't go to another clinic and she didn't go to another hospital or home.

[26] Dr. Richards had not told him to ask other people. Later he told me that he used his name so that people would feel obligated to tell him.

187

MYRA: She was very sick, much sicker than you are, and she died.

BENJAMIN: She had bad nosebleeds. They packed her. I had nosebleeds, but mine stopped.[27]

4. NELSON: (*After a woman who had lost her son left*) Do you drive to the hospital?

MYRA: No, I walk.

NELSON: Do you walk at night?

MYRA: Yes. (*Noting the look on his face*) You wouldn't?

NELSON: No, you would get shot.

MYRA: (*Silence.*)

NELSON: An ambulance would come and take you to the funeral home. And then they would drain the blood out of you and wait three days and bury you.

MYRA: That's what happens?

NELSON: I saw them do it to my grandmother.

MYRA: To your grandmother? I thought you told me you were here when your grandmother died. [He was.]

NELSON: (*Quickly*) It was my grandmother. They wait three days to see if you're alive. I mean they draw the blood after they wait three days. [NELSON had been in the hospital three days. They had drawn blood and done a bone marrow that day.] That's what happens when you die. I'm going to get a new medicine and blood put *in* me tonight.

Establishment of the cause of death was a major focus of conversations in which the children disclosed their awareness of the prognosis. Regardless of what the other party in the conversation might say, the children adhered to the

[27] Benjamin asked everyone he saw that day what happened to Maria. Later, when I asked him why he asked everyone, he said, "The ones who tell me are my friends. I knew Maria died. I saw the cart come for her. They told everyone to go in their rooms. I wanted to see if you were really my friend."

same general format. In the just-cited examples, the children opened the conversation by mentioning either an individual who had died or someone in danger of dying. In following statements, the children attempted to establish the cause of death either by asking a question or stating a hypothesis and assessing the other party's reaction. Having established the cause of death in their own minds, the children ended the conversation by comparing the deceased to themselves.

If the children had recently discovered their prognosis, they would, when making the comparison, call attention to how they were different from the deceased (e.g., Benjamin in example 3). If the children had been aware of their prognosis for some time, they would, like Mary (in the burial of the paper dolls), talk about how much they resembled the deceased. Thus, while Benjamin's speech about Maria and Mary's doll burial are both conversations in which children disclose their awareness of the prognosis to someone else, Benjamin's conversation is more typical of children who have just entered stage 5. Mary's, on the other hand, is more typical of children who have been at stage 5 for some time.

There were children in stage 5 who, for a variety of reasons (see chapter six), felt they could not speak freely, even with people they trusted, about their awareness of the prognosis. These children would not engage others in a conversation about the prognosis or another child's death. They would simply state their awareness and terminate the discussion. One six-year-old boy announced, "I'm not going to school anymore," and turned over on his side, refusing to speak to me. A seven-year-old girl blurted out to her brother, "I won't be here for your birthday," and crawled under the sheets.

These statements accomplish the same thing as disclosure conversations.[28] To say, for example, "I'm not going to school anymore," is to say, "I'm not like other children, I am dif-

[28] This method of interpretation is described by Garfinkel (1967: 24-30) and based on work by Sacks (1972a and b), Bar-Hillel (1954), and other ethnometho-dologists.

189

ferent."[29] All other children must go to school. When you are dying or dead you do not have to go to school anymore. Or, "I won't be here for your birthday," is a way of saying, "I'm leaving this earth."

It is also interesting to note that disclosure statements were a telegraphic form of disclosure conversations. That is, while the content varied slightly, the same three parts were represented. The statement began with an announcement of a death, but it was one's own. The cause of death, the illness itself, was not established in detail, but implied. And one's own status was compared to a living child's rather than to a leukemic's.

In all the examples of disclosure of awareness of the prognosis given, there are no references to Heaven. Heaven was only part of one five-year-old Spanish-American's view of death: "Do children play in Heaven?" When her mother told her they did, she responded, "Good, now I can play with Julio and Jorge [two Spanish children who had died that summer]." The other children never took death beyond the grave. Grave imagery was far more prevalent than Heaven imagery. The children's views of death were expressed in terms of what they would miss on earth (school, birthdays, TV shows) rather than what would be "waiting for them in the afterlife." They were concerned with leaving the world, people, and things they knew, not with going to another world.

Disclosure statements and conversations differed from other kinds of statements and conversations. For example, when discussing drugs and their side effects, children tended to deliver monologues, going into great detail at length. When they disclosed their awareness, however, their remarks were brief and to the point. There was also a period of silence before the opening utterance and a period of silence at the end. This gave one the feeling that the con-

[29] Many of the doctors took statements like this and the one that follows as an indication of a child's awareness of impending death.

versation came out of nowhere, or was inappropriate to the ongoing action, all of which added to the dramatic effect. My conversation with Scott (example 1, above) came while we were walking around the hospital during clinic. Benjamin (example 3, above) started his conversation when I was rushing past his room, loaded down with shopping bags. Tom (example 2, above) started his conversation with the nurse when she came to make sure he was still sleeping.

A dramatic and inappropriate quality marked many of the statements and responses children made at stage 5. The subject did not even have to be disease- or death-related for the children to respond as if it were. For example, I asked an eight-year-old girl if she wanted to play "Pirates and Travelers." Her response was not yes or no, but rather, "That's hard to play with an I.V. in your arm." A six-year-old boy waking up from a long nap and seeing two interns by his bed said with a strained smile, "I fooled you, I didn't die." A five-year-old boy, lying uncomfortably on his back, when asked if he wanted to be turned over, said, "No, I'm practicing for my coffin."

Death and disease were by this time constantly on the children's minds. Their world, their thoughts, hence their statements and actions, were permeated with death and disease imagery. In general, as this imagery increased in conversations and play, other topics decreased or were never discussed.

Conversations about the drugs and their side effects declined noticeably,[30] which was not surprising since the children now realized that the drugs were not the answer they and their parents had once thought them to be.

[30] Only one child was an exception to this. His parents talked about drugs and new treatments up until the last day of the child's life. The child, to save his parents' face (see chapters five and six), did the same. Except for conversations he had with his parents, however, he conformed to the general pattern. If his parents were not around, he did not talk about drugs and side effects.

191

Further, when the drugs ran out death became imminent. Likewise, little reference was made to one's progress. What was there to say? It was only an indication of further deterioration, of approaching death. Mary, for example, became quite upset when an X-ray technician scolded her for "taking so long to get up on the table." The reprimand did not bother her so much as the fact that she was forced to realize once more her increasing debilitation. "Does she think I want to be like this? I don't like people staring at me. I don't want to make in my pants. I just can't help it."

It was not unusual to hear the children make a series of remarks about what they could no longer do, "messed up" plans, and how they differed from other children. This far along in the disease-process, such remarks were not about the children's condition *per se* as much as their awareness of what it all indicated—a poor prognosis.

Furthermore, children in early stages of the disease had discussed their progress in terms of going home, but since they "were not going home" now, there was no sense discussing progress. They felt they were never really going home, that at best they might have a "few breaks" between hospitalizations. They did not differentiate between the days in the hospital until they were told that they might be able to go home, and even then they were never as excited about it as they had been in the early stages.

They were, however, just as *anxious* about going home as they had ever been, although for very different reasons. Formerly, their anxiety had stemmed from fears of poor lab reports coming in or infections appearing when they were about to leave the hospital.

I might get to go home if my blood tests are all right. I just have to have one blood test before I go and if it's OK, then I can go. My platelets are still low, but they'll let me go even if they're still low, 'cause it's only in the test. I'm not bleeding.

192

I'm getting the I.V. out tomorrow and then they are going to watch me for a day and then maybe I can go home.

In the early stages, they had talked about going home, about their progress, in a particular way. When admitted for relapse with complications, they had talked about the procedures. When their condition had seemed to improve and it seemed possible they might go home, they had talked about lab reports and the efficacy of various drugs and treatments. Finally, when going home had been assured, even though they remained in relapse, they had talked about different things than they had in the past (but usually with reference to the disease)—about the way the disease had limited, but not totally curtailed, their activities; about what they could do when they left the hospital—and they had expressed hope they would not have to return for a while.

But when they knew they were dying, when going home was only a few-weeks break from hospitalization, they were no longer interested in indications that they might go home (e.g., good counts, absence of infection), or in what they could do when they got there. They were not even concerned about how long it would be before they would have to return to the hospital, or what complications would make the return necessary. They feared going home, because they might not be as comfortable there as they were in the hospital: "I want to stay here"; "I'm comfortable here. They can give me more pain medicine here." The flurry of activity that once surrounded going home was now reserved for getting ready to come back to the hospital. Mary, who had not helped pack to leave the hospital, did so the night she came to the hospital to die.

About the future, conversations declined noticeably, usually limited to the next holiday or occasion (Halloween, Christmas, start of school, a birthday). Also, the children

193

tried to rush these holidays and occasions, to bring them closer. One five-year-old boy asked for his Christmas presents in October; another wanted to buy a winter coat in July. In June, several children at stage 5 asked their doctors if they could go back to school in September. Even the doctors who doubted that children could know their prognosis without being told thought these actions showed the children were suspicious, perhaps even probing for information about how much longer they had to live.

The children, who knew that holidays and special events had a new significance for parents as well, would often talk about the ways a given occasion used to be celebrated, and the way it was celebrated since they had been sick.

> On my birthday now I get to pick what I want to do.
> . . . My birthday this year comes on a Tuesday.[31]

> I get more presents now than before I got sick. My sister gets the same, she's not sick.

The children no longer spoke of former long-range goals and plans. They never again mentioned what they were going to be when they grew up, and became angry if anyone else did. A six-year-old boy was angered when his doctor tried to get him to submit to a procedure by explaining it and saying, "I thought you would understand. You once told me you wanted to be a doctor." He screamed back, "I'm not going to be anything," as he threw an empty syringe at her. She said, "OK, OK," but a nurse present asked, "What *are* you going to be?" "A ghost," he replied, and turned over.

The children's lack of interest in future plans did not reflect a lack of interest in the passage of time. They were concerned about the time they had remaining, often pushing themselves to get things done. They would also get angry when people took "too long" to remember things, to answer

[31] This statement was made four months before the child's birthday. The child died a few weeks after the statement.

194

questions, to bring things to them. Parents and staff often commented on such behavior: "They demand because they know time is short"; "It's as if they know that if they wait too long they might be dead by then. They're not just being difficult, Mary included.[32] That child knows something."

The children often verbalized this fear of wasting time. When they wanted something and people did not move quickly, they would often say, "Don't waste time," "We can't waste time." One day after clinic, Seth's father was talking to another parent in the waiting room. Seth wanted to leave. Pulling on his father's pant leg he said, "Come on, you're wasting time." The father looked at him, replying, "No, I was just talking to these people," and continued talking. With some urgency, Seth then exclaimed, "Come on! We can't waste time!" This is not the usual way a five-year-old gets his father's attention when he wants to leave a place.[33] While his intent was not necessarily to communicate the fact that he would soon die, he was, even in such seemingly unrelated moments, expressing an awareness of his condition and of the time factor involved. Time took on a meaning not usually found in children this age: Time was not endless, as it is for most children, as it once had been for these leukemics.

This attitude toward life, toward what it had become, was reflected in the children's overall behavior. Previously cooperative during procedures, even when in great pain, they suddenly began to balk, to cry, and to scream before, during, and after all procedures. They would argue whenever doctors and nurses wanted to do a bone marrow or

[32] Mary was a demanding child who never directly said anything about her prognosis. Those who thought she was aware of it, however, based their claim on her demanding behavior. They felt it was not just a matter of being spoiled, as she "does it now with all of us. It used to be just for her mother's benefit. Now it's because time is running out and she knows it."

[33] Again, there is a notable inappropriateness in the speech of the child aware of his prognosis.

just change an I.V. Some would also try to talk personnel out of doing routine procedures, and complain if a nurse just wanted to make the bed. They did not want to be touched, poked, or prodded any more. If the staff tried to "reason with them" ("It will make you feel better, so you can go home"), children often blurted out, "You know I can't go home," or "I'm dying."

At such times, the staff would often relent. Some fled the room in such haste that they left the medical apparatus behind. Such behavior reinforced the children's conclusions about their prognosis, and hence the futility of various treatments. The motivation for children to play the role of proper, well-behaved patients (the view of themselves as getting better) no longer existed.

A more subtle yet definite change in the childen's behavior was their failure to talk to people close to them, even about things that mattered to them. They would withdraw from family and friends, either through expressions of anger or through silence. "Then she [Mother] won't cry so much and be sad." Eventually, even conversations about the disease came to an end. The children asked no questions. They knew the answers. They stopped responding or even listening to others.

Paradoxically, to maintain relations the children behaved the way people ordinarily do to sever them. Silence, withdrawal, and open displays of anger and hostility were among the few modes of behavior left to them, through which they could avoid disrupting the order into which they had been socialized. In chapter five, I explain the rules for maintaining that order.

The view and approach to socialization found in the modern perspective (see chapter one) has been used in this chapter to answer the question of how the terminally ill children become aware of their world and their place in it. The modern perspective was chosen over the traditional perspective for two reasons. First, its underlying view of children is consistent with the view of children in this research. Second, the traditional view is not applicable to terminally ill children.

The modern perspective in socialization requires that we consider four factors in studying the socialization of children: acquisition of information about the world, self, and others; experiences with others and with oneself in that world; changes in self-concept; and the order to which one is being socialized. The study of the first three factors was undertaken in this chapter.

CHAPTER FIVE

Knowing and Concealing

It should now be clear that the terminally ill children knew they were dying before death became imminent. What remains unclear, however, is why they kept such knowledge a secret. The few admissions of awareness, made to non-staff and nonfamily members, were often couched in symbols with vague references. Why was this the case? Why didn't the children reveal their awareness to parents and those who took care of them? It is especially puzzling given the gravity of what the children knew. Their consistent impenetrable silence in the face of ultimate separation and loss requires an explanation, which lies in understanding the social order of which the children were a part and their reasons for preserving that order.

The children and those they interacted with were part of a social order that could only be preserved through the practice of mutual pretense. In this chapter I explain what mutual pretense is and how it was practiced.

1. MUTUAL PRETENSE:
THE CONTEXT OF AWARENESS

According to Glaser and Strauss (1965b:9ff), the behavior of the dying patient, particularly his behavior in interaction with others, can best be understood in terms of the "awareness context" in which it takes place. An awareness context is "what each interacting person knows of the patient's defined status, along with his recognition of the others' awarenesses of his own definition. . . . It is the context within which these people interact while taking

198

cognizance of it" (Glaser and Strauss 1965b:10). Glaser and Strauss identified four types of awareness contexts: closed awareness, suspected awareness, mutual pretense awareness, and open awareness.

In the closed awareness context, "the patient does not recognize his impending death, even though everyone else does" (Glaser and Strauss 1965b:11). In the suspected awareness context, "the patient suspects what the others know and therefore attempts to confirm or invalidate his suspicion" (Glaser and Strauss 1965b:11). In the mutual pretense context, each party defines the patient as dying but acts otherwise, "when both agree to act as if [he] were going to live" (Glaser and Strauss 1965b:64). In the open awareness context, "personnel and patient both are aware that he is dying, and . . . they act on this awareness relatively openly" (Glaser and Strauss 1965b:11).

Glaser and Strauss argue that understanding the awareness context in which interaction occurs is essential because of its effect on the interplay between the patient, staff, and family. "People guide their talk and action according to who knows what and with what certainty" (Glaser and Strauss 1965b:11). As we see in chapter seven, section 2, much of the children's behavior at stage 5 can be viewed as tactics for maintaining the mutual pretense context of awareness. Why the children behaved as they did becomes clearer.

Glaser and Strauss (1965b:11) also argue that "as talk, action, and the accompanying cues unfold, certain awareness contexts tend to evolve into other contexts." This occurs when one of the parties to the interaction violates the rules necessary for maintaining the stated context. For example, if the suspected awareness context is to be maintained, individuals must take care to do nothing that would confirm a patient's suspicions that he is dying. If the individuals do something that confirms the patient's suspicions and the patient perceives the action as such, the context will shift to either mutual pretense or open awareness. In the same way, if the patient, family, and staff are engaging in mutual pretense and one of the parties violates one of the rules for maintaining it (e.g., mentions the patient's prognosis), open awareness ensues.

Glaser and Strauss (1965b:74ff) claim that because mutual pretense is such a "delicately balanced drama," with a plethora of rules to be followed, it inevitably breaks down, and open awareness becomes the new context for interaction. Notably, however, in the case of leukemic children, once they became aware of their prognosis (stage 5), they practiced mutual pretense to the end, in spite of others' violations of the rules.[1] Breaches in the rules of mutual pretense did not lead to open awareness, as they did with the terminally ill adults Glaser and Strauss studied.[2]

2. THE DEVELOPMENT AND MAINTENANCE OF MUTUAL PRETENSE

The conditions necessary for development of mutual pretense were present from the moment the children entered the hospital, even before the diagnosis was made. The staff was already predisposed to keep information from patients, guarding against "leaks" and covering up in the face of unavoidable leaks. For example, when the children were admitted, the nurses marked the children's charts "Possible WBC (White Blood Cell) Disease," the notation for leukemia. This notation was used lest patients or unsuspecting family members inadvertently see the charts and from them learn the diagnoses. It also served as a warning to other nonpediatric staff members, who might come in contact with the children, that they had leukemia, but had not been and should not be told. The notation on the chart

[1] There were two children who tried to change the context from mutual pretense to open awareness. For a variety of reasons, discussed in chapter 6, they failed. Mutual pretense remained the dominant mode of interaction.

[2] While Glaser and Strauss did not study terminally ill children or adolescents, all examples that they give of terminally ill children and adolescents (e.g., John Gunther's son in *Death Be Not Proud*) indicate these children practiced mutual pretense until their deaths.

provided more than medical information; it told how one should interact with the patients, what questions should be avoided, and what kind of information could be given, or, if a procedure had to be explained, what the procedure would involve, not why it was being done or what the results might indicate. If the children asked questions that might force the staff to reveal the prognosis ("What happens when the drugs run out?"), the staff members showed their unwillingness to talk about the matter by leaving the room, reprimanding the children, or by simply ignoring the question.

The parents also helped to set the stage for mutual pretense. As indicated in chapter four, as early as stage 3, when children started to ask probing questions about their condition, the parents began to signal their unwillingness to talk about it. They volunteered very little information and explained as little as possible. The children, noting these and other signals of unwillingness to deal with their condition (long absences from the room, brief interactions, avoidance of disease-related topics of conversation), obeyed them. When they realized they were dying and that people were no more willing to talk about their condition than they had ever been, the children started to practice mutual pretense.

> The patient, as remarked earlier, picks up these signals of unwillingness, and the mutual pretense context has been initiated. . . . Both sides play according to the rules implicit in the interaction. Although neither the staff nor patient may recognize these rules as such, certain tactics are fashioned around them, and the action is partly constrained by them. (Glaser and Strauss 1965b:69-70 and 72)

(1) *All parties to the interaction should avoid dangerous topics* (Glaser and Strauss 1965b:72)

The children and staff or family members avoided dangerous topics in their conversations in case such topics

201

would force them to reveal their awareness of the prognosis, and thus bring an end to the mutual pretense. Dangerous topics they avoided were: the children's condition (since they were dying); the drugs (since there were "none left"); the children's appearance (since it was deteriorating); other children's deaths (since they are reminders of impending death); future events and holidays (since they would not "be around" for them); and future plans (since they would not be able to see them through).[3]

(2) *"Talk about dangerous topics is permissible as long as neither party breaks down"* (Glaser and Strauss 1965b:72)

The children could talk to family and staff about dangerous topics yet maintain the pretense if they couched the conversation in other terms. When one six-year-old boy and a staff member talked about the upcoming Christmas holiday, she spoke as if the child were going to be alive to celebrate the holiday. They talked about past Christmas plans as if these were for the coming Christmas. In this way, each was able to keep the other from focusing on "the Christmas that he [the child] won't have, and bawling," bringing an end to the mutual pretense they were trying to sustain. A more obvious example was the time Mary was able to talk about her prognosis, the most dangerous topic, and maintain mutual pretense by focusing on the doll rather than on herself. When Mary died and I questioned her mother about the incident, she stated that Mary was trying to tell her "something," but "she knew I didn't want to hear that kind of talk." She also admitted to crying about it later that day when she looked at Mary's paper dolls.

(3) *All parties to the interaction should focus on safe topics and activities* (Glaser and Strauss 1965b:73)

The children, staff, and family members endeavored to center the action around safe topics and activities. In con-

[3] For examples of the children's following this and the other rules that follow, I refer the reader to appropriate parts of chapter four, and Act V of "The World of Jeffrey Andrews."

trast to dangerous topics, safe topics of conversation were devoid of disease reference, relatively uncontroversial when undertaken by well people, and had a timeless quality about them. The children, staff, and family often tried to engage each other in discussions about the daily routine, ward activities, the zoo, politics, restaurants, movies, TV programs, books, and sports.

Safe activities were those that did not remind the children of their incapacity. People encouraged them to color, watch TV, and play table games, and the children often invited people into their rooms for these activities.

(4) *Props should be used to sustain the "crucial illusion"* (Glaser and Strauss 1965b:71)

Various props were used that gave the illusion that although the children were quite ill, at least they were not dying. For example, the children often brought school books to the hospital and would on occasion take them out, as if to say, "I am going back to school, I am not dying." Likewise, the staff continued to give medications and left the I.V.s intact, even when it was clear that they were no longer of any help. If they had not done so, the mutual pretense would certainly have broken down, for the pulling of I.V.s from a terminal patient was a clue to everyone that the patient was dying and that there was nothing more to do.

(5) *"When something happens, or is said that tends to expose the fiction that both parties are attempting to sustain, [i.e., that the patient is not dying, is going to get better] then each must pretend that nothing has gone awry"* (Glaser and Strauss 1965b:73)

The four rules so far described were extremely difficult to follow because the tactics used to carry them out could as easily have shattered the illusion as sustained it. There was always the risk of slips and leaks. When the occupational therapist suggested to a seven-year-old boy that he draw a picture, a safe activity, the child responded, "OK, let's draw graves." Care then had to be taken to mend the break, if the mutual pretense was to be maintained. Several methods could be used. The one chosen depended on which rule had been violated.

When a dangerous topic, such as the child's condition, came up or pierced what either party thought was a suitable amount of veiling, the pretense was maintained either by ignoring the slip and shifting the topic of conversation, or by acknowledging the slip and then doing something that contradicted it. For example, after a discussion of an eight-year-old girl's incontinence, a definite sign of advanced deterioration, she walked to the bathroom as if nothing had happened. When a seven-year-old boy's Christmas presents arrived three weeks early and Santa came to visit him, suggesting that the boy would not live to Christmas, he turned to his choked-up family and the staff members around his bed, saying, "Santa has lots of children to see, he just came here first."

Doing or saying something that discounted what had just been said or done was also common when a safe topic backfired. A nurse was talking to one seven-year-old boy about baseball players, and he said, "I can't play baseball any more." She was able to maintain the mutual pretense context by quickly rejoining, "That's right, no ball playing in the rooms—hospital rules." The child could then not follow, as she feared he might, with "because I'm dying," and thereby break the mutual pretense.

The use of props to maintain mutual pretense was also problematic. Children at stage 5 often refused their medications and would not let procedures be done. They could, however, sustain the mutual pretense by refusing the procedure in the way normal children would, by crying, rather than by countering with, "Well, I'm dying anyway," or "It won't do any good." Many of the children who had never cried in the face of procedures started to when they reached stage 5. By doing so, they were able to express their feelings and at the same time prevent the breakdown of mutual pretense.

(6) *All parties to the interaction must strive to keep the interaction normal* (Glaser and Strauss 1965b:74)

While the need to maintain an aura of normalcy existed when the children first became ill, it was never as great as when they were close to death. In the early stages of the disease there was hope. Acting "sick" was not as threatening then as it was in the terminal stage, when there was virtually no hope left. The children had to "act normally" and staff and family had to support those normal actions and reciprocate, if the pretense was to be maintained.

In some families, with some staff members, the limits on "normal" were more constrained than with others. The more constrained the limits, the greater the number of dangerous or potentially dangerous topics of conversations and activities, and hence the greater the chances of breaking down the mutual pretense. Mary, for example, in contrast with Arthur, could not talk about anything (drugs, side effects, treatments, procedures, appearance) that called attention to her illness if she was to keep the situation normal, if the pretense was to be continued. Arthur was allowed to talk about the drugs, for to his parents they represented the possibility of getting better, of freedom from the disease.[4] By extension then, Arthur felt the need to act bravely in the face of procedures when his parents were around, to try to go through with them and not balk. Jeffrey, in contrast with Arthur and Mary, could keep the situation normal by simply avoiding direct admission about the prognosis.

(7) *All parties must strive to keep the interaction brief.*

The requirements for maintaining mutual pretense placed tremendous burdens on those involved. The major respon-

[4] Although this kind of behavior indicates that the parents accept the fact that the child has leukemia, it does not mean they accept the prognosis. In fact, Arthur's parents, as well as all parents who focused on the drugs (studied them, tried to get experimental ones), believed that fatal prognosis could be avoided if more or different drugs were used.

sibility shifted back and forth, but each party shared it to some degree. When one used a strategy to maintain mutual pretense, there was always the risk of having it backfire, necessitating employment of another strategy to mend the break. The longer the encounter, the greater the chance of breakdown. For this reason, the children, staff, and families tried to keep interactions brief.

(8) *When the rules become impossible to follow and the breakdown of mutual pretense appears imminent, avoid or terminate the interaction.*

At times, however, individuals felt that they could not follow the rules necessary for the maintenance of mutual pretense, yet they did not want to terminate the mutual pretense context. Consequently, one of the parties to the interaction employed a tactic that prevented interaction altogether. I refer to these tactics as "distancing strategies."

Glaser and Strauss (1965b) never mention the use of distancing strategies as tactics for maintaining mutual pretense. In part, this might be because they did not focus on terminally ill children, among whom such strategies are used with greater frequency than among terminally ill adults. It should be noted, though, that some of the behavior Glaser and Strauss observed in the few terminally ill children they did study could be accounted for as an attempt to avoid or to terminate interaction, much like distancing strategies.

The parents and staff members used different distancing strategies from those of the children. When they felt that they could no longer maintain the pretense, they would avoid the children's rooms, or, if already in a room, make excuses to leave (answer a page, smoke a cigarette, make a phone call). These were alternatives not open to the bedridden children. If adults chose to stay, the children could not get out of their sight or leave the room, so they relied on one of several other distancing strategies to terminate interaction.

The distancing strategies used, by some of the children

named in this book were: refusal to talk (Sandy), feigning sleep (Mary), continual lashing out or crying out (Jeffrey), withdrawal (Tom), and engaging in practically inaudible or superficial conversation (Lisa). In contrast with the strategies used to establish relationships or bring individuals closer (exhibition of wounds, questions about medical procedures, side effects and conditions), the strategies used for maintaining distance weakened and destroyed relationships. The children then had fewer people with whom they had to keep up the pretense. They managed to decrease the possibility of breakdown in a way that reinforced normalcy.

These avoidance and distancing strategies, like all other tactics used for maintaining mutual pretense, harbored the possibility of ending mutual pretense. If the staff or the parents avoided the children's rooms too much, the children sensed it was because the adults were uncomfortable about their condition and "afraid that the subject of his prognosis might come up." "No one comes to see me anymore. I'm dying and I look bad." "They don't make me get needles no more. Roberta didn't come for two days." Similarly, the children's avoidance of adults, through the various strategies for inhibiting conversation, aroused the staff's suspicions that the children knew, but were not telling. "She knows. She just doesn't want to talk about it." "He yells so I can have an excuse for leaving."

As with crying, the children risked being deserted for the action, but they also reinforced the adults' belief that the children were normal. Normal children let off steam. They resist passivity. The leukemics' yelling and screaming was seen as fighting, as throwing off passivity, as living and not dying.

> See she's fighting. When they stop fighting they die. Just look at Maria. That kid should have been dead three weeks ago, bleeding that way, all over. But she goes to the bathroom herself and she tells you if you're welcome or not.

207

A leukemic's refusal to speak was interpreted in a similar way. By employing such a strategy, they were showing that they had some control, if not over what was happening to them, at least over the nonmedical people they had to deal with.

MRS. HILL: Has Reggie talked to you at all this hospital-ization?

MYRA: Yeah, but not since Saturday when he got mad at me. I think he might feel bad about it.

MRS. HILL: I can't understand it. He likes you and asks for you.

MYRA: Well, maybe it's because I'm the one person they know they can push around. Everyone else they have no choice about, with me they can do as they please. Besides, they know I'll come back.

MRS. ANDREWS: I think that's it. Jeffrey knows that if he wants to talk you'll listen and if he doesn't want to talk you'll shut up.

MRS. HILL: Yeah. They have to have someone or some-thing they feel they have control over, because they certainly do not have control over themselves and what is done with them.

Mutual pretense, then, was a "delicately balanced drama." One had to shift back and forth, give and take, reveal and cover, if the pretense was to be maintained, for in the very rules by which it was staged were the possibilities for the drama's end.

Following Glaser and Strauss (1965b), the concept of mutual pretense has helped illuminate how interaction at stage 5 proceeds. We have a better understanding of why the children at stage 5 behaved as they did. But the questions remain: Why did they, their parents, and the staff follow the rules? Why, when a slip was made, did individ-uals go to such great lengths to cover it up? Why did they go even further to devise strategies that minimized contact and hence made opportunities for breakdown? Why, in spite of the length of time it had to be maintained, did mutual pretense never give way to open awareness, as Glaser and Strauss found it does among adults?

In essence, we have established that the leukemic children were aware of their prognosis, that they concealed this awareness from others, and we know how they did so. We have not established *why* they concealed their awareness, and why others concealed their awareness from them. For the solution to these problems we must look at the fabric of society.

CHAPTER SIX

Mutual Pretense:
Causes and Consequences

The most frequently offered explanation for the practice of mutual pretense is that death is taboo and must be kept from intruding (cf. Glaser and Strauss 1965b, Fulton 1966, Kalish 1969, Hoffman and Futterman 1971, and Hendin 1973). I contend that simply labeling death as taboo and the mentioning of it as forbidden is not adequate to explain this practice. The leukemic children, their parents and the staff that attended them, I argue, practiced mutual pretense because it offered each of them a way to fulfill the roles and responsibilities necessary for maintaining membership in the society, in the face of that which threatened the fulfillment of social obligations and continued membership.

1. THE CHILDREN

Children in American society are molded for their futures. We ask of them, demand of them, train them, so that they will "turn out all right." They are creatures to be socialized, to be readied. "In their efforts to socialize the child, parents are guided, however fallibly, by their awareness of such social expectation and their image of what the child must become if he is to live successfully in the world as the parents envision it will be at the time the child becomes an adult" (Inkeles 1968:75). Parents have definite ideas about their children's futures and what should be done to ensure that they meet the demands of adulthood. "Few parents appear to be casual about their offspring" (Clausen 1968b:138). While some parents work quite actively on almost all aspects of behavior, there are certain areas towards which all parents direct some major attention.[1]

From a very early period, parents work on their children's sexual identity. Boys and girls are given toys and clothes, and taught games, appropriate to their sex; they are discouraged from using and playing with others. Boys are given pants, boots, boats, and trucks. Girls are given dresses, slips, dolls, and tea sets. "Boys are in general trained to attain quite different objectives than girls are" (Inkeles 1968:107).

Each child, then, is prepared to assume the appropriate sexual role, as defined by the society. This preparation includes instruction in sexual conduct. Children are generally discouraged from such activities as masturbation or sexual play with others of the same and opposite sex. They are reprimanded in the first two instances, because one "shouldn't do those things," "it's not the way a child should enjoy himself"; and in the latter instances because that is for later, after one is married, after one has "earned it."

The parent is also in part responsible for training children by example, by direct instruction, through affirmation, and through correction, how to carry on social relations and what to do in various social situations. Children learn to be "reasonably responsive to the pattern of social order and to the personal needs and requirements of the other individuals with whom [they are] in immediate contact" (Inkeles 1968:87). They are expected to be well mannered, to tell the truth, to be cooperative, to show respect for adults, and to pay attention to them.

"The parents' evaluation of the child's behavior proceeds, however, not only by direct extrapolation, but also by

[1] The areas of behavior most parents direct their attention to in the socialization of offspring are also those that many sociologists and anthropologists consider when studying children. However, they are studying only one aspect of being a child—childhood socialization by adults—the consequences of which are discussed in chapter one, above.

vaguer and less conscious processes, in which the connection between present and future behavior is more indirectly and symbolically reckoned" (Aberle and Naegele 1968:189). When children succeed, they are rewarded; when they fail, they are punished or ignored. All of these actions are done "for their own good." This justification for discipline is also the rationale for withholding certain things from children, and for not indulging them materially or nonmaterially. Many goods, rights, and privileges are for a later time, when they are older, when they have earned them. Complete gratification is for the future, after one has "made it."

In American society, responsibility for children's socialization is shared by the school, which nurtures their intellectual, physical, and emotional development. From kindergarten, they learn bodily, social, and intellectual skills—how to count and bounce a ball, how to pledge allegiance to the flag and share toys. When they deviate, they are punished (verbal or social ostracism, loss of playground privileges). They are labeled by their teachers according to adult perceptions of intellectual and social accomplishments.

The very act of going to school marks one as a child in this society; just as having a job in the case of men, or being a homemaker in the case of women, marks one as an adult.[2] When two adults meet, they often inquire about what the other is doing. "What are you doing these days?" or "What do you do for a living?" Whereas, when adults encounter a child, they usually ask something like, "What grade are you in?" or in the summer months, "What grade are you going into?" Such questions are often followed by, "And what are you going to be when you grow up?"

Children, in American society, are "in process," "not yet fully formed," as childhood is a period of formation, of becoming. Socialization is by definition forward-looking

[2] Students are not considered full-fledged adults, even if they are over twenty-one.

212

(Inkeles 1968: 76, Aberle and Naegele 1968:89), not a period of concluding or of summing up.

Dying children, however, do not fit comfortably into such a view. Although, like other children, they are sensitive, intelligent, kind, willful, and young, they will not "become," they have no future. Participation in the institutions that mark one as children in this society are not for them. They do not go to school, they go to the hospital. They do not wear sexually, or even socially, appropriate clothing, but nondescript hospital gowns that are either immodestly short or unbecomingly large, and they go about without underwear. Boys are not discouraged from masturbating, and girls are not discouraged from punching. Little is withheld materially, and reprimands usually come only when tempers are short.

Dying children are more like the elderly than their own healthy peers—without futures, worried, often passive, unhappy, burdened with responsibilities for others and their feelings. They even resemble old people—either bald or disheveled, emaciated or bloated, incapacitated, generally sickly, and most of all losing, failing with time. Their worth can only be measured by what they do now, unlike other children, who have time to prove themselves.

By practicing the rules of mutual pretense, these children keep the parent/child, doctor/patient relationship from breaking down. By assuming the role of child or patient, as adults define it, they allow the parent or doctor to assume the reciprocal role and all the behavior that follows from it. Each time the dying children use a prop that other children use (rule 4 of mutual pretense) or do something that other children do (rule 6 of mutual pretense), they not only follow those rules, but also give credence to the illusion of their normalcy, thereby allowing others to do what is expected of them.[3] Further, by practicing mutual pretense,

[3] For examples, see chapter five, section 2, above.

213

they demonstrate awareness of their social obligations and responsibilities and their competence in social relations. They show, as Inkeles (1968:87) states, they are "responsive to the pattern of social order and to the personal needs and requirements of the other individuals with whom [they are] in immediate contact," and thereby gain in social worth that which they would otherwise be deprived of by death.

2. THE PARENTS

Parents are shapers, the agents entrusted with molding their offsprings' formlessness and potential. To this end, parents are supposed to guide children in the right direction and correct them when they are wrong. As the authorities, the sources of knowledge, parents should be able to tell children what to do and what to expect. They are viewed as being in control of themselves and of their progeny.

Parents are also nurturants in our society, which means that they are supposed to spend time with the children, expending effort on their upbringing (Wolfenstein 1955:73). They are the providers for the helpless young, whom they are supposed to protect physically and emotionally from want, pain, and fear. In exchange for fulfilling these roles, as society defines them, parents are promised "fun and happiness" (Wolfenstein 1955:173).

In the face of terminal illness, mothers and fathers are systematically stripped of these parental roles and the consequent pleasures. Further, as Futterman and Hoffman (1971:15) point out, "the onset of leukemia in a child represents an assault on a parent's sense of adequacy as guardian of his child and, more generally, as a person with a meaningful control over his own and his family's destinies."

Such parents cannot be rearers, for to what end can they rear the terminally ill? "Why should I toilet train him? It's not like he's going to . . ."; "Why should I make her go to school?" Parents gradually lose their standing as authority figures for these children. "Amazement was noted as to how

214

children learned who were the authority figures in the hospital and to bypass their parents" (Hamovitch 1964:7). But not even the loss of this stature bothered the parents as much as their loss of authority and control over what was happening to their young. Many parents thought that they did not know very much, too little to answer their own questions, not to mention the children's.

> I just don't know what to tell Laura, I don't even know. When Laura first went down to surgery we told her that she had a mass that might have to come out. She didn't expect "the works" and, well, neither did we.

The parents saw themselves as powerless before the disease, the doctors, the machines used for treatment, and, most important, their children.

They felt that they could not care for their children on a day-to-day basis, let alone in the future. The hospital became the provider. "Mothers complained about having to relinquish their maternal responsibilities to nurses" (Hamovitch 1964:5). It seemed to them that the nurses were taking over their nurturing responsibilities. In many mothers, this led to feelings of, "Why bother to do anything?"

> I'm not sure who I am reading this book for, her or me. She's just lying there. At least before I could give her a pill. I can't even do that now.

Activities that were supposed to be fun or used to be fun for the family, like holidays and outings, were not any more. Many parents felt pressured to squeeze everything in. They were often so anxious about whether the children were enjoying themselves that they could not share the enjoyment. There was always the cloud of "Well, this might be his last. . . ."

Like any other, these mothers wanted to cuddle their children, but the pain often made the children unwilling to be hugged or touched (see play, Act II, Scene 6).

"Another common problem was that of the younger child

215

[I also saw this in older children] who openly rejected his parents, made them feel guilty, and gave them a sense of failure. This seemed to be particularly true after the children had been in the hospital for some time, and there was an implied accusation that the parent had failed to protect them" (Hamovitch 1964:9). Parents often expressed their feelings of failure to protect, in the face of procedures; they tended to express guilt during the induction of the first remission.[4]

Maybe if I brought him in sooner, when he got that cold. Oh, I don't know.

MRS. WELDER: (*After leaving* FAITH's *room during a procedure*) It's times like this when I think about what she knows and how sick she is. She's in there screaming her head off, and there's nothing I can do.

The way he kept screaming, "Don't leave me." And I couldn't help him.

Their inability to protect the children from procedures and pain also made it difficult for parents to spend time with their children as "good" parents are supposed to do. "Sometimes I just can't take it in there any more. Seeing him in the bed there like that. I keep seeing him in the . . . [coffin] you know."

Far worse, of course, than taking from parents their "sense of mastery and worth" (Hoffman and Futterman 1971:73), leukemia took their children—an irrevocable separation. To some extent, mutual pretense helped parents prepare for this final severance by pacing it out, and by allowing them to rehearse the separation in an acceptable manner. By their use of distancing strategies, children gave parents an excuse (rule 8 of mutual pretense); parents could then leave without feeling they were deserting the children, who, by their actions, were asking them to leave.

[4] This was also noted by the doctors. See the play, Act I, Scene 16.

"He knows I'll leave if he yells at me."[5] Also, if a procedure then occurred while the parents were out of the room, as was often the case, they did not have to feel that they had failed to protect the children.

Some parents felt that protection also meant shielding the children from knowledge of the prognosis. They rationalized withholding information (observing rule 1 of mutual pretense), even using deception with statements like "You'll get better" (observing rule 5 of mutual pretense) on grounds that this protected children from unhappiness and the possibility of an inadvertent premature death. They reasoned that knowledge might make children give up (Hoffman and Futterman 1971:34-5).

> I don't believe in telling my child everything like some mothers. Look at Jennifer Handleman. You know why that kid always looks so unhappy? [the speaker's child did not look any happier] I'll tell you—because her mother tells her everything.

> I think if we told Cherry everything she'd stop taking her medicine.[6] She'd quit. You know what I mean?

It should be noted that parents who assume this position and let their children know it (by nonverbal cues) are also not put in the position of having to answer difficult questions, because by rule 1 of mutual pretense, questions about one's condition cannot be asked. In this way, their authority cannot be undermined. Much of what sustained mutual pretense, then, also allowed the parents to retain the parental role.

3. THE HOSPITAL STAFF

The task of doctors in our society is to cure, or at least to restore, patients to some measure of social functioning as

---

[5] The child later confirmed his parent's remark.

[6] This mother believed at the time that the medicines could keep her child alive.

prescribed by society (Wilson 1963:278).[7] Physicians are used to seeing themselves, and being seen by others, as capable of meeting these demands. They are also used to the feelings of authority and control that derive from such a view. As medical students, doctors learn "not to kill patients through error, and to save patients' lives through diagnosis and treatment, but their teachers emphasize very little, or not at all, how to talk with dying patients, how or whether to disclose an impending death, or even how to approach the subject with the wives, children, and parents of dying patients" (Glaser and Strauss 1965b:4). They are taught detachment for the sake of objectivity, so that they can carry out the essentials for terminal cases without bogging down.

The same can be said about nurses' training. While they share the responsibilities for care of the terminally ill, and are often the ones the patients and their families turn to for information, nurses are taught very little about how to deal with such matters (Glaser and Strauss 1965b:40).

In general, medical personnel are never taught what to do when medicine fails. Graduates leave medical school believing that if they do what they are supposed to and make no mistakes, patients will at least improve, if not totally recover. The ramifications of such a view are greatest when patients die. Doctors often wind up seeing themselves as failures. One doctor (*Philadelphia Inquirer*, August 14, 1972) commented, "Death represents failure to a physician and it's hard for him to deal with it." As Glaser and Strauss (1965b:240) found, "Some physicians purposely specialize in branches of medicine that will minimize their chances of encountering dying patients. Many nurses frankly admit preference for wards or fields where there is little confrontation with death, where people get better." As one nurse re-

[7] For a complete discussion of the education of medical personnel and its effects on their ability to cope with various psychosocial problems that arise in treating the terminally ill, see Becker et al. 1961, Glaser and Strauss 1965b and 1968, and Quint 1967.

marked to me when more than half of the children on the floor were near death, "I never thought pediatrics would be like this."

Leukemics are an affront to the doctors' sense of mastery, to their training, their profession, and their self-concept. They do not have all the answers. They can neither cure these children nor, as the disease progresses, insure their comfort. In their bags are very few tricks for the terminally ill, and by the time the children are failing, no tricks are left.

DR. SMEDLEY: (*During a resuscitation of a child*) Any more tricks in your bag?

DR. LANG: Yes, but not for this child.

STUDENT: Why?

DR. SMEDLEY: She has leukemia.

INTERN: Then what are we doing this for?

DR. SMEDLEY: For ourselves, I guess.

At the same time, even detachment proves difficult. The basic assumptions and instructions that underly the doctor/patient relationship run amuck.

Mutual pretense allows physicians to salvage some of what is expected of them, to fulfill their definitions as healers. As long as they support the illusion that the children will get better, or at least can be made more comfortable, they can carry out the procedures and duties that in part define them as physicians. They can carry on "business as usual" (rule 4 of mutual pretense).[8] Further, by observing the seventh rule of mutual pretense, keeping the interactions brief, they can avoid becoming too involved, and thereby retain an idea of themselves as objective.

It is evident that the practice of mutual pretense allows participants to fulfill their role expectations, and retain social membership in the face of a threat to such membership.

[8] It should be noted that the staff was the first to initiate mutual pretense.

To explain further the dominance of mutual pretense, however, and to illustrate more clearly how such a practice insures continued membership with its benefits, we should study what happened to individuals who did not participate, but who practiced "open awareness."

4. OPEN AWARENESS: THE ALTERNATIVE

According to Glaser and Strauss (1965b:79), open awareness comes about "whenever both staff [and/or family member involved in the interaction] and patient know that he is dying and acknowledge it in their actions." If one party discloses his awareness of the prognosis but the other party refuses to acknowledge the disclosure, open awareness does not exist. Both parties must agree. For example, Larry Helman kept screaming "I'm dying, I'm dying." His mother insisted, "No. You're getting better." Larry rebuked her with, "No I'm not. I have the same thing as Dennis [his brother who died of leukemia]." His mother shouted, "Stop talking like that!" The argument continued until Larry relented. The Helmans returned to the practice of mutual pretense for the remainder of Larry's life.

Only two children in my study were able to bring about open awareness. Except for the fact that their disclosure speeches were more direct and less couched in symbolism than the other children's, they disclosed their awareness in the same manner. They made the same speech to everyone they attempted open awareness with. One eight-year-old girl simply stated to her parents, "You see, I'm going to die." Another seven-year-old girl commented to her parents, to certain staff members, and to me, "I'm going to die soon. They are trying to help my blood, but it's [the medicine] making my liver bad." In both cases, the parents acknowledged their child's admission with hugs and tears, followed by verbal assent.

The parents who practiced open awareness were different from the others studied in two major respects. First, a large part of their identity was not tied to being parents. As the psychiatrist who studied these parents explained, much of their identity and sense of self-worth or self-esteem seemed to come from other sources, like jobs, not from the parent role. Second, these parents were more unconventional in their behavior and less concerned with society's judgment of their behavior than the other parents studied.

Staff members who practiced open awareness (there were only two) were also different from their co-workers. For one R.N., open awareness was a cause célèbre, the reason and justification for working with terminally ill patients. An aide who practiced open awareness identified herself as "a child-care person" rather than as "a medical person." Open awareness was not practiced by any of the doctors.

Although these parents and staff members acknowledged the children's disclosures, in both cases it was the children, not the adults, who brought it about. Further, the shift to open awareness did not result from a breakdown in the mutual pretense context, when someone could no longer maintain it.

I would argue that even in cases where it does happen this way, there is a danger in regarding open awareness as a *result* of a breakdown in mutual pretense, as Glaser and Strauss (1965b) do. It gives the impression that open awareness is the end of a long continuum, something striven for, and marking a kind of acceptance. The people who practiced open awareness did not accept the prognosis any more than those who practiced mutual pretense. Furthermore, when open awareness was achieved, it was not necessarily final or complete in every area. There were lapses back into mutual pretense when the children achieved a remission, or when a procedure had to be performed that did not seem necessary for dying patients. There were also long lapses with no mention of the prognosis. In other words, open awareness should not be interpreted as "a sudden clearing of the air."

Finally, the practice of open awareness did not necessarily

mean that the individuals felt any more comfortable around each other. The parents who practiced open awareness were as frequently absent from their children's rooms as parents who practiced mutual pretense. Staff avoided the rooms of the children known to practice open awareness just as much, if not more so, than the rooms of the children who practiced mutual pretense.

In all other respects, children who practiced open awareness behaved just like those who practiced mutual pretense. They avoided the names of deceased children and their belongings, were preoccupied with death and disease imagery in their play, art, and conversations, refrained from non-disease related discussion and play as well as from discussions about going home and future plans, and continued to practice distancing strategies.

Parents who practiced open awareness often suffered from problems not shared by parents who practiced mutual pretense. Often staff members would not want to do as much for them as they would for other parents. They were often ostracized, even called "bad parents" by peers and staff, for not protecting their offspring from unhappy news.

Even parents who did not criticize those practicing open awareness were not sure they would ever want to be "open" with their children; "openness" might not make things any easier, and in fact might make them more difficult—if not for the children, at least for themselves.

The open parents felt that being honest with their children helped them all, if not to accept, at least to cope, with the prognosis. They felt that the honesty aided in bringing them all closer in the face of that which would ultimately pull them apart. But these parents, as well as others that have been studied (cf. work of Comerford 1974, Naimen 1971-1974, Hamovitch 1964, Karon and Vernick 1968), were quick to point out that open awareness did not free them from constant conflicts and dilemmas, which, it is important to note, were essentially the same as those of the other parents. Aside from problems of separation, delegation of responsibility, and feelings of guilt, anger, and frustration already discussed, all the parents were also faced with more concrete problems of how to treat the children and what to tell them.

A constant dilemma was whether to treat the children as if they were normal or special. Treating the children "normally" required the parents to demand of their offspring what they had before the illness, i.e., that they go to school, help around the house, and be able to defer gratification. These demands, and subsequent discipline when expectations were not met, had been justified before on the premise that if the children did not do what was expected they would not grow up to be responsible adults. In other words, correction and some measure of restraint were necessary for their own future good. But since the leukemics would not grow up, why deprive them of what comes with growing up, the privileges of maturity? Why not indulge them with special treatment?

Many mothers argued that special treatment was wrong because it was not fair to the other siblings, who had enough problems already as a result of the attention that the leukemic child required. Furthermore, special treatment might make the leukemics all the more aware of differences between themselves and other children, and they were different enough as it was.

> I remember the first time I spanked her. After she was home awhile from the hospital (after the first terrible visit). I could see she was delighted, for the spanking meant she was not "different." (Comerford 1974:148)

Mrs. Handleman finally let Jennifer stay out of school when going to school was making her more, rather than less, conscious of how different she was from other children. Some mothers felt that special treatment was wrong, because the children might live for some time and become spoiled or difficult to handle.

I don't tell them what Jenny's got. They don't all have to know. They'll start treating her special and I don't need anymore of that.[9]

I don't like the way my mother's spoiling the baby. I have a niece the same age and Mom makes a difference. I don't want that. I don't want her to grow up to be a freak or something. She'll be spoiled enough. She's the baby and I have three older boys. After all, she's going to be growing up here, here in the clinic, and she'll know things are different for her.

I thought I would have tremendous feelings of guilt later for having spanked her, but I knew that if she did survive, we did not want a spoiled "brat" for a daughter, and that she must learn that one does not always get one's own way in life. (Comerford 1974:148-149)

These three statements were made by mothers of children in their first remissions, or doing well. Underlying all these statements is a belief that the children will get better, perhaps even grow up, and that they should be prepared for this outcome as well as for a fatal one.

Continuous relapses and the deaths of other children in the clinic shatter such hopes and weaken such arguments for discipline. But they do not remove the dilemma or permit total indulgence. Besides the problems such a course would pose siblings, to indulge children is to admit that they no longer need rearing. One can only do without rearing if one is going to die, and, as we have seen, such a view has consequences for overall care and treatment.

---

[9] Parents felt that other people were inclined to treat the child special, in part because they did not know what else to do, and also to make themselves feel better.

I think people just give them things so they'll feel better, I don't like them to do it. It's just not good for Adam or for Stephen. I used to tell them so, but I'm tired of telling them. If that's what they have to do, well. . . .

Therefore, in view of the parents' ambivalence, whether they disciplined or indulged the children, their course of action seemed to reflect more how they viewed the children than what arguments they put forth. Such changes in parental attitudes, related to the children's conditions, are reflected in the play. When Jeffrey Andrews was admitted to the hospital, his parents treated him as they always had. He was expected to eat and to do as he was told, to understand when they had to leave the hospital. After the Andrews were told the diagnosis, they began to indulge their son. All his mother could think about was the prognosis. "A neighbor's child died and it started the same way." But after Jeffrey achieved a remission, they began to treat him "normally." They stopped giving him special treatment, indulging him, and began rearing him again. This continued until the final stages, and even then not every whim was indulged. In general, the more one was aware of the child's imminent death, the greater the indulgence. The more one thought of the child as possibly recovering, the less the indulgence.[10]

By extension then, the parents' behavior could also be looked at as a more accurate reflection of how they viewed the child than was anything they said. For example, the staff felt that Mrs. Costin denied Mary's illness because she refused to use the word *leukemia* or discuss the possibility of Mary's dying, and instead talked about future plans and how well Mary looked. Her behavior toward Mary, however, reflected acknowledgment of the prognosis, not denial. The Costins indulged their daughter and justified it in terms of her illness. A mother who indulges for this reason is not one who is hopeful. Mrs. Costin even admitted that she

---

[10] The doctors I spoke with during the study point out that this kind of approach to indulgence can become problematic, because the parents often want to do things (e.g., take trips to Disneyland) when the child is really "too sick to do them." It would have been better to carry out these projects right after the first remission, but the parents did not fully accept the end at that time.

treated Mary differently in the beginning, when she had hope: "Yes, we gave in to her a lot and gave her presents all the time, but she still had to practice [the piano] and help out, you know, clean up her room and all. But now, what for?" A more accurate assessment of Mrs. Costin's attitude would have been that her statements about how well Mary looked and future plans were a front to help her in dealing with Mary and the staff. What she really felt was, as she herself said, "I know what Mary's got, but I don't have to accept it."

Another dilemma that persisted throughout the course of the illness was what to tell the children. Parents gave most thought to the problem during the induction of the first remission, when another child died, and when their own child was dying. These were problematic times for all the parents.

Those who practiced mutual pretense saw every question as a search for information about the prognosis, so it was best to answer as few questions as possible. Mrs. Andrews asked Mrs. Smith what she had told her son:

> MRS. SMITH: It's pretty hard to keep things from them, no matter how hard you try.
> MRS. ANDREWS: Have you told your son?
> MRS. SMITH: He knows he has a blood disease, and, well, I don't know. But they do pick up quick.

Similarly, when I asked Mrs. Costin how she answered Mary's questions about the other children in the clinic, and what was happening to her, as well as what she told Mary when another child died, the only question to which Mrs. Costin responded was the last.

> MYRA: Doesn't she notice the other kids in the clinic and ask about them, what's wrong with them, or what happened to them, or when they don't come back to clinic anymore?
> MRS. COSTIN: Yeah, sure. But I just tell her that they went to another clinic.

Although questions about the prognosis might have been foremost in the parents' minds and have motivated their questions about procedures, the disease process, and other children, they were not necessarily as important to the children. The children were not always asking about the prognosis, for as discussed in chapter four, it was quite some time before they became aware of it, and by then they had stopped asking about much of anything.

For the parents who practiced open awareness, there were questions about whether or not the child should be told how imminent death was and about impending procedures and side effects of drugs before they were employed. If a child is told of a possible procedure or drug side effect, which does not then materialize, the child might be more anxious than if the explanation had been given later.

To a large extent, the problem of what to tell children revolved around the issue of protection. Does one protect them most by telling them nothing or everything? What are adults protecting children from when they decide to tell or not to tell? The parents remained ambivalent and, as in the breakthrough to open awareness, it was up to the children to make the first moves. Parents rarely, if ever, volunteered any information.

The more one admits to children what is happening, the more there is to deal with, the greater the problems of "acknowledging ultimate loss of the child and maintaining hope" (Hoffman and Futterman 1971:69). This is seen most clearly in the terminal stages. How does one, after acknowledging the fact that the child will die, make the child go through with painful procedures, especially when there is no guarantee that the relief will compensate for the pain of the procedure?

This is the conflict that the doctors and nurses felt most keenly. On one hand, how does one carry out painful procedures on children riddled with pain when there is not even a guarantee of relief? On the other hand, how does one stop procedures without feeling that all that went before (and that one is currently doing for others still in their first remission) was in vain? There is always the dilemma of the prolongation of life in the hope of cure—as justification for what has been done for this child, and what will be done for other children—versus the acknowledgment of loss necessary for the preparation of the family, and the maintenance of the patient. This dilemma was not any more successfully resolved by staff members who practiced open awareness than by those who practiced mutual pretense.

As we have seen, the children, regardless of which form of interaction they practiced, were not free from conflict either. They were faced with constant conflict. Even the decision to reveal one's awareness directly was fraught with questions of to whom and when. There were always risks involved. If the children used a distancing strategy that other people did not like, or if they attempted to reveal their knowledge and others did not accept it, they might be abandoned. And for the children, physical isolation was far worse than psychological isolation (i.e., the inability to share one's innermost thoughts and fears). Furthermore, open awareness did not guarantee less isolation. As we saw, children who practiced open awareness were avoided just as much, if not more, than those who practiced mutual pretense.

Mutual pretense, then, was the dominant mode of interaction between the terminally ill and those that attended them, because it offered individuals a way to do what society expected of them. It enabled them to fulfill various social roles and responsibilities necessary for maintaining membership in the society in the face of a threat to continued membership. The cases of the children, the parents, and the medical staff and what happened to each of them when they chose to practice mutual pretense or open awareness were considered.

The onset of leukemia challenged the children's ability to meet the hopes of parents and society. They would not be able to become, to demonstrate their worth in future achievements, for they would have no future—that which defines one as being a child. The practice of mutual pretense allowed them to act as if they had a future, to act like children. By following the rules necessary for maintaining mutual pretense, they showed themselves responsive to the needs of others. The rewards for such behavior were great. They gained a sense of achievement, satisfaction, and worth in their own eyes and in the eyes of their caretakers (parents and medical staff). By reinforcing the adults' hopes, the children thereby guaranteed their continued presence. They were not left alone.

The children's practice of mutual pretense allowed the caretakers to play their reciprocal roles. Parents in this society are responsible for nurturing, protecting, and rearing children. These three tasks became increasingly impossible in the face of terminal illness, and yet they define being a parent. Through the tactics that they fashioned to follow rules 1, 4, and 6 of mutual pretense, the parents were able, to some extent, to play these roles. In fact, the strategies used to follow rule 8 helped parents "to rehearse" ultimate separation from their children, and they were supported in their actions by other parents.

Physicians in our society are charged with curing, or at the very least "caring" (a term whose meaning is quite ambiguous). They see themselves, and are seen by others, as masters. Leukemia challenges this sense of mastery and worth. They feel like failures. Through the practice of mutual pretense (rule 4 in particular) they could salvage some of their self-esteem and continue to work. They too were supported for their actions by parents and colleagues who wanted to see them as "curers."

When the children and caretakers practiced open awareness (mutual acknowledgment of the prognosis), they were unable to fulfill their social roles and responsibilities: The children could not act as if they were going to become; the parents could not see themselves as protectors and rearers;

the medical personnel were unable to feel themselves part of the curing process. As mentioned earlier, the adults who practiced open awareness were not tied to their role definitions.

For those who practiced openness, there was the reward of "feeling good for being honest," but apparently that was too high a price to pay for the abandonment and ostracism which followed. Open awareness did not free parents from conflicts (e.g., separation, delegation of responsibility, how to treat the children, what to tell them), or make them more accepting of the prognosis. Many of those who practiced open awareness tried to revert back to mutual pretense. And while they could never totally sustain the mutual pretense context, they could not continually practice open awareness either.

In essence, mutual pretense is the individual's attempt to maintain the social order. As Durkheim, Goffman, and Garfinkel have argued, the social order is a moral order. Individuals will go to great lengths to maintain it. For to violate it, to break the rules necessary for its maintenance, is to risk exclusion and abandonment, "a fate worse than death itself." The practice of mutual pretense reflects a human dilemma far more fundamental than the fear of "breaking a taboo"—the existential dilemma.

CHAPTER SEVEN

Conclusion

Death is not merely a biological phenomenon, but a social and cultural one as well. Our manner of facing our own death, and, in the case at hand, the death of a child, has as much to do with our view of ourselves and with our social relationships as it does with the biological inevitability of death. The death of a child poignantly underlines the impact of social and cultural factors on the way that we die and the way that we permit others to die.

Seeing death as a sociocultural phenomenon was critical to my understanding of what was happening to the terminally ill children, and more specifically, to how they became aware of the fact that they were dying and why they concealed that knowledge from their caretakers. In this concluding chapter, I focus on the importance of viewing death as a social and cultural phenomenon, not only to answer the questions underlying this research, but also to come to grips with the problem of how to treat terminally ill children.

1. DEATH, SELF, AND SOCIETY

The children lay before their caretakers as members of society unable to remain members. There they all were: children with futures to be molded; parents charged with this responsibility; medical practitioners trained to cure. Leukemia now threatened everyone's ability to fulfill their socially defined roles. Moreover, it threatened their ability to carry on social interaction.

Interaction proceeds on the basis of the ideas that we have of ourselves and others have of us, on the basis of our

231

identities (cf. Mead 1970, Goffman 1959). These identities are linked to our social roles. To take away the roles is to take away the identities. The possibility of social interaction is negated. If this is the case, how could interaction continue for those facing the loss of social role and identity—for the terminally ill and their caretakers?

Interaction could take place as long as everyone acted as if they still had their social roles. It could be maintained as long as the children, parents, and medical practitioners fulfilled the social obligations and responsibilities necessary for the maintenance of those respective roles. And, as demonstrated in chapters five and six, this is precisely what happened, what the practice of mutual pretense made possible.

Everyone could retain their identity and membership in society, except those who did not practice mutual pretense; they were ostracized and abandoned. To put it another way, as long as individuals fulfill their obligations and responsibilities and do not violate the social order, they are granted continued membership in the society and all that comes with it—freedom from fear and abandonment. No one seemed to know this better than the terminally ill children; for they practiced mutual pretense unto death.

Ironically, these children came to see their own task in life as supporting others. They showed themselves to be responsive to the needs of their parents. Through the tactics they fashioned to follow rule 8 of mutual pretense, they gave their parents the opportunity to rehearse the ultimate separation.

MYRA: Jeffrey, why do you always yell at your mother?
JEFFREY: Then she won't miss me when I'm gone.
MRS. ANDREWS: Jeffrey yells at me because he knows I can't take it. He yells so I can have an excuse for leaving.

In essence, the children's ability to practice mutual pretense marked them as able to meet the most fundamental demand that society places on all its members—preservation of the social order. For those who can live to a ripe old age, there are more concrete ways to demonstrate support of society's order. One can amass great fortunes, succeed professionally and raise "good" children. These ways were not open to the terminally ill children, so they managed in the way they knew best. They contributed to society and its order in a fundamental and no less great sense by allowing the living their identities, their sense of self-worth, derived from their roles.

The funeral is for the living, and so is the dying. The way we are permitted to die, and the way that we permit others to die, is to enable the living to continue the process of their lives. The dying have to be fitted into this scheme of the living, there is no separate way for them. Perhaps this is why, when we think of a "happy death," we think of dying suddenly or in our sleep. It is not just the physical pain of a long and lingering illness that we seek to avoid; for today we can almost guarantee people freedom from pain. No, it is the social pain, the pain that comes in the limbo phase, the pain of living with death, the pain that comes from committing an antisocial act, which we do not wish to endure.

2. RELATING TO TERMINALLY ILL CHILDREN

For medical professionals who care for terminally ill children, the foremost question about social and psychological management of these patients is, What does one tell them?

Basically, the decision should be made by the same rule of thumb that is applied in deciding what to tell children about sex: Tell them only what they want to know, what they are asking about, and on their own terms.

As we have seen (chapter four), leukemic children had different questions, concerns, and needs at different stages of their illness. When first diagnosed, they were concerned about the seriousness of the illness, about the fact that they were sicker than they had ever been. When they began to achieve the first remission, they wanted to know about the

233

drugs used in the treatment and their side effects. They were heartened by the fact that although they had been ill, they were now recovering. However, during the first relapse, old doubts returned. They wondered if they would always be sick. They tried to learn everything they could about procedures and treatments they had to endure. After further relapses, they asked about the chronic nature of the illness. They wanted to know if and when the suffering would end. At such a time, the death of a friend provided the needed information. They knew that, like their friends, they too would die.

Often children will decide to conceal their knowledge of the prognosis from adults. It is, however, possible to measure children's awareness by examining their behavior. Reviewing briefly from chapter six, nine types of behavior were exhibited by the terminally ill children studied.

1. Avoidance of deceased children's names and belongings.
2. Lack of interest in nondisease-related conversation and play.
3. Preoccupation with death and disease imagery in play, art, and literature.
4. Engagement of selected individuals in either disclosure conversations or disclosure speeches.
5. Anxiety about increased debilitation and about going home, but for different reasons than earlier on in the disease process.
6. Avoidance of talk about the future.
7. Concern that things be done immediately.
8. Refusal to cooperate with relatively simple, painless procedures.
9. Establishment of distance from others through displays of anger or silence.

When any such behavior occurs, the question most often asked, if it has not already been asked, is, "Should I tell the child that he is dying?" Since the children discover the prognosis whether adults reveal it or not, perhaps the question should be rephrased, "Should I acknowledge the prognosis with the child?" This question is far more difficult to answer, because of the many factors involved. The needs of the children, the parents, and the staff must all be taken into account; for one dies as a member of society, linked to other individuals. Often these individuals' needs are conflicting.

The children need to share their knowledge, but they also need to have their parents with them (see chapter six, section 1). The parents likewise need to be with the children, but they also need to avoid discussion of the prognosis with them (see chapter six, section 2). The staff need to treat the children, but to do so they also need to view them as treatable (see chapter six, section 3). How then can the conflicting needs of each individual be met to permit their continued relationship with one another?

The answer lies in devising a policy that allows the children to maintain open awareness with those who can handle it, and at the same time to maintain mutual pretense with those who want to practice it. This is not at all abnormal. It is widely known that to be accepted in some groups, one must act differently than in others. The children know this and act accordingly.

The children know both what their parents know and what they want to hear. They are more concerned with having parents around than with telling them the prognosis. Children will do whatever is necessary to keep their parents near, but they would often like to share their knowledge with someone else as well.

That person should listen to what the children say, taking cues from them, answering only what they ask, and on their terms. Remember, children will honor whatever rules are set up.

The issue then is not whether to tell, but how to tell, in a way that respects the children and all of their many, often conflicting needs.

235

Doing the Fieldwork:
A Personal Account

When people would ask me the subject of my doctoral research, I would begin by saying that I studied terminally ill children. Before I could say much more, I would usually be interrupted by questions like, "How did you do it?" "Whatever made a nice young girl like you want to study dying children?" "What was it like?"

This essay sets out to answer these questions. It should also explain what I, the researcher, brought to the situation and what I took away. I present some of the details (e.g., the quirks of fate that led me to undertake the study, details of getting the project off the ground, obtaining consent, forming relationships, and my personal feelings about the project). All these factors made a significant difference in what information was and was not available to me. ·

In the process, I am also answering some other basic questions that often follow any discussion of my fieldwork: What is it like to do fieldwork in one's own culture? How do you study a subject that people do not necessarily want to talk about? What is it like to study children?

In a sense, this essay is a brief account of my socialization to a sector of our culture in which I had never previously participated, but one that is nonetheless a major feature of that culture. It is my socialization to a situation at once like and unlike any other I have known. It may be seen also as what happens when one has to deal with a universal aspect of human existence in a society that seems to want to deny its universality.

To write this essay in the spirit of the questions asked, I

have abandoned the more formal style of the preceding chapters for plain talk about the fieldwork experience, what happened to me and to the people I studied. Detailed examples of many things touched on here are found in the play and in the conversations recorded in various chapters.

When I thought about a dissertation topic, the possibility of studying dying children did not occur to me. I was unaware, or perhaps chose to ignore, that there was such a thing as a dying child. With millions of other Americans, I shared the belief that in our country children do not die except perhaps in accidents.

When I undertook the research, I was twenty-two years old and had never experienced the death of a close friend or relative. I had never even attended a funeral. My experiences with death were limited to the theater, movies, television, and literature.

These bits and snatches do not seem the necessary inspiration for a study of terminally ill children. They had, in fact, nothing to do with the selection of the project, but everything to do with its execution.

In the spring of 1971, I had decided to write my thesis on childhood socialization, with particular attention to the nature and development of self-concept and identity. My fieldwork, I decided, would be done on the Hopi reservation, comparing the socialization of Hopi schoolchildren in BIA schools run by whites and Navajos (traditional enemies of the Hopi) with that of Hopi schoolchildren in a Mennonite day school and a new Hopi-run day school. I had applied for a grant for the pilot study in the summer of 1971, as well as a year's study in 1972. Although the grant money came through, I decided not to do the study. Various groups wanted copies of my field notes. Realizing that some of the data could be used against the Hopi-run school and various families, I decided, as a matter of conscience, to abandon the project.

That spring, as part of a course in medical anthropology,

237

I was doing research on health as an idiom of communication in preschool children. Questions that concerned me included: To what end do three-, four-, and five-year-old children use phrases like: "I'm sick," or "I don't feel good"? How do adults and other children respond to such phrases? At my instructor's insistence, I conducted a comparative study of hospitalized children at the same hospital where I later undertook my doctoral research.

There I became increasingly interested in how sick children's use of health and illness idioms was related to their self-image. Many of the children I studied were "professional patients."[1] That is, in the nine short years of their lives, they had been hospitalized, as many as fifty times. In the process of socialization to the patient role, they had learned a great deal about how the hospital operated, how to manipulate various people, and the meanings of various kinds of staff behavior and expressions. Several children told me, "When they tell you to get in your room and it's not lights out, somebody died and they're coming for him." In their conversations and their play, these patients also revealed very sophisticated knowledge about their disease, its treatment, and its course; the views others had of them; the way they were treated; and the way they wanted to be treated. One said, "I'm very small for my age. Dr. Green is going to give me some growth hormone to make me grow. It'll take awhile, but then kids won't make fun of me and treat me like some freak or something."

I was struck by how totally unaware, or in what a state of denial, the staff was about the extent of these children's knowledge. The most striking example was in the oncology clinic. There, in front of the children, some doctors and parents would exchange information about cancer cures, blood tests, deaths of other children; then they would deny

[1] One of the pediatricians arranged for me to observe and interview chronically ill and terminally ill children on the wards and in the pediatric specialty clinics (e.g., hematology, oncology, renal and cystic fibrosis).

that the children knew anything about what was happening. Many adults stated that there was no way for the children to know anything about their diagnosis because they had not been told anything.

At this point, it seemed to me that the pediatric service, and more particularly the pediatric oncology clinic, were in many ways far better places than the Hopi reservation to study socialization and the development of self-concept. Factors contributing to the development of a particular self-concept or role definition would stand out in bold relief in the hospital. One would be better able to control for the specific kinds of information that were necessary for a particular self-concept and the actions taken appropriate to that role. But, in part because of the problems discussed in the conclusion of this essay, I remained committed to a study on the reservation. Only after the Hopi project collapsed did I decide to study terminally ill children.

I wrote a new summer research proposal. The scope of the problem was "limited" to determining whether or not terminally ill children are aware of the fact that they are dying, and if so, how they become aware and why the topic is taboo. Unlike the Hopi proposal, this was not a proposal for a pilot project leading to a long-term study and ultimately to a dissertation. Many members of my committee seemed to regard the project as something that would at best give me some field experience, but certainly not material for a dissertation. Also, the committee was somewhat concerned about my undertaking a study of dying children.

I decided to do the research on terminally ill children in the same hospital where I had done the initial study, because it was not a cancer research hospital; I was already familiar with the hospital and some staff members; and it had been the site of other related studies of terminally ill children and their families. But before I could begin research, I had to obtain research clearance. I sent a copy of my research proposal to the pediatrician who had taken me around the hospital during my initial study, and I asked him to put it into proper channels.

A few days later, the pediatrician phoned me and suggested that I come to the hospital and meet with members of the psychiatry department who had studied parents of terminally ill children. When I heard this, I thought that the proposal must have cleared the pediatric hematologists (those pediatricians who treat the leukemics in the pediatric oncology clinic), and that I would be able to proceed.

However, when I arrived at the hospital for the "scheduled" meeting with the psychiatrists, it became obvious that this pediatrician did not share my idea of the first step in starting the project (i.e., clearing the research with the patients' doctors). The proposal had not even been seen by the pediatric hematologists. To him, the first step was an evaluation of me and the proposal by individuals involved in related research. If they felt that I was incompetent, mentally or emotionally to do the research, or if it overlapped with what was already planned or being done, I would not receive permission.

I went to the psychiatry department at the appointed hour. I was told that no one in the department expected me. In fact, they were expecting another visitor (Joel Vernick of Karon and Vernick 1968) and would not have time to talk to me at all that day. I should come back in a week to discuss my proposal, they said, but if I wanted to "stick around" and listen to what Vernick had to say it was all right with them. Vernick was to meet with members of the psychiatry department and "FATIS group" to discuss the waiting-room program that they had designed for the pediatric oncology clinic.[2] Later in the day, Vernick was to

[2] FATIS is an acronym for Family Adaptation to Terminal Illness. The group was formed when two psychiatrists and a psychologist began their research on anticipatory grief in parents of terminally ill children. The group consisted of the two psychiatrists and the psychologist who were conducting the research, the pediatric occupational therapist who worked with the children in the oncology clinic

240

give a talk open to the entire hospital staff. I decided to accept their invitation, and try to see the pediatric hematologists, unannounced, after Vernick's lecture.

Listening in during the FATIS meeting, I began to feel even more strongly that it was most important to get consent from the pediatric hematologists. Whether I would be able to do the study or not hinged on their say-so, regardless of what the FATIS members would say.

Vernick's presentation that afternoon did not help my cause at all. As he spoke and the pediatricians argued with him, it did not seem likely that the hematologists would welcome anyone who wanted to study awareness in terminally ill children. There was Vernick, insisting that all children knew and should be told; there was I, wanting to study the process; and there was the majority of the pediatricians, claiming that the children did not know, but even if they did, they should not be told.

I knew that I had to do something immediately. At the end of the meeting I approached the head of the pediatric oncolocy clinic, who was already in animated discussion with the social worker in charge of the parents' group, and stated my case. The two began arguing, and new people from whom I would need consent were mentioned. My

---

waiting room, the psychiatric social worker and the family therapist who led the parents' group, the head of social service for the hospital, and several members of the child psychiatry department. An interesting note: None of the pediatric hematologists, residents, interns, or nurses who treated the children were ever members of the FATIS group. The group met regularly until late fall 1971, when it was disbanded at the request of the occupational therapist and the co-leaders of the parents' group, who felt the group was no longer necessary, since the research had been completed and the researchers were not involved in the play and parent groups in the oncology clinic. The others agreed, stating that the group had served its purpose and that only those actively engaged in research and treatment should continue to meet. There were in fact other more significant, if not overtly stated, reasons for dissolving the group, but a discussion of these is beyond the scope of this book.

suspicions were confirmed. The power lay with the pediatric hematologists. I followed the two of them back to the pediatric department and explained that I was rather confused. Their immediate reaction was one of an "in-joke." They were helpful and gave me a ride to the train.

I still wanted some explanation, or closure, so later that evening I called the chief oncologist at home. She said that she and the other pediatric hematologists would make a decision and let me know the following day. It was clear that the psychiatrists were out of the picture, whether they realized it or not.

The chief oncologist called the following day. She told me that she and the other hematologists thought it would be "OK" if I did the study, and she gave me some helpful suggestions for my project. Then she told me that I should wear a nurse's uniform when I worked with the children, that the nurses would probably want it that way. I told her that I did not want to wear a nurse's uniform, or any other for that matter, because I felt that doing so would skew my data. She agreed to let me come in street clothes.

I remember thinking, though, why a nursing uniform and not a lab coat? In other medical sociology studies, the researchers have worn lab coats (cf. Becker and Greer et al. 1961; Sudnow 1967). Was it because I was female, and nurses are females and doctors are male? But the chief oncologist is female. Or was it because nurses are "helpers," "they have time to talk to children," and I was being seen as an educated helper and talker? Or was it that they needed to assign me a place in their social structure, and "nurse" was an appropriate unambiguous status? There was the female occupational therapist, who wore only street clothes and talked with the children, but her status with the "medical team" was somewhat more ambiguous than mine. The "medical team" did not come in direct contact with her as much as they would with me. Also, she worked out of a nonmedical department. Her presence was not determined by the physicians.

It was decided that I should begin the following Monday, and that the chief oncologist would introduce me to the parents' group in order to get their consent to my study. But as one of the other doctors put it, "If we tell our patients that we want them to cooperate, they will." While in a sense this pleased me, it also concerned me. Not only because of the ethics involved, but also because it would affect my data. From what I had read and seen during my preliminary study, I was aware of the covert and overt hostility between many parents and the staff members. Granted, some of the hostility was misplaced because of parents' feelings about their children, but some was generated by their belief that the doctors were not treating the patients properly. At this time, the big issue at parents' group meetings was how the parents felt about the way doctors and the nurses treated them and their children.

The chief oncologist told me to meet her on Monday at 10 a.m. in her office.[3] Ever the eager anthropologist, I arrived before 10 a.m. and stationed myself outside her office door, observing the activity on the floor when colleagues meet colleagues after the weekend. The first person I saw was one of the foreign pediatric fellows that I had met during my preliminary study. She welcomed me and wished me good luck. As soon as she turned I took out my notebook and jotted down the encounter. No wonder everyone was slightly paranoid. There I was, as one mother remarked later that day, "with my blue book, with carbon paper, unflinchingly jotting everything down." One doctor remarked later, "What happened to that little red book?"[4]

Doctors whose patients were not involved in the study were friendlier than those whose patients were. Many smiled and exchanged greetings as if to say, "Thanks for not

[3] The pediatricians' research labs and offices are located on the floor below the pediatric wards. Patients are rarely seen on this floor.

[4] During the initial study I silently stood against hospital walls, jotting down notes in a small red notebook, like a wall fixture with mobile hands.

studying my patients." Two hematology fellows collected their bags and file folders and proceeded down the hall toward the elevators. They stopped at the refrigerator and took something out. One remarked, "You got the poisons?" Noting the little rabbit with big ears that had jumped up behind, he quickly retracted, "I mean the vincristine."

When the chief oncologist finally arrived, I followed her obediently, pencil poised. After a very brief exchange of pleasantries, she began to tell me about the parents and the parents' group. Although my study dealt with awareness and communication in terminally ill children, she never mentioned the children. I could not have deduced from that conversation what her position was on the subject. As we entered the clinic, she briefly introduced me to the occupational therapist working with the children and hurried me along.

We stood in the entryway to the treatment rooms. Here the hematologists gathered and drew up patients' medications. One of the leaders of the parents' group made coffee for the parents' group meeting. Standing near the entryway was a little boy I thought I recognized from my earlier study, but I was not quite sure. If it was the boy I remembered, he had changed a great deal, for the boy who stood before me was bald and quite heavy. Another boy whom I remembered quite vividly from the preliminary study was noticeably absent. I later learned that he had died in the interim, a finding that would add a good deal of urgency to any fieldwork I undertook from then on.

What followed on my first day in the field is reported in the play (Act II, Scene 4). Most important, I addressed the parents' group and received their permission to do the study. I did not feel that this was enough; perhaps they consented because it all happened so rapidly. They had no idea I was coming, and they really did not have time to consider the implications of my research, or even of my being there. Also, people feel relatively secure when their child is coming to the clinic, less vulnerable than when their child is in the hospital. There, I might be more in the way than in the clinic, and they might not want me around. In the clinic, I could be seen as just another "play lady," not necessarily as someone studying their children. So I decided to take their agreement at the meeting only as an indication that I could study their children in the clinic. I would explain my project and its implications to each set of parents again when their child was hospitalized. I also decided that if the parents consented, but appeared uncomfortable or told someone else that they would rather I did not study their child, I would not do so. I would never take any statement of consent as final, since I felt that the parents needed a way of getting out of the study any time they desired.

Not all of the parents attended the meeting. I spoke to those who did not attend individually in the waiting room before I included their children in the study, and again when their children were hospitalized.

What disturbed me most during this initial permission-getting period, however, was that the group I felt I needed permission from, the children—the object of the study—still had not been asked. No one seemed to feel it was necessary to obtain their permission. No one even thought about it until I mentioned it; it was not even an issue. To me this indicated several things about the way these people viewed children in general, let alone dying children.

Goffman (1961) and others have talked about how mental patients, deprived of their rights, are treated like children. They are not considered to be their own agents. What is to be done to them and for them must be cleared through the caretakers (in this case the parent or medical staff), even though it may in no way directly affect the caretakers. This was the case with these children. They were deprived of rights over their bodies as well as their minds.

To me the situation was bad enough. I was not going to contribute to such behavior. I decided that I would ask each of the children for permission to speak with them about their thoughts and feelings. It would be up to each child to

245

decide whether to speak to me or not. I did not assume the right to study any child simply because the parents or the staff said I could. I often put this belief ahead of what the parents or the staff felt "was the right thing to do." If a child did not want to talk, I did not force the issue. It was the children, not parents or staff, I was interested in. My allegiance was to the children.

Many would argue with my approach; but I felt it was a critical factor in enabling me to learn as much as I did, and, perhaps, help some of these children. Of course, the problem of conflicting allegiances is not new to anthropologists. In the field, the anthropologist often feels torn between the various groups he or she is studying (e.g., families, tribes, colonial governments). And even though the children I studied were a "children's group," they formed a group, nonetheless, with all the attendant rights and privileges.

I believe my relationships with the children were based on mutual trust and understanding, established very early in the relationship, and constantly reinforced through mutual giving, taking, and testing. When I first met a child, I would say I was an anthropologist, that I studied children and was interested in what children thought and did. The children would respond by telling me where and how they had been pinched, poked, or prodded that day.[5]

Whenever I went to visit children in their hospital rooms, I asked permission before entering. I did so even if the children saw me in the hall and invited me in, or if the mother asked me to come in while she went home or went out to eat.

When I entered their rooms, I would take my cues from the children. If they wanted to watch TV or color pictures, I watched TV or colored. Often, children would talk in the

[5] This response is discussed in great detail in chapter four, under stage 1 in "The Stages of Awareness." It is part of a kind of formal introduction the children used when encountering someone for the first time. I refer to this special act as "exhibition of wounds."

course of the program or while coloring. It also became apparent later that the children asked me to watch TV to test the relationship. As one eight-year-old boy said to me after I watched TV for one solid hour without a word, "All right. You're OK. What do you want to know?" In general, I moved slowly and cautiously. There were times when I wanted to pursue a question, but refrained from doing so for fear of breaking off communication.

The children regarded me differently, and hence treated me differently, than they did other adults. I did not fit into any of the conventional categories of persons that saw them in the hospital (e.g., doctor, nurse, social worker, parent, relative). As one seven-year-old girl described me, "You're like a big kid, but you're no kid. I mean you go to school, but that's different school." It also seemed important to them that I was not married and that I had no children. It was as if then I could belong more completely to them.

Another feature of my relationship with the children was that I was, as one mother put it, "the one thing that they [the children] have any control over." Regardless of how the children acted (and we did have some bad times together), I would not desert them. They could scream and yell at me, play or fight with me, talk to me or kick me, share secrets or refuse to speak, ride piggyback, stroke my hair, borrow my jewelry, or cry, and I always came back. I was there for them and they knew it.

They came to expect and even to demand my presence on various occasions, and became extremely angry if I could not be there when they wanted me. Although I was different things to different children, I was a definite part of their world of dying children. Of all the nonfamily persons, I was the only one who was always there, in a variety of situations, places, and roles.

Perhaps because I did not fit any existing hospital category, I could function in several ways for the children (e.g., sounding board, source of information, confidante, and friend). In my role as a source of information, many questions were addressed to me; through this I discerned what kinds of things the questioning child knew and/or wanted to know more about. In exchange, though, I was expected to volunteer information back that I might not feel right about giving (e.g., news of a death). In my role as friend, I was allowed to ask questions and pursue various matters, but I was also expected to participate in some activities that I might not want to be part of.

In the face of these conflicts, I tried to be honest and yet act in a way that would not present problems for the children or their families. I wanted to make sure the children felt free to express themselves. To this end, I tried to avoid suggesting there was anything they could not say or feel. In brief, I wanted to know what was on their minds, but not at the expense of themselves or their families.

The parents were extremely helpful to me throughout the course of my research. Aside from the fact that they allowed me to study their children, they often provided me with information necessary for interpreting many of the discussions I had with their offspring. They would even stop me in the hall or call to tell me something they thought I might be interested in.

This kind of exchange was intensified as a result of a talk I gave to the parents' group in September. While the parents were surprised, shocked, and even somewhat upset at how much their children knew and expressed, directly as well as indirectly, they were nevertheless quite responsive. They began offering other kinds of evidence that corroborated my report. Interestingly, much of this information was about children who had already died and whom I did not know. The parents also began to piece together remarks their children had made whose full significance had escaped them. Many parents thought that they had failed to understand such remarks earlier because, as one mother put it, "I know I couldn't bear it if I knew that he knew." Another mother said frankly, "I know we're [she and her child] in a protection game."

Toward the end of this meeting, some of the mothers suggested that I come and observe their children at home, "away from the hospital." We also planned to continue the discussion the following Monday. That discussion never took place. A child died on the weekend, the first to die in a long time, and that was what the parents wanted to talk about. We did not get a chance to meet in any of the succeeding Mondays either, for a series of deaths followed, involving the children of parents who had expressed interest in further meetings. By the time I could have attended another parents' meeting, the majority of the children involved in the study had died; I was getting ready to terminate the project and return to school.

The parents reacted to me in various ways; they were ambivalent over the long term. They did not always perceive and treat me consistently. For some I was, on various occasions, a baby sitter or a nurse's aide; for others, or at different times for the same parent, a sounding board or a source of information. The latter role proved the most difficult, because the parents often wanted information about other parents and children, which I refused to give. When questioned, I would simply say "I don't know." After awhile, it became a standing joke. When parents asked me something I obviously did not want to share, they would then say, "I know. . . . You don't know."

In general, the parents' reactions to me were based on their opinion of me and my work, as well as their child's situation at the moment. If the parents liked me, approved of my work, and the child was doing well, I could be anything from a sounding board to a baby sitter. If the parents did not like me or my work and the child was doing well, I was at best allowed to be a nurse's aide.

The parents vacillated between respect and anger. Although they respected my research, as the time of my departure approached, they became angry with me and sometimes would not even speak to me. I had become a constant, and my leaving, they felt, was a desertion of them: "the way everyone else does," as their child would (this analysis was by the psychiatric social worker working with the parents).

One reaction I never got, although I had somewhat expected it, was, "How could you know anything? Your child isn't dying." Perhaps this was because, unlike other investigators who reported such responses, I was not studying them or their children through them, and they knew it.

All staff members are members of the "Medical Team." As members of the team, they share certain characteristics that affect all their relationships. In a sense, these characteristics form the backdrop for the development of relationships. First, staff members represent the institution that one chooses to participate in. As a participant, but nonetheless an outsider, one is a guest in their home—their place of work. Second, they are in control. One depends on them for entrance and continued access to subjects. Third, they have a job to do that may or may not be at variance with one's purposes. What can be accomplished depends to some extent on how, in their view, one's goals mesh with theirs, and how one fits into their work and social scheme.

As explained earlier, my relationship with the hematologists began to develop even before I started my fieldwork. Briefly, I changed in their eyes from an object of teasing and joking, to an object of increasing curiosity, to a source of information, to a consultant and researcher, and finally, to someone capable of going to medical school (the highest honor they could bestow). In other words, one of them.

As a result of my own upbringing and observations, I tended to see the pediatric hematologists as the persons in charge. But while they granted permission for the study, and set the tone, if I had depended solely on them I would have failed. The day-to-day work on a hospital floor depends on the nursing staff and the house staff (residents and interns). What I could accomplish depended to a great extent on my relationship with them. For example, the hematologists might say I could look at records, but it was up to the nurses to get them for me. Or the hematologists might tell the residents and nurses to help me gather data, but if they did not want to, there was no way the information would be forthcoming.

In spite of what many nurses said about being glad to have me do the research ("Now there will be someone to spend the time with the leukemics that we just don't have"), I felt that initially they were not too thrilled. They were extremely suspicious about what I was really studying— understandably, since most studies of the dying to date had dealt in large part with the way staff managed the dying (cf. Glaser and Strauss 1965b; Strauss and Glaser 1967; Sudnow 1967; Quint 1967).

At first, they treated me like an educated volunteer worker, an attitude compounded by the fact that I appeared in the summer, when there is a great influx of volunteers. They spent much time instructing me in proper handwashing techniques and the procedures for entering various types of isolation rooms. Part of the treatment was probably a result of my conduct. Like a volunteer, and like most anthropologists in the field, I willingly did whatever they told me. I played with the children, helped with the meals, accompanied the children to various parts of the hospital, and assisted in procedures. What they did not realize until I had had an opportunity to speak with many of them was that my behavior was research-motivated. Because I was interested in the children's thoughts and feelings, I explained, I wanted to see what they did in a variety of situations. Only later when my plans and purposes were fully understood did the staff treat me as a researcher and a consultant.

With a few of the nurses, problems of jealousy developed that forced me to stop studying certain children extensively.

As others have reported, pediatric nurses often become very protective of their patients. They begin to feel and to act as if no one, including the child's mother, can care for the child as well as they can; in fact, the others interfere with proper care.

Although the house staff continued to suspect my motives, they never stopped helping me. They would often share information with me about various patients' conditions, tell me their interpretations of various children's behavior, notify me at home if something was happening at the hospital that they thought I should know about, and include me in rounds.

Other personnel played a part in my research—the pediatric occupational therapist, the psychiatric social worker and the psychologist who led the parents' group, and the members of the FATIS group mentioned earlier. All of them understood my intentions from the outset and treated me accordingly. They offered advice as one would to any researcher. Later, as the time came for me to leave the field, they began to offer other kinds of advice, whether I wanted it or not. Some admitted they had become dependent on me to a degree. Rather than try to form a relationship on their own, they had used me as the link between the medical staff and themselves. Also, since I was always available to parents and children, they did not feel guilty about not being around (e.g., on the floors in the evenings), as they usually did.

My relationships shifted in many ways, through good times and bad, through periods of friendship and open hostility, yet none of the staff were ever uncooperative. At all times, they tried to be helpful and accommodating, more so, I believe, than I could ever have been to a guest in my home, especially one who did not always follow house rules.

There is a tacit assumption that to do a study of the terminally ill is to be constantly concerned and involved with death. On the contrary, there is something quite paradoxical about studying the dying. It is not morbid. The difficulties and hard times come not when the children are dying, but when they are alive and you know what is ahead.

Such times included the moment when Lynn, her pigtails flopping behind her, came down the hall shouting as she jumped into my arms, "I'm going home today." Involuntarily I thought, "How long before she is back here again?" Or when Seth, his body riddled with pain, I.V.'s running in both arms, his nose packed, tried to sway with some rock-and-roll music, because he knew that both he and I needed to see him living. Or when Scott, hearing that one of his friends died over the weekend, came and hugged me, and simply said, "I hope that doesn't happen to me." Half defensively and half longingly I replied, "I hope that doesn't happen to you either."

I am like the parents and, at times, the doctors too. Perhaps this child will be different; perhaps a cure will be found in time—I want to believe it. Mentally, I review the child's case history, attending only to those aspects that make his history different from the other leukemic children who have already died. "Well, he never had a major bleed," or, "Look how well she responds to the chemotherapy." I ignore all the bad signs. I think of the progress in cancer research, of the advertisements from research centers showing "cured" children. I push contradictory evidence out of my mind.

But then reality hits, because I know deep down that this child will not be different. Perhaps he never had a major bleed, but then there are the times when they have to stop the drugs because of the side effects. She responds well to chemotherapy, but her liver no longer functions properly because of long-term drug damage. Progress *has* been made. There may even be a cure tomorrow. It will not be for these children, however, for the toxic effects of the drugs have marked them. In fact, it is said that some children have already been cured, but of what have they been cured, and for how long?

Anger quickly replaces these thoughts and feelings. Why this child? What did he do? Why can't something be done? The anger builds and is often directed at strangers, people too busy to know that a child is living with dying. I walk through the toy section of a large department store, crowded with Christmas shoppers, full of Christmas cheer. While two ladies argue about the best style bike for a nine-year-old boy, I try to find a toy for Jack that will not remind him of the bike he can no longer ride and may never see again. Another woman is pushing ahead in line so she can be home in time to help her grandchildren decorate the tree. I muse to myself. I am in a hurry too. I promised Andy an angel for his tree, and I am spurred by a different urgency.

The anger soars. It wells up into an indictment of this country for its priorities on spending. It is thrown up to a God I am not quite sure exists, but who deserves to be blamed just the same. I have to blame someone, something; how can I explain to myself the death of a child? I must do something, and what can I or anyone else do? Dr. Abrams said to the residents, "What makes you think that your medicine is any more powerful than that novena?"

The feeling of impotence is overwhelming. But the rage has passed. No one heard me. I really did not say or do anything. I am tired. Guilt always seems to follow the rage and anger. I can walk out of the hospital, I can leave it all behind, I can intellectualize it all, I can even profit from it. For out of this experience will come a dissertation, perhaps even a Ph.D. I will become an anthropologist. But these children will *not* become.

They have done for me in so many ways, but I wonder what I have done for them. It was always so hard to do something for them. How we all talked about the Marias who right up until the end asked to be taken to the bathroom, about the Jeffreys who shouted us out of their rooms, and about the Seths who would not let us in; all because they knew when we could not take it.

They constantly did for me. They were my teachers, and are so even in death. For most of their lives, even when they were sick, they were caught up in the business of living. There were people to talk to, games to play, houses to build, pictures to draw. There was so much to do, and so little time to do it in. Then again, there never really is enough time. Life is a terminal illness for all of us. It is just that some know the end before others.

I caught the children's sense of urgency, their fear of wasting time, their knowledge of the finitude of things. I felt that I had to get every word down, as if it were the last. At the same time, I realized that I had entered into a relationship with these children which required that I take my time and not push them.

At the end of the day I was always afraid to leave them. I might miss something. They might not be there when I got back. But I had to leave. After all, I was there to learn as much as I could. I had notes to write, work to analyze; tasks made more difficult by the depression and fatigue that often came at the day's end.

My feelings vacillate from day to day. If I had it to do again, would I? I have changed since the time I did the study. I am older, married, and have experienced the deaths of some of my closest friends and relatives. When I did the research, I had not had these experiences; my "innocence" was in many ways essential to my doing the study as I did and accomplishing what I did. I am haunted by another question: How many were helped and how many were hurt by my study? When one does such research, contributions to science are not sufficient justification, in my view. I have failed unless this study contributes to the memory of the children, to those who cared for them, and to children who still must suffer.

LITERATURE CITED

Aberle, David and Naegele, Kaspar
    1968   Middle-Class Fathers' Occupational Role and Attitude toward Children. In *A Modern Introduction to the Family*. Edited by Norman Bell and Ezra Vogel. New York: Free Press.

Agranoff, J. H. and Mauer, A. M.
    1965   What Should the Child with Leukemia Be Told? *American Journal of Diseases of Children*, 110:231.

Alexander, Irving and Alderstein, Arthur
    1960   Studies in the Psychology of Death. In *Perspectives in Personality Research*. Edited by Henry David and J. C. Brengelmann. New York: Springer Publishing Co.
    1965   Affective Responses to the Concept of Death in a Population of Children and Early Adolescents. In *Death and Identity*. Edited by R. Fulton. Chicago: Aldine.

Anthony, Sylvia
    1940   *The Child's Discovery of Death*. New York: Harcourt, Brace and Co.
    1968   The Child's Idea of Death. In *The World of the Child*. Edited by Toby Talbot. New York: Anchor Books.

Axline, Virginia
    1947   *Play Therapy*. New York: Ballantine Books.

Bain, R.
    1936   The Self—and Other Worlds of a Child. *American Journal of Sociology*, 41:767-775.

Bard, Morton
    1970   The Price of Survival for Cancer Victims. In

Where Medicine Fails. Edited by Anselm Strauss. Chicago: Aldine.

Bar-Hillel, Y.
1954   Indexical Expressions. *Mind*, 63:359-379.

Barker, Roger
1963   *Stream of Behavior.* New York: Appleton-Century-Crofts.

Becker, Howard
1958   Problems of Inference and Proof in Participant Observation. *American Sociology Review*, 23:652-657.

Becker, Howard and Greer, Blanche
1957   Participant Observation and Interviewing: A Comparison. In *Symbolic Interaction: A Reader in Social Psychology.* Edited by J. Manis and B. Meltzer. Boston: Allyn and Bacon, Inc.
1963   Medical Education. In *Handbook of Medical Sociology.* Edited by Howard Freeman, Sol Levine, and Leo Reeder. Englewood Cliffs, New Jersey: Prentice-Hall.

Becker, Howard, Greer, Blanche, Hughes, Everett C., and Strauss, Anselm
1961   *Boys in White: Student Culture in Medical School.* Chicago: University of Chicago Press.

Berger, Peter
1963   *Invitation to Sociology: A Humanistic Perspective.* New York: Anchor, Doubleday and Co.

Bergman, A. G. and Schulte, C. J. A.
1967   Care of the Child with Cancer. *Pediatrics*, 40 (Part 2):492-546.

Binger, C. M., Ablin, A. R., Feurerstein, R. C., Kushner, J. H., Zoger, S., and Mikelsen, C.
1969   Childhood Leukemia: Emotional Impact on Patient and Family. *New England Journal of Medicine*, 280:414-418.

Blom, Gaston
1958   The Reactions of Hospitalized Children to Illness. *Pediatrics*, 22:590-600.
Bluebond-Langner, Myra
1974   I Know, Do You? A Study of Awareness, Communication, and Coping in Terminally Ill Children. In *Anticipatory Grief*. Edited by Bernard Schoenberg, Arthur Carr, David Peretz, Austin Kutscher, and Ivan Goldberg. New York: Columbia University Press.
1975   *The Dying Child Speaks, But Do We Hear Him?: Awareness and Communication in Leukemic Children*. Paper presented at the 1975 meeting of The Society for Applied Anthropology. Amsterdam, Holland.
1977   Meanings of Death to Children. In *New Meanings of Death*. Edited by Herman Feifel. New York: McGraw-Hill.
Blumer, Herbert
1969   *Symbolic Interaction*. Englewood Cliffs, New Jersey: Prentice-Hall.
Borstein, Irving and Klein, Annette
1974   Parents of Fatally Ill Children in a Parents' Group. In *Anticipatory Grief*. Edited by Bernard Schoenberg, Arthur Carr, David Peretz, Austin Kutscher, and Ivan Goldberg. New York: Columbia University Press.
Bowlby, John
1961   Process of Mourning. *International Journal of Psychoanalysis*, 42:317-340.
1969   *Attachment and Loss*. 2 volumes. New York: Basic Books.
Bozeman, Mary F., Orbach, Charles, and Sutherland, Arthur
1955   Psychological Impact of Cancer and Its Treatment. III. The Adaptation of Mothers to the Threatened Loss of Their Children through Leukemia: Part I. *Cancer*, 8:1-19.

Braroe, Niels
  1970   *Change and Identity: Patterns of Interaction in an Indian-White Community.* Unpublished Ph.D. thesis, University of Illinois.

Brim, Orville
  1966   Socialization through the Life Cycle. In *Socialization after Childhood.* Edited by O. Brim and S. Wheeler. New York: John Wiley and Sons, Inc.

Brukman, Jan
  1972   Lectures transcribed by author for "Modern Perspectives in Culture and Personality." Department of Anthropology, University of Illinois.
  1973   Lectures transcribed by author for "Language and Culture." Department of Anthropology, University of Illinois.

Burnett, F. H.
  1911   *The Secret Garden.* New York: J. B. Lippincott Co.

Cain, A. and Cain, Barbara
  1962   On Replacing a Child. *American Journal of Orthopsychiatry,* 32:297-298.

Cain, A., Fast, I., and Erikson, M.
  1964   Children's Disturbed Reactions to the Death of a Sibling. *American Journal of Orthopsychiatry,* 34:741-752.

Capes, Mary
  1956   The Child in the Hospital. *Mental Hygiene,* 40:107-157.

Cappon, D.
  1959   The Dying. *Psychiatric Quarterly,* 33:466.

Caprio, F. S.
  1946   Ethnological Attitudes toward Death: A Psychoanalytic Evaluation. *Journal of Criminal Psychopathology,* 7:737-752.

Carpenter, Kathryn and Stewart, J. Marion
  1962   Parents Take Heart at City of Hope. *American Journal of Nursing,* 62:82-85.

259

Chodoff, P., Friedman, S. B., and Hamburg, D. A.
1964   Stress, Defenses, and Coping Behavior: Observations in Parents of Children with Malignant Diseases. *American Journal of Psychiatry*, 120:743-749.

Cicourel, Aaron
1964   *Method and Measurement in Sociology*. New York: Free Press.
1970   The Acquisition of Social Structure: Toward a Developmental Sociology of Languages and Meaning. In *Understanding Everyday Life*. Edited by Jack Douglas. Chicago: Aldine.

Clausen, John
1968a   A Historical and Comparative View of Socialization Theory and Research. In *Socialization and Society*. Edited by J. Clausen. Boston: Little, Brown and Co.
1968b   Perspectives on Childhood Socialization. In *Socialization and Society*. Edited by J. Clausen. Boston: Little, Brown and Co.

Cobb, Beatrix
1956   Psychological Impact of Long Illness and Death of a Child on the Family Circle. *Journal of Pediatrics*, 49:746-751.

Comerford, Brenda
1974   Parental Anticipatory Grief and Guidelines for Caregivers. In *Anticipatory Grief*. Edited by Bernard Schoenberg, Arthur Carr, David Peretz, Austin Kutscher, and Ivan Goldberg. New York: Columbia University Press.

Cooley, Charles H.
1970   Self as Sentiment and Reflection. In *Social Psychology through Symbolic Interaction*. Edited by G. Stone and H. Farberman. Waltham, Massachusetts: Xerox College Publications.
1972   The Looking Glass Self. In *Symbolic Interaction: A Reader in Social Psychology*. Edited by J.

Manis and B. Meltzer. Boston: Allyn and Bacon, Inc.

Dager, Edward (ed.)
1971   *Socialization: Process, Product, and Change.* Chicago: Markham Publishing Co.

Dalton, Melvin
1959   *Men Who Manage.* New York: John Wiley and Sons, Inc.

Davis, Fred
1963   *Passage through Crisis: Polio Victims and Their Families.* New York: Bobbs-Merrill Co., Inc.

Dennis, Wayne
1966   *Group Values through Children's Drawings.* New York: John Wiley and Sons, Inc.

Denzin, Norman
1970a   Symbolic Interactionism and Ethnomethodology. In *Understanding Everyday Life.* Edited by Jack Douglas. Chicago: Aldine.
1970b   *The Research Act.* Chicago: Aldine.
1973   *Children and Their Caretakers.* New Brunswick, New Jersey: Transaction Books.

Desmonde, William
1970   The Position of George Herbert Mead. In *Social Psychology through Symbolic Interaction.* Edited by G. Stone and H. Farberman. Waltham, Massachusetts: Xerox College Publications.

Dewey, John
1972   Communication, Individual, and Society. In *Symbolic Interaction: A Reader in Social Psychology.* Edited by J. Manis and B. Meltzer. Boston: Allyn and Bacon, Inc.

Dimock, Henry
1960   *The Child in the Hospital.* Philadelphia: F. A. Davis, Inc.

Diskin, Martin and Guggenheim, Hans
1967   The Child and Death as Seen in Different Cul-

tures. In *Explaining Death to Children*. Edited by Earl Grollman. Boston: Beacon Press.

Douglas, Jack
1970   *Understanding Everyday Life*. Chicago: Aldine.

Drake, Donald
1972   How Do You Tell a Child He Is Dying of Leukemia? In *The Philadelphia Inquirer*, August 14:1.

Dreitzel, Hans P.
1973   Introduction. In *Childhood and Socialization*. Edited by H. Dreitzel. New York: Macmillan Co.

Duff, Raymond S. and Hollingshead, Arthur
1968   *Sickness and Society*. New York: Harper and Row.

Easson, W. M.
1970   *The Dying Child*. Illinois: Thomas Press.

Elkin, Frederick
1960   *The Child and Society: The Process of Socialization*. New York: Random House.

Fast, Irene and Cain, A.
1964   Fears of Death in Bereaved Children and Adults. *American Journal of Orthopsychiatry*, 34:278-279.

Feifel, Herman (ed.)
1965   *The Meaning of Death*. New York: McGraw-Hill.

Friedman, S. B., Chodoff, D., Mason, J. W., and Hamburg, D. A.
1963   Behavioral Observations on Parents Anticipating the Death of a Child. *Pediatrics*, 32:610-625.

Friedman, S. B., Karon, M. E., and Goldsmith, G.
1965   *Childhood Leukemia—A Pamphlet for Parents*. U. S. Government Printing Office.

Freidson, Eliot
1961   *Patient's View of Medical Practice*. New York: Russell-Sage Foundation.
1964   *The Hospital in Modern Society*. New York: Free Press.

Fulton, Robert (ed.)
  1966   *Death and Identity.* New York: John Wiley and
          Sons, Inc.
  1967   On the Dying of Death. In *Explaining Death to
          Children.* Edited by E. Grollman. Boston: Beacon
          Press.

Futterman, Edward and Hoffman, Irwin
  1970   Transient School Phobia in the Leukemic Child.
          *Journal of the American Academy of Child
          Psychiatry,* 9:477-494.
  1971   *Crisis and Adaptation in the Families of Fatally
          Ill Children.* University of Illinois Hospital: Chi-
          cago, Illinois. (Mimeographed)

Garfinkel, Harold
  1967   *Studies in Ethnomethodology.* Englewood Cliffs,
          New Jersey: Prentice-Hall.
  1972a   Common Sense Knowledge of Social Structure:
          The Documentary Method of Interpretation. In
          *Symbolic Interaction: A Reader in Social Psychol-
          ogy.* Edited by J. Manis and B. Meltzer. Boston:
          Allyn and Bacon, Inc.
  1972b   Conditions of Successful Degradation Ceremo-
          nies. In *Symbolic Interaction: A Reader in Social
          Psychology.* Edited by J. Manis and B. Meltzer.
          Boston: Allyn and Bacon, Inc.

Gartley, William and Bernasioni, M.
  1967   The Concept of Death in Children. *Journal of
          Genetic Psychology,* 110:71-85.

Geist, Harold
  1965   *A Child Goes to the Hospital.* Illinois: Thomas
          Press.

Gergen, Kenneth J.
  1971   *The Concept of Self.* New York: Holt, Rinehart,
          and Winston.

Gesell, Arnold and Ily, Francis
  1946   *The Child from Five to Ten.* New York: Harper
          and Row.

Glaser, Barney and Strauss, Anselm
1964   Awareness Contexts and Social Interaction. *American Sociology Review,* 29:669-679.
1965a   Temporal Aspects of Dying as a Non-Scheduled Status Passage. *American Journal of Sociology,* 71:48-49.
1965b   *Awareness of Dying: A Study of Social Interaction.* Chicago: Aldine.
1967   *Discovery of Grounded Theory.* Chicago: Aldine.
1968   *Time for Dying.* Chicago: Aldine.
1970   Dying on Time. In *Where Medicine Fails.* Edited by Anselm Strauss. Chicago: Aldine.
Goffman, Erving
1959   *The Presentation of the Self in Everyday Life.* Garden City, New York: Anchor, Doubleday and Co.
1961   *Asylums.* Garden City, New York: Anchor, Doubleday and Co.
1963   *Stigma: Notes on the Management of Spoiled Identity.* Englewood Cliffs, New Jersey: Prentice-Hall.
1967   *Interaction Ritual.* Garden City, New York: Anchor, Doubleday and Co.
1971   *Relations in Public.* New York: Harper and Row.
Goodman, Mary Ellen
1970   *The Culture of Childhood.* New York: Teachers College, Columbia University.
Gore, Geoffrey
1965   *Death, Grief and Mourning.* Garden City, New York: Anchor, Doubleday and Co.
Greene, W. A. and Miller, G.
1958   Psychological Factors and Reticuloendothelial Disease. *Psychosomatic Medicine,* 20:124-144.
Grollman, Earl (ed.)
1967   *Explaining Death to Children.* Boston: Beacon Press.

Gunther, John
  1949   *Death Be Not Proud.* New York: Harper Publishing Co.
Hamovitch, Maurice
  1964   *The Parent and the Fatally Ill Child: A Demonstration of Parent Participation in a Hospital Pediatric Department.* California: City of Hope Medical Center.
Havighurst, R. J. and Neugarten, B.
  1955   *American Indian and White Children: A Sociopsychological Investigation.* Chicago: University of Chicago Press.
Hendin, David
  1973   *Death as a Fact of Life.* New York: W. W. Norton and Co., Inc.
Henry, Jules
  1964   Death, Fear, and Climax in Nursery School Play. In *Concepts of Development in Early Childhood Education.* Edited by Peter Neubauer. New York: Random House.
  1971   *Pathways to Madness.* New York: Random House.
Hinton, John
  1967   *Dying.* London: Penguin.
Hoffman, Irwin and Futterman, Edward
  1971   Coping with Waiting: Psychiatric Intervention and Study in the Waiting Room of a Pediatric Oncology Clinic. *Comprehensive Psychiatry,* 12 (1):67-81.
Howell, Doris A.
  1966   A Child Dies. *Journal of Pediatric Surgery,* 1:2-7.
Hutschnecker, Arnold A.
  1968   Personality Factors in Dying Patients. In *The Meaning of Death.* Edited by H. Feifel. New York: McGraw-Hill.
Inkeles, Alexander
  1968   Society, Social Structure, and Childhood Sociali-

zation. In *Socialization and Society*. Edited by
John Clausen. Boston: Little, Brown and Co.

Irwin, R. and Weston, D.
1963   Preschool Child's Response to Death of Infant
Sibling. *American Journal of Diseases of Children*, 106:564-567.

James, William
1962   *Essays on Faith and Morals*. New York: The
World Publishing Co., Meridan Books.

Jensen, R. A. et al.
1955   The Hospitalized Child: Roundtable 1954. *American Journal of Orthopsychiatry*, 25:293-318.

Joffee, Carole
1973   Taking Young Children Seriously. In *Children
and Their Caretakers*. Edited by Norman Denzin.
New Brunswick, New Jersey: Transaction Books.

Kalish, Richard
1963   An Approach to the Study of Death Attitudes.
American Behavioral Scientist, 6:684.

1969   The Effects of Death upon the Family. In *Death
and Dying: Current Issues in the Treatment of
the Dying Person*. Edited by H. J. Pearson. Cleveland: Case Western Reserve Press.

Kaplan, B.
1961   *Studying Personality Cross-Culturally*. New York:
Harper and Row.

Kardiner, A.
1945   *The Psychological Frontiers of Society*. New
York: Columbia University Press.

Karon, Myron and Vernick, Joel
1968   An Approach to Emotional Support of Fatally Ill
Children. *Clinical Pediatrics*, 7:274-280.

Kastenbaum, Robert
1967   The Child's Understanding of Death: How Does
It Develop? In *Explaining Death to Children*.
Edited by E. Grollman. Boston: Beacon Press.

Kastenbaum, Robert and Aisenberg, Sylvia
   1972   *The Psychology of Death.* New York: Springer
          Publishing Co.
Kliman, Gilbert
   1968   *Psychological Emergencies of Childhood.* New
          York: Grune and Stratton, Inc.
Knudson, Alfred G. and Natterson, Joseph
   1960   Participation of Parents in the Hospital Care of
          Fatally Ill Children. *Pediatrics,* 26:482-490.
Kubler-Ross, Elizabeth
   1969   *On Death and Dying.* New York: Macmillan Co.
Langsly, D. G.
   1961   Psychology of a Doomed Family. *American Jour-
          nal of Psychotherapy,* 15:631.
Layman, E. M. and Lourie, R. S.
   1958   Waiting Room Observations as a Technique for
          Analysis of Communication Behavior in Children
          and Their Parents. In *Psychopathology of Com-
          munication.* Edited by P. Hoch and J. Zubin. New
          York: Grune and Stratton, Inc.
Lifton, Robert Jay
   1969   *Death in Life.* New York: Random House.
Lindeman, Erick
   1944   Symptomatology and Management of Acute
          Grief. *American Journal of Psychiatry,* 101:141-
          148.
Linton, R.
   1945   *The Cultural Background of Personality.* New
          York: Appleton-Century.
Lourie, R. S.
   1963   The Pediatrician and the Handling of Terminal
          Illness. *Pediatrics,* 32:477-479.
Maccoby, Eleanor
   1968   The Choice of Variables in the Study of Socializa-
          tion. In *Selected Studies in Marriage and the
          Family.* Edited by Robert Winch and Louis Good-
          man. New York: Holt, Rhinehart, and Winston.

MacKay, Robert
1973   Conceptions of Children and Models of Socialization. In *Childhood and Socialization.* Edited by Hans P. Dreitzel. New York: Macmillan Co.

Manis, Jerome and Meltzer, Bernard (eds.)
1972   *Symbolic Interaction: A Reader in Social Psychology.* Boston: Allyn and Bacon, Inc.

Mayer, Philip (ed.)
1970   *Socialization: The Approach from Social Anthropology.* A.S.A. Monographs, vol. 8. London: Tavistock Publications Ltd.

McCall, George and Simmons, J. L. (eds.)
1969   *Issues in Participant-Observation.* Reading, Massachusetts: Addison-Wesley Publishing Co.

McHugh, Peter
1968   *Defining the Situation: The Organization of Meaning in Social Interaction.* Indianapolis: Bobbs-Merrill Co., Inc.

McMichael, Joan
1971   *Handicap: A Study of Physically Handicapped Children and Their Families.* Pittsburgh: University of Pittsburgh Press.

Mead, George Herbert
1970   *Mind, Self, and Society.* Chicago: University of Chicago Press.

Mead, Margaret
1928   *Coming of Age in Samoa.* New York: Wm. Morrow and Co.
1930   *Growing Up in New Guinea.* New York: Wm. Morrow and Co.

Mead, Margaret and Wolfenstein, Martha (eds.)
1955   *Childhood in Contemporary Culture.* Chicago: University of Chicago Press.

Meltzer, Bernard
1972   Mead's Social Psychology. In *Symbolic Interaction: A Reader in Social Psychology.* Edited by J. Manis and B. Meltzer. Boston: Allyn and Bacon, Inc.

Meltzer, Bernard and Petras, Jerome
1972   The Chicago and Iowa Schools of Symbolic Interactionism. In *Symbolic Interaction: A Reader in
Social Psychology*. Edited by J. Manis and B.
Meltzer. Boston: Allyn and Bacon, Inc.

Menninger, K.
1959   Hope. *American Journal of Psychiatry*, 116:481.

Miller, S. M.
1969   The Participant-Observer and Over-Rapport. In
Issues in Participant-Observation. Edited by
George McCall and J. L. Simmons. Massachusetts: Addison-Wesley Publishing Co.

Moellenhoff, Fritz
1939   Ideas of Children about Death. *Bulletin of Menninger Clinic*, 3:148-156.

Morrissey, James
1965   Death Anxiety in Children with a Fatal Illness. In
Crisis Intervention: Selected Readings. Edited by
H. J. Parad. New York: Family Service Associa-
tion of America.

Murstein, Bernard
1958   Attitudes of Parents of Hospitalized Children toward Doctors, Nurses, and Husbands. *Journal of
Clinical Psychology*, 14:184-186.

Nagy, Maria H.
1965   The Child's View of Death. In *The Meaning of
Death*. Edited by Herman Feifel. New York: Mc-
Graw-Hill.

Naimen, Laurence
1971-
1974   Case History Notes Discussed in Personal Conversation with the Author.

Natanson, Maurice
1963   *Philosophy of the Social Sciences*. New York:
Random House.
1970   *The Journeying Self: A Study in Philosophy and
Social Role*. Massachusetts: Addison-Wesley Publishing Co.

Natterson, Joseph M. and Knudson, Alfred
  1960   Observations Concerning Fear of Death in Fatally Ill Children and Their Mothers. *Psychosomatic Medicine,* 22:456-465.
Nelson, Waldo, Vaughn, Victor, and McKay, R. James
  1969   *Textbook of Pediatrics.* Philadelphia: W. B. Saunders Co.
O'Neill, John
  1973   Embodiment and Child Development: A Phenomenological Approach. In *Childhood and Socialization.* Edited by Hans P. Dreitzel. New York: Macmillan Co.
Opie, Iona and Opie, Peter
  1959   *Lore and Language of School Children.* London: Oxford University Press.
  1969   Children's Games in Street and Playground. Oxford: Clarendon Press.
Orbach, Charles
  1959   The Multiple Meanings of the Loss of a Child. *American Journal of Psychotherapy,* 13:906-915.
Orbach, Charles, Sutherland, Arthur M., and Bozeman, Morey
  1955   Psychological Impact of Cancer and Its Treatment. III. The Adaptation of Mothers to the Threatened Loss of Their Children through Leukemia: Part II. *Cancer,* 8:20-23.
Parkes, Colin Murray
  1973   *Bereavement: Studies of Grief in Adult Life.* New York: International Universities Press.
Parsons, Talcott
  1968   Youth in the Context of American Society. In *Selected Studies in Marriage and the Family.* Edited by Robert Winch and Louis Goodman. New York: Holt, Rinehart, and Winston.
Pearson, Leonard (ed.)
  1969   *Death and Dying: Current Issues in the Treatment of the Dying Person.* Cleveland: Case Western Reserve Press.

270

Pelto, Pertti
1970   *Anthropological Research: The Structure of Inquiry.* New York: Harper and Row.

Piaget, Jean
1952   *The Language and Thought of the Child.* New York: Harcourt, Brace and Co.

Pitcher, Evelyn and Prelinger, Ernest
1969   *Children Tell Stories: An Analysis of Fantasy.* New York: International Universities Press.

Prugh, Dane G.
1963   Toward an Understanding of Psychosomatic Concepts in Relation to Illness in Children. In *Modern Perspectives in Child Development.* Edited by A. Solnit and S. Provence. New York: International Universities Press.

Psathas, George
1972   Ethnomethods and Phenomenology. In *Symbolic Interaction: A Reader in Social Psychology.* Edited by J. Manis and B. Meltzer. Boston: Allyn and Bacon, Inc.

Quint, Jeanne
1967   *The Nurse and the Dying Patient.* New York: Macmillan Co.

Rafky, David
1973   Phenomenology and Socialization: Some Comments on the Assumptions Underlying Socialization Theory. In *Childhood and Socialization.* Edited by Hans Dreitzel. New York: Macmillan Co.

Redl, F.
1959   Strategy and Telling of Life Span Interview. *American Journal of Orthopsychiatry,* 29:6.

Richards, Audrey I.
1970   Socialization and Contemporary British Social Anthropology. In *Socialization: The Approach from Social Anthropology.* Edited by Philip Mayer. A.S.A. Monographs, vol. 8. London: Tavistock Publications Ltd.

Richmond, Julius B. and Waisman, Harry A.
1955   Psychologic Aspects of Management of Children
        with Malignant Diseases. *American Journal of
        Diseases of Children*, 89:42-47.
Robertson, James
1958   *Young Children in Hospitals*. New York: Basic
        Books, Inc.
Rochlin, Gregory
1967   How Younger Children View Death and Them-
        selves. In *Explaining Death to Children*. Edited
        by E. Grollman. Boston: Beacon Press.
Russell, Bertrand
1929   Your Child and the Fear of Death. *Forum*, 81:174-
        178.
Sacks, Harvey
1972a   On the Analyzability of Stories by Children. In
        Sociolinguistics. Edited by J. Gumperz and D.
        Hymes. New York: Holt, Rinehart, and Winston.
1972b   An Initial Investigation on the Usability of Con-
        versational Data for Doing Sociology. In *Studies
        in Social Interaction*. Edited by David Sudnow.
        New York: Free Press.
Schilder, Paul and Wechsler, David
1934   The Attitudes of Children toward Death. *Journal
        of Genetics and Psychology*, 45:406-451.
Schutz, Alfred
1962   *Collected Papers*, volume I, *The Problem of So-
        cial Reality*. The Hague: Martinus Nighoff.
Schwartz, Morris and Schwartz, Charolette Green
1955   Problems in Participant Observation. *American
        Journal of Sociology*, 60:343-354.
Sewell, William H.
1970   Some Recent Developments in Socialization The-
        ory and Research. In *Social Psychology Through
        Symbolic Interaction*. Edited by G. Stone and H.
        Farberman. Waltham, Massachusetts: Xerox Col-
        lege Publications.

Snedeker, L. et al. (Committee on Hospital Care of the American Academy of Pediatrics)
1960   Care of Children in Hospitals. Illinois: American Academy of Pediatrics.

Solnit, Albert and Green, Morris
1959   Psychological Considerations in the Management of Death on the Pediatrics Hospital Service: I. The Doctor and Child's Family. Pediatrics, 24: 106-112.
1963   The Pediatric Management of the Dying Child: Part II, The Child's Reaction to the Fear of Dying. In Modern Perspectives in Child Development. Edited by Albert Solnit and Sally Provence. New York: International Universities Press.

Solnit, Albert and Provence, Sally
1963   Modern Perspectives in Child Development. New York: International Universities Press.

Speier, M.
1970   The Everyday World of the Child. In Understanding Everyday Life. Edited by Jack Douglas. Chicago: Aldine.

Stebbins, Robert
1972   Studying the Definition of the Situation: Theory and Field Research Strategies. In Symbolic Interaction: A Reader in Social Psychology. Edited by J. Manis and B. Meltzer. Boston: Allyn and Bacon, Inc.

Strauss, Anselm
1969   Mirrors and Masks. Mill Valley, California: Sociology Press.
1970   Anguish. Mill Valley, California: Sociology Press.

Strauss, Anselm and Glaser, Barney
1967   Time for Dying. Chicago: Aldine.

Sudnow, David
1967   Passing on: The Social Organization of Dying. Englewood Cliffs, New Jersey: Prentice-Hall.
1969   Studies in Interaction. New York: Free Press.

Swanson, Guy
  1972   Mead and Freud: Their Relevance for Social Psychology. In *Symbolic Interaction: A Reader in Social Psychology*. Edited by J. Manis and B. Meltzer. Boston: Allyn and Bacon, Inc.
Thomas, W. I.
  1928   *The Child in America*. New York: Alfred Knopf.
Tisza, Veronica
  1962   The Management of the Parents of a Chronically Ill Child. *American Journal of Orthopsychiatry*, 32:53-59.
Toch, R.
  1964   Management of the Child with a Fatal Disease. *Clinical Pediatrics*, 3:418.
Van Gennep, Arnold
  1969   *The Rites of Passage*. Chicago: University of Chicago Press.
Vernick, Joel and Karon, Myron
  1965   Who's Afraid of Death on a Leukemia Ward? *American Journal of Diseases of Children*, 109: 393-397.
Wahl, Charles W.
  1959   The Fear of Death. In *The Meaning of Death*. Edited by Herman Feifel. New York: McGraw-Hill.
Wallace, Anthony
  1970   *Culture and Personality*. New York: Random House.
Waller, Willard
  1970   The Definition of the Situation. In *Social Psychology through Symbolic Interaction*. Edited by G. Stone and H. Farberman. Waltham, Massachusetts: Xerox College Publications.
Wheeler, Stanton
  1966   The Structure of Formally Organized Socialization Settings. In *Socialization after Childhood*. Edited by A. Brim and S. Wheeler. New York: John Wiley and Sons, Inc.

White, E. B.
  1952   *Charlotte's Web.* New York: Dell Publishing Co.
Whiting, John and Child, Irvin
  1953   *Child Training and Personality.* New Haven, Connecticut: Yale University Press.
  1966   *Field Guide for a Study of Socialization.* New York: John Wiley and Sons, Inc.
Wolf, Richard
  1963   The Hospital and the Child. In *Modern Perspectives in Child Development.* Edited by A. Solnit and S. Provence. New York: International Universities Press.
Wolfenstein, Martha
  1955   Fun Morality: An Analysis of Recent Child Training Literature. In *Childhood in Contemporary Culture.* Edited by M. Mead and M. Wolfenstein. Chicago: University of Chicago Press.
Wright, Herbert
  1967   *Recording and Analyzing Child Behavior.* New York: Harper and Row.
Wylie, Ruth
  1961   *The Self-Concept: A Critical Survey of Pertinent Research Literature.* Lincoln: University of Nebraska Press.

INDEX